8/22/91

To Ruth Ham....,

Towards a "common
humanity" — one day!

Tony Platt.

E. Franklin Frazier Reconsidered

E. Franklin Frazier Reconsidered

Anthony M. Platt

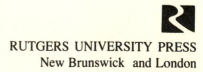

RUTGERS UNIVERSITY PRESS
New Brunswick and London

"A moral life is a life of activity in society."
–*E. Franklin Frazier, 1918*

"Scholarship is a choice of how to live as well as a choice of career."
–*C. Wright Mills, 1959*

"To accept one's past—one's history—is not the same thing as drowning in it; it is learning how to use it."
–*James Baldwin, 1962*

Library of Congress Cataloging-in-Publication Data
Platt, Anthony M.
    E. Franklin Frazier reconsidered / Anthony M. Platt.
        p.   cm.
    Includes bibliographical references and index.
    ISBN 0-8135-1631-5
        1. Frazier, Edward Franklin, 1894–1962. 2. Sociologists—
United States—Biography. 3. Sociology—United States—
History.   I. Title.
    HM22.6.U6F736   1991
    301'.092—dc20
    [B]   90-36223
                              CIP
British Cataloging-in-Publication information available

Grateful acknowledgment is made to the following to reprint previously unpublished material: Excerpts from letters, memoranda, diaries, essays, and other materials by E. Franklin Frazier by permission of the Moorland-Spingarn Research Center, Howard University; correspondence from G. Stanley Hall and Frank Hankins, and Frazier's graduate school transcript courtesy of Clark University; Frazier's transcript of his doctoral courses by permission of the University of Chicago.

Grateful acknowledgment is made to the following to reprint previously published material: E. Franklin Frazier, "New Role of the Negro Woman," which previously appeared in *Ebony* 15 (August 1960); Langston Hughes, "Cross," copyright 1926 by Alfred A. Knopf and renewed 1954 by Langston Hughes, reprinted from *Selected Poems of Langston Hughes* by permission of the publisher. Chapter 7 is an expanded and revised version of Anthony Platt and Susan Chandler, "Constant Struggle: E. Franklin Frazier and Black Social Work in the 1920s," reprinted with permission from *Social Work* 33 (1988): 293–297, copyright 1988, National Association of Social Workers, Inc. Chapter 11 is a revised version of Anthony Platt, "E. Franklin Frazier and Daniel Patrick Moynihan: Setting the Record Straight," *Contemporary Crises* 11 (1987): 265–277, reprinted by permission of Kluwer Academic Publishers.

Contents

Preface and Acknowledgments

This book, which has been many years in the making, has two important origins. First, it comes out of my intellectual interest in modern U.S. history, especially the revisionist tradition with its explicit efforts to debunk and deconstruct official mythologies. Second, it reflects my personal decision to live as a politically committed intellectual in an academic milieu that generally frowns on such efforts when they emanate from the left.

I have lived with Edward Franklin Frazier for some twenty years. I first thought about the possibility of this book when I was working for the National Commission on the Causes and Prevention of Violence and discovered Frazier's unpublished report on the 1935 Harlem riot. It was a marvelously original and bold study that stood apart from the conventional wisdom of the collective behavior literature. It was difficult to fit this Frazier with the Frazier who "pathologized" the Afro-American family. This contradiction sparked my curiosity. All biographers, especially one who has related to a subject for as long as I have, run the risk of identification and romanticism. I readily confess to the first charge. I admire Frazier and have learned much from how he lived his life. As to the second charge, it helps that Frazier himself was an antiromantic who hated being treated as a "Negro saint." I hope that my respectful appreciation of his life and work has not contributed to new mythologies.

Many people have played a part in helping me write this book since its germination in the early 1970s. Of the numerous research assistants who spent too many hours in libraries tracking down elusive leads, my special thanks to Susan Chandler, June Kress, and Renetia Martin, all of whom went far beyond the tasks of data collection and helped to shape my interpretations.

Several people—notably Elizabeth Martinez, Ed McCaughan, and all my other colleagues at Global Options in San Francisco—generously gave the moral and intellectual support that enabled me to keep going when I had my doubts about the project. Special thanks to Rod Bush and Gerda Ray, who read an early draft and were more than encouraging, and to Piri Thomas for getting my writing to flow. Pat and Dennis Sherman (in and around New York) and June Kress and Dennis Soiberman (in Washington, D.C.) provided homes away from home during my research trips back east. Indispensably critical readings of a close-to-final manuscript were given by John Horton and Walter Jackson. Marlie Wasserman (Rutgers University Press) and Sydelle Kramer (Frances Goldin agency) proved that publisher and agent can work in harmony. Thanks to both for their enthusiastic support of this book. As always, Cecilia O'Leary did the right thing: She stayed out of the kitchen and demanded historical rigor.

For their advice, encouragement, and appreciation of Frazier's life and work, I want to acknowledge especially G. Franklin Edwards and Michael Winston at Howard University, plus all the other people who gave interviews, responded to letters and phone calls, and dug into their memories and old files in order to bring Frazier to life with all his complexity and contradictions. Special thanks to Herbert Blumer, St. Clair Drake, Morris Ernst, Marie Brown Frazier, Everett Hughes, Dorothy Porter, and A. Philip Randolph; and Herbert Aptheker, John Bracey, Jr., David Carmichael, Herbert Gutman, David Hellwig, Norman Hill, Eugene Holmes, Inabel Lindsay, Rayford Logan, Gordan Morgan, John Morsell, James Nabrit, Alvin Schorr, John Stanfield, and Frederick Stielow. Without the helpful intervention by Congressman Ronald Dellums, no doubt I would still be waiting for the FBI to release Frazier's files.

Books like this one are made possible by the hidden and generally unglamorous work done by librarians in stacks and back offices. My thanks to the unsung archivists and librarians at Howard University, California State University (Sacramento), California State Library, University of California (Berkeley), New York Municipal Archives, Schomburg Collection of Negro Literature and History, New York Historical Society, Arthur Garfield Hays Papers (Princeton University), National Archives, Clark University Archives, YMCA of the USA Archives (University of Minnesota), and Afro-American Newspapers and Archives Research Center (Bowie State University). I owe a special debt of gratitude to Esme Bhan and the dedicated staff of the Moorland-Spingarn Research Center, Howard University, who served as my guides to the Frazier Papers. I hope I did justice to their work.

I am very grateful to my colleagues at California State University, Sacramento, for their encouragement and, not least, for funding a semester's leave in spring 1989, thus taking away my last excuse for any further delay of this book.

And to Edward Franklin Frazier, appreciation and respect for teaching me that "a moral life is a life of activity in society."

E. Franklin Frazier Reconsidered

Prologue

Neither Saint nor Stone

This study calls for a reconsideration of the life, work, and contributions of Edward Franklin Frazier (1894–1962), Afro-American intellectual, sociologist, and activist. Why a reconsideration and what needs to be reconsidered?

Some time in the early 1920s, shortly after Frazier had moved from the North to Atlanta to teach sociology at Morehouse College, he wrote a bitter essay about life on the southern side of the "Styxian Potomac," a region characterized by "Jim Crow, Disenfranchisement, Lawlessness, White Supremacy, Religious Intolerance, Peonage, and Anti-Evolutionism or Respectable Ignorance." To Frazier, one of the most terrifying aspects of the institutionalized racism he found so deeply entrenched in the South was the monolithic, one-dimensional reduction of Afro-American people to "saints or stones."[1] Not lynching nor impoverishment nor job discrimination but rather "the denial of personality to the Negro," he wrote in his first article for *Crisis* in 1924, was "the greatest crime of the age."[2]

It is ironic that since his death in 1962 Frazier similarly has been subjected to assessments that generally deny the complexity and contradictions of his life's work. His negative image in progressive circles derives from his posthumous association with *The Negro Family: The Case for National Action*—better known as the Moynihan Report, published three years after his death. Accepting at face value the derisive nomination of Frazier as father of the Moynihan Report, several commentators then set out to trace this attribution back to Frazier's alleged cooptation by the University of Chicago, where, in the late 1920s, he went to complete a doctoral degree in sociology. According to this view, Chicago was the site of Frazier's original sin which, despite his best efforts and good intentions, he was never able to expiate.[3] By the time of his death, the prevailing political assessment was that his work was not to be taken too seriously. It was even something of an embarrassment in an era of civil rights and black liberation movements. Charitably, Frazier's detractors reduced him to a stone and left him alone.[4]

The other prevailing view of Frazier elevates him to sainthood. This is Frazier the "distinguished Negro sociologist" who as the first black president of the American Sociological Association in 1948 succeeded against all odds, who pulled himself up by his working-class bootstraps to become a leading academic intellectual. The advocates of this perspective similarly return to Frazier's graduate training in Chicago but, unlike his detractors, commemorate him as a loyal and capable disciple of Robert Park and other white academics who were generous enough to recruit Afro-American students despite the prevalence of racism in academia. Here he is remembered primarily for his contributions as a sociologist, a *Negro sociologist*.[5]

This study attempts to break through these two perceptions and characterizations of Frazier. I will argue that the association with Moynihan is essentially wrong, while the idealization of Frazier is insufficient and incomplete. Once we break the molds that imprison Frazier as saint or stone, we find a highly talented, original, multifaceted, and contradictory intellectual who bequeathed us an extraordinary legacy of writings ranging from scholarly texts to savage polemics and who forged an exemplary record of sustained political activism against the horrors and injustices of racism at considerable personal risk.

This study is in part an assessment of Frazier's intellectual and political contributions, in part a chronological narrative of his life and accomplishments. But these aspects are not its central focus or goal. Instead I will draw on Frazier's biography and milieu in order to argue several revisionist interpretations.

First, Frazier made sufficient contributions, intellectually and politically, to be taken seriously in his own right. Clearly, he was influenced by his academic mentors and by leaders in the militant black movements that erupted after World War I, but he was much more than a follower of W.E.B. Du Bois or Park's "most complete student."[6] The tendency to understand Frazier only through a series of dependent relationships denies his unique contributions and the impact he had on other intellectuals and activists. True, he had great respect, for example, for Du Bois and Park (his 1949 textbook was dedicated to them), but he was also among their fiercest critics.

In particular, I will assess Frazier's role in the New Negro movement of the 1920s. Because of the prominence of other figures, such as Du Bois, Paul Robeson, Langston Hughes, and Alain Locke, Frazier's contributions have been overshadowed or relegated to the margins. Moreover, scholars have tended to ignore the "early" Frazier in favor of the "mature" Frazier, who published *The Negro Family in the United States* (1939), *The Negro in the United States* (1949), and *Race and Culture Contacts in the Modern World* (1957). By the end of the 1920s, however, Frazier had lived more than half his life, and the main contours of both his ideas and activism were well established. This study, therefore, will focus more on these early, formative years, than on the later years.

Second, Frazier is remembered primarily for his academic writings, notably on the Afro-American family and race relations. His polemical and explicitly politicized work, such as *Black Bourgeoisie,* is generally regarded as a forgettable and somewhat unreasonable, even slightly disreputable, detour from his "real" accomplishments. However, Frazier's statement in 1951—"I consider myself primarily a scholar [and] I do not consider myself a Negro leader or an interracial leader"—has sometimes been taken too literally and narrowly.[7] Frazier certainly hated interracial politics, which he considered superficial and hypocritical, and he stayed far away from the organizational aspects of politics.

However, Frazier's work and self-identity were consistently driven by a sense of moral outrage at any kind of social inequality and a relentless, burning hatred of racism. Although his contributions were much more modest, Frazier was no less political than Du Bois. They made different kinds of contributions and operated in different arenas, but, like Du Bois, it was a rare day when Frazier did not think about the struggle against inequality. From his first publication as an undergraduate in the student newspaper at Howard University in 1916 (in which he advocated suffrage for women) to his last essay in 1962 (in which he railed against the obsequious conformity of black intellectuals), Frazier was a self-conscious ideologue who expressed his politics primarily in the combat of ideas.

Whatever Frazier's personal preference, he was not allowed to restrict his politics to academic discourse. Simply by virtue of being an Afro-American intellectual in the United States after World War I, he joined a small and privileged cadre who, irrespective of their political beliefs, by necessity had to fight racism in order to practice their craft—to get jobs, to gain access to resources, to travel, to attend conferences, to be published, to be taken seriously. Frazier, more so than most, made a point of fighting the ubiquitous restrictions and petty humiliations that barred him from full participation in academia. This determination, some call it stubbornness, nearly cost him his life on at least one occasion.

Frazier's problems were compounded by the political content of his ideas, for he went far beyond the liberal sensibilities of most of his peers. As a self-professed and unswerving atheist with a commitment, however vaguely and inconsistently expressed, to socialist ideas, he was a ready target for racists, fundamentalists, and redbaiters. Frazier very well may have preferred to be left to his research, teaching, and writings, but he chose to follow a set of principles that regularly and persistently put him into the limelight of political controversy.

Third, regarding Frazier's intellectual contributions, his work on the Afro-American family has been rightfully noted as one of his major contributions. I will suggest, however, that it is inaccurate, as well as racist, to credit the Chicago School with being the decisive influence on Frazier's ideas about the family. He spent only two years as a full-time graduate student at the University of Chicago. When he arrived in 1927, he was thirty-three years old, an experienced and traveled intellectual, and an independent and strong-willed thinker who had already formulated his initial ideas about the family, partly as a result of studying Du Bois's book on the topic, partly in the course of his firsthand experience constructing a curriculum (including courses on the family) at the Atlanta School of Social Work. The Chicago sociologists certainly played their part in Frazier's intellectual development—and Frazier was the first to acknowledge their contribution—but they were one influence among many.

Fourth, the most serious charge made against Frazier in the wake of the controversial Moynihan Report was that he negated Afro-American culture and was a soulless environmental determinist who had no respect and certainly no love for the spiritual and artistic contributions of black communities.[8] Reading only the Moynihan Report and selected paragraphs from Frazier's writings, one can easily reach this conclusion. Frazier certainly had strong, unambiguous views on cultural issues and, in the 1920s especially, was quite suspicious of the fashionable cultural nationalism of the Negro Renaissance because, as he put it in 1928, "it basks in the sun of white capitalism."[9] He was also unyielding, even dogmatic, in his position that African cultural bonds were decisively severed in the course of slavery (a position that, by the way, Du Bois also held at one time). But in the 1960s he received the most criticism for his view that black families were "disorganized" by racism and exploitation when they relocated to the urban ghettoes in search of jobs and equality after Reconstruction.[10]

But these positions did not constitute a negation of culture. On the contrary, Frazier was more sensitive to cultural issues than most social scientists, and in his writings in the 1920s and 1930s he was preoccupied with restoring and recognizing the cultural integrity of Afro-American communities. His concern about the instabilities in family life generated by slavery, migration, and capitalist urbanization was at least matched by his appreciation of the toughness and resilience of the black family in all its variety and complexity. This topic was not a fleeting interest of Frazier's. The last series of essays he wrote, between 1959 and 1962, addressed profound issues of cultural identity. Consider some of his last published words: "It may turn out that in the distant future Negroes will disappear physically from American society. If this is our fate, let us disappear with dignity and let us leave a worthwhile memorial—in science, in art, in literature, in sculpture, in music—of our having been here."[11] Moreover, although Frazier spent a lifetime disagreeing with Melville Herskovits about the impact of African culture on black Americans in the nineteenth century, his final political statement—bequeathing his library to the University of Ghana—indicated that he was more than receptive to Kwame Nkrumah's revolutionary nationalism as a model for black Americans in the twentieth century.

Fifth, the reconstruction of Frazier's life by his critics has tended to depoliticize his contributions and overestimate his cooptation by the University of Chicago. "His professional career," wrote Oliver Cox in one of the more scathing denunciations of Frazier, "had to be contrived on the tightrope set up by the associational establishment. He won many prizes and honors, but the exigencies of winning involved his soul and his manhood."[12]

The image of a tightrope is fitting, but how well Frazier managed to stay on it is an open question. He was an activist, even an adventurist from time to time, who continually tried to broaden the definition,

responsibilities, and obligations of an intellectual. There is no indication that he was any less pugnacious or class conscious after his two
years at Chicago than he was before, as Cox and others have implied.
In fact, it might be argued that his political persona was most visible
and most uncompromised in the years following the awarding of his
doctorate in 1931.

This is not to suggest that Frazier's activism was consistent or that
his political views were always explicit and easily identified, as compared, for example, with those of Du Bois, whose dramatic shifts in
political allegiance were a matter of public debate. But whatever his
political marginality and ambivalence, however unclear he was about
his vision of socialism and equality, Frazier remained an ideologically
committed intellectual before and after his entry into academic life.

He supported the left wing of the Socialist Party but abandoned it in
disgust when he felt that it had lost its revolutionary militancy. He was
both a product and a critic of the Negro Renaissance in the 1920s. He
was perceived to be enough of a fellow traveler of the Communist Party
in the 1930s (even though he had profound differences with the party's
line on the National Question) to be redbaited and investigated as a
security risk for at least the last twenty years of his life. He was an
advocate of strategies of integration pursued by liberals from Franklin
D. Roosevelt to John F. Kennedy, but he was always concerned—and
more so at the end of his life—that, in James Baldwin's memorable
allusion, too high a price might be paid for incorporation into a "burning house."[13] He was a committed sociologist who devoted considerable
energy to building up professional associations and to defending his
life's work, but he quietly and occasionally not so quietly despaired
about the trivial preoccupations, stupidity, and political cowardice of
his peers. It may not be easy to fit Frazier into a convenient political
category or to decipher his ideological world-view, but academia did
not "turn" or depoliticize him. Quite the contrary, academia was his
political milieu, more of a battle ground than a marketplace of ideas.

Sixth, Frazier may not have been religious, but he was a dedicated
believer in the Protestant ethic; individual responsibility, hard work,
and self-reliance were a matter of faith and of practice. He was a loner
more than a joiner, a thinker more than an organizer, an intellectual who
produced largely through his own efforts eight books, well over one
hundred articles and reviews, and countless speeches and essays. In the
1920s and 1930s he essentially constructed two academic departments

(the Atlanta School of Social Work and Howard University's sociology department) and still found time to speak his mind wherever he was invited—at church clubs and women's organizations in the Deep South, farmers' cooperatives and unions in the Midwest and North, as well as distinguished gatherings of Pan-Africanists in Paris and New Negroes in New York. Throughout his life, Frazier maintained this furious pace of activities, as though life were far too short and precious for him. He was rarely between projects and even more rarely refused a request for an article or speech or guest lecture.

It is crucial to understand that this prodigious productivity took place despite continual restraints, restrictions, and impositions on, for want of a better term, Frazier's academic freedom. Frazier may have been sufficiently conventional to become the first Afro-American president of the American Sociological Association, but for most of his life he was subject to harassment or humiliation by university administrators, boards of trustees, racist organizations, right-wing politicians, McCarthyist inquisitors or the FBI. We need to understand the magnitude of these repressive contraints not to excuse Frazier's deficiencies and limitations but rather to appreciate how much he accomplished against enormous odds.

This study invites you to reconsider Edward Franklin Frazier, not as a saint or a stone, but as somebody who tried, as he put it, "to provide answers to important questions" about the persistence of racism and social inequality.[14] Even though he was essentially a man of ideas, he tried to practice what he thought by fighting for the right to have his ideas taken seriously. During Frazier's lifetime this struggle for legitimacy was difficult for white intellectuals who challenged the status quo.[15] For an Afro-American intellectual or artist, even one who remained primarily within the bounds of propriety, it was almost impossible, as we know from the price paid by Hughes, Baldwin, Zora Neale Hurston, Robeson, and countless others whose ideas made them renegades.

This is a fitting time to reconsider Frazier. Confronted by deepening racial and ethnic divisions in the United States, a ferocious renewal of mean-spirited racism, and a resurgence of longstanding debates about integrationist and nationalist strategies for achieving social equality, we cannot afford to lightly dismiss or underestimate somebody who devoted a lifetime to grappling with these issues.

Roots

I

Son of the Crossways, 1894–1912

Edward Franklin Frazier was a war baby. Born in 1894, the year in which Du Bois was completing his doctoral degree at Harvard and 135 blacks were being lynched in the South, Frazier entered a world on the brink of war and a country characterized by deepening racial antagonisms, increasing violence against Afro-Americans, and the rise of militant movements for civil rights and self-defense. The 1890s witnessed the birth of U.S. expansionism and military interventions in Latin America and other parts of the Third World. Following the U.S. defeat of Spain in 1898, the Pax Americana was imposed on Cuba, Puerto Rico, Hawaii, Guam, and the Philippines,[1] prompting Du Bois to note sadly in 1903 that U.S. militarism against "weaker and darker peoples" now made it difficult for Afro-Americans to escape racism by emigrating to another country. "Where in the world may we go and be safe from lying and brute force?"[2]

Edward Frazier was born into a cadre of activists who after World War I would come together from vastly different regions of the country to form the cutting edge of a social, political, and cultural movement that would irrevocably change conceptions of race and the politics of race relations. With the exception of Du Bois, who was already in his mid-twenties when Frazier was born and who outlived many of Frazier's contemporaries, the generation of New Negroes was born in the last decade of the nineteenth and first decade of the twentieth centuries.

Progressive Afro-American intellectuals, writers, and future academic colleagues of Frazier's born during this era included Jesse Fauset (1884), Charles Johnson (1893), Jean Toomer (1894), Rudolph Fisher

(1897), Oliver Cox (1901), and Ralph Bunche (1904). A. Philip Randolph, the socialist labor leader, was born in 1889; Elijah Muhammed, who eventually would take over leadership of the Nation of Islam, in 1897; Marcus Garvey and Claude McKay, future immigrants from Jamaica who would have a unique impact on politics and literature, in 1887 and 1890, respectively; Paul Robeson, the multitalented singer, actor, and activist, in 1898; and soon after came Zora Neale Hurston (c. 1901), Sterling Brown (1901), Arna Bontemps and Langston Hughes (1902), Countee Cullen (1903), and Richard Wright (1908), all of whom helped to transform American literature and to forge the Negro Renaissance.[3]

Early Years

Relatively little is known about Frazier's family background or childhood. It is ironic that one of the leading experts on the sociology of the family and a pioneer in Afro-American history left almost no records, memoirs, or documents about his own formative years. He began a serious, reflective diary in December 1950, which lasted less than a month. His diaries from the 1920s are filled only with addresses, travel information, and budgets. He kept official certificates documenting his educational achievements, and he preserved three scrapbooks of newspaper clippings (1900–1903) bequeathed by his father. Other than a striking photograph of a young Edward Frazier, with long black curls flowing over his formal suit, he left few autobiographical remnants of his childhood and family in Baltimore.

This same man was a meticulous recorder of the world around him, a scholar who took every opportunity to collect stories, folklore, and family histories. He was the first social scientist to fully document the history, variety, and status of the Afro-American family in the United States.[4] Almost everybody he knew—his wife's family, his friends, students, business contacts—was asked to record his or her past in great detail. "Dear Dad," he wrote in a typical letter to his father-in-law in 1928, "I am writing to ask you to help me . . . by writing your family history for me." Frazier encouraged him to "go back as far as you can and to comprise all the memories of your ancestors which have been handed down to you. I want it to include all the hopes and ambitions and struggles of you and your parents."[5] Frazier never put himself to this written test.

Given that Frazier collected hundreds of such life histories and carefully maintained them in his files along with some forty years of correspondence (including carbon copies of his own letters), first drafts of manuscripts, even old shopping lists, it is unlikely that he would have thrown out his own memoirs. More likely, he never wrote them. Consequently, for Frazier's early years, we must rely primarily on the recollections of his wife, relatives, and friends after his death in 1962, plus scattered autobiographical comments buried in his publications.

According to Marie Brown Frazier, his wife of forty years, Frazier lost interest in his own family after his parents died. Occasionally, he would talk about going over to the Eastern shore of Maryland "to see if I can find some of my relatives," but he never did. He stayed in touch with his three brothers and sister—and when she died took responsibility for his nephew's education—but "he wasn't a great family man," said his wife. In fact, he was closer to and more knowledgeable about his wife's interesting family, pillars of black society in North Carolina, than his own. Frazier's philosophy, recalled his wife, was that blood relations are accidental. "Friendship is the thing in this world that counts," he used to say. The fact that somebody is your brother "doesn't mean anything."[6] To underscore this point, when one of his brothers died and left him some money, Frazier refused it, saying he had done nothing to earn or deserve the legacy.[7]

Some facts about Frazier's childhood and youth are clear and uncontested. He was born in Baltimore on September 24, 1894, the son of James Edward Frazier, a bank messenger, and Mary Clark Frazier. His paternal grandfather was a self-emancipated slave who had bought his family's freedom, and his mother had been born a slave.[8] As a child and teenager, Edward was slight, handsome, and dark-skinned. In his college yearbook, he is serious, distinguished, still slim. Soon after, he begins to fill out, a "big, strong" man for his five feet and nine inches. Marie Brown Frazier remembered him in his twenties "with a thick mop of hair standing up on his head. Sort of built like Fred Douglass." He was also black and burly enough that Marie's friends warned her against marrying a "Negroid" who was the "wrong color."[9]

Edward was close to both his parents and retained strong, vivid memories of his father even though James died when his son was ten years old, four years before he completed elementary school. James was a frugal and hard-working patriarch who believed in the virtues of education and self-discipline and who, as his son recalled, "never went to school, taught himself how to read and write and . . . set an example by the fact that he was a voracious reader."[10]

The Fraziers owned the small house they lived in, and after James's death in 1905 the whole family worked to maintain their standard of living. Edward's mother worked as a maid to keep the family together and her children in school.[11] Although Edward drifted apart from his brothers and sister after he went to college in 1912, he maintained contact with his mother until her death in 1928. By the time Edward (or E. Franklin as he was now known) was thirty-four years old, he had lost both parents and his sister, and had cut himself off from his brothers. Moreover, about this time his wife Marie found out that she could not bear children herself. Thus, Edward, who by his own account grew up in a tight and loving family, and E. Franklin, who devoted many years to studying the Afro-American family, spent his own adult life outside the conventions of a traditional or extended nuclear family. Perhaps his father's emphasis on the importance of being a self-made man also stamped Edward with the character of a loner, a person who valued independence almost to the point of isolation and who, in his nephew's words, "wore no man's collar."[12]

In the Frazier family, education was stressed as both an instrument and a virtue in itself, especially for the boys. James "had an almost religious faith in the importance of education," recollected Arthur Davis, a longtime colleague of Frazier's at Howard University. "At the nightly family gatherings which took place after supper, he never tired of pointing out to his children that they could avoid the kind of humiliation he occasionally endured by getting an education."[13] Each of the boys apparently followed his advice, becoming successful as a lawyer, physician, businessman, and professor.

Edward, the future professor, was bright and from an early age did well in school, finishing grammar school at the head of his class. In June 1912 he graduated one of the top three in his class at Colored High School and received the school's only annual scholarship to Howard University in Washington, D.C.[14] When he completed his bachelor's degree in 1916, graduating *cum laude* from the College of Arts and Sciences, Alain Locke, one of his professors and soon after a leader of the New Negro movement, wrote a reference for Edward, describing him "as one of the most consistently competent and painstaking students I have taught in four years of experience at the institution." Also, he added, "Mr. Frazier's mental endowment is exceptional somewhat."[15] A few years later, after he completed his master's degree at Clark University, he received a reference from its president, who gave him the highest praise possible for a black student in a predominantly white university in 1920. "Mr. Frazier . . . seems to me to be quite gentlemanly and mentally white," wrote G. Stanley Hall.[16]

Race Man

Everybody who knew Frazier remarks about his moral toughness, independent spirit, determination, and pugnacity. To Davis he was a "nonconformist, a protester, a gadfly."[17] According to Adelaide Cromwell Hill, he was "a man of wit and humor" who was "always extremely impatient with stupidity, conformity, and hypocrisy."[18] One obituary noted that he was "outspokingly blunt in expressing unpopular views."[19] A "maverick" and "iconoclast" was how the sociologist St. Clair Drake remembered him.[20] Even Frazier recognized this trait in himself when in the 1920s he chose *Enfant Terrible* as his pseudonym for a column that he proposed to the Chicago *Daily Defender.*[21]

Was there any indication of these character traits during Frazier's formative years? When Shirley Graham Du Bois presented Frazier's library to the University of Ghana in 1963, she attributed the following autobiographical comment to Frazier:

> As far back as I can go on my mother's side I remember my great-grandmother. Her parents were born in Africa. The one thing she must have told my grandfather for he told me, was that his people on the African side were Ibos. We didn't know what he was talking about when he told us, but I have found out since that the Ibos were hard to manage and that they stopped bringing them here as slaves. I remember that my great-grandmother was hard to manage and grandfather had to build a separate house for her. She lived to be ninety-six years old.[22]

Although it was a fitting story for the ceremony, it was just not true. The words were not Frazier's but rather those of a young woman whom he had interviewed in the 1930s.[23] But Marie Brown Frazier verified at least one part of the apocryphal story. Frazier did not talk much about his grandparents, but "he claimed that he was of Ibo descent and he was very proud of it. He used to hear his grandmother use some Ibo words," recalled Mrs. Frazier in 1975.[24] Given Frazier's longstanding antipathy to the thesis that African customs played a decisive role in the development of Afro-American culture, maybe he was unwilling to credit his grandmother with any responsibility for his own rebellious character.[25]

As we shall see in the next chapter, we know that eighteen-year-old Edward was already receptive to the left-wing politics and militant currents that he found at Howard University when he arrived there as a freshman in 1912. Clearly this receptivity was nourished during his childhood, and we must assume that he inherited much more than a serious interest in education from his father. According to Marie Brown Frazier, James Frazier "was very race conscious and kept up with all the misfortunes that Negroes were going through at that particular time. His father used to just walk and talk to him all the time about what was going on racially in the world."[26] In 1895, the year after Frazier's birth, Booker T. Washington gave his infamous Atlanta Compromise speech, urging Negroes to suspend the battle for equality. About the same time, Homer Plessy was arrested and convicted for riding in a white railroad car in Louisiana. In *Plessy v. Ferguson* the U.S. Supreme Court legitimated segregation in the guise of "separate but equal." Clearly, there was no lack of misfortunes to discuss.

Frazier himself was clear about how he became a race man.[27] He "swears that he got his first stimulation from these walks with his father. . . . He had great respect for his father."[28] Davis also confirmed the significant influence of his father. "Like his son, the elder Frazier was a protester; he was an inveterate writer of letters-to-the-editor. Frazier's own militant character was formed in large measure, he believed, by the example and indoctrination of his father."[29] The scrapbooks of newspaper clippings left by James Frazier to his children were carefully preserved by Frazier throughout his life. The clippings covered a range of topics about developments in politics, education, and religion, and other contemporary issues.[30]

Somewhere in this childhood, from a combination of parental influences, a racist milieu, and his own inner resources, Edward developed an uncompromising racial self-consciousness. So effective was this conditioning, he told one interviewer, that "as a boy walking to school, he habitually spat upon the Johns Hopkins University buildings because he knew he could not aspire to enroll there."[31]

Later, after he left Howard University in 1916, Frazier carefully recorded the insults, degradation, and physical attacks that he experienced as a result of racism. Growing up in racist Baltimore, attending school in a thoroughly segregated system, and listening to his father's monologues about indignities, as a young man he already knew he was born on the wrong side of the "color line." He was also, in the words of Drake, "a son of the 'crossways,'" growing up in a community that embodied all the contradictions of rural life in the Deep South and urban life in the rapidly expanding ghettos of the upper South and North.[32] His childhood in Baltimore must have given him a solid foundation for his later insightful essays about the subtle gradations of color prejudice within Afro-American communities and about the Byzantine rituals and etiquette of race relations.

Double Consciousness

Frazier was also an unusually class-conscious race man. Coming from a working-class family, he knew the meaning of hard work from an early age. He had regular jobs by the time he was ten years old, after his father's death, selling papers in the morning before school, delivering groceries after school, contributing his "little pittance" to the survival of the family. Even with a scholarship to Howard University, he was up at five o'clock in the morning washing dishes, stoking boilers, and doing odd jobs to supplement his income.[33] "While going through college," recalled Frazier in 1942, "I was a waiter and bell-hop in hotels and on boats. I was a stevedore for a few weeks in Norfolk, Virginia, and I have done everything in a steel mill except run a crane and press steel."[34]

The economic insecurity of his early years remained a preoccupation throughout his life. When he married Marie Brown in 1922, he insisted on supporting both of them, even though she came from North Carolina's black bourgeoisie and was a strong-willed, independent woman with a college education. In the 1920s he was constantly looking for paid speaking engagements and research jobs to augment his meager faculty salary. "We budgeted our lives," said Frazier's wife. "It wasn't until we went to Fisk in 1929 that things got easier for us." For the next thirty years, they lived a comfortable life, eventually owning their home in Washington, D.C., and a nearby summer cabin. Frazier's frugality and shrewd sense of money in the 1920s and 1930s allowed them to travel and enjoy life in their later years. Nevertheless, until the day he died, he was "completely obsessed" with saving enough money "to leave you," he told his wife, "so you can live well without working."[35]

No doubt this concern about making a living and his familiarity with the world of work from an early age gave Frazier the basis for his class consciousness—an unusual sensitivity to economic nuances and the determining influence of economics on social relations—which characterized his research and writings throughout his life. Moreover, he found it easy to talk to poor and working people, and he made them feel at ease with him. When he began to visit his wife's family in North Carolina, he was more comfortable in conversations with their servants than with their "society" friends. "He would go out and talk to the washerwomen and get them to laugh and they'd have the best time in the world," recalled Marie Brown Frazier. He was "always learning something. . . . People would just open up, just tell him everything they knew."[36] Word about Frazier's ability to relate to rural blacks must have reached Du Bois, then editor of *Crisis* magazine, back in New York in the early 1920s, for Du Bois hired Frazier to do field research in the Deep South, thus beginning a collaboration that would endure until Frazier's death in May 1962.[37]

Somehow and somewhere in his adolescence Frazier also developed a contempt for organized religion and, soon after, a resolute and unwaivering atheism. Both attitudes were unusual and dangerous for a black intellectual prior to the 1920s. Moreover, Frazier did not keep these subversive views to himself. One of his first publications, a pamphlet that he had printed at his own expense during World War I, was a scathing denunciation of the all-too-intimate ties between religion and militarism.[38] By the time he met Marie Brown's friends in 1922, he had a reputation for being an "infidel" with "strange ideas."[39]

Although Frazier was familiar with the central role of religion and the church in Afro-American communities, and he wrote extensively on these topics,[40] he himself was never a believer, not even in his later years. "What intelligent and intellectually honest person believes in the immortality of the soul or that we shall be punished after death for our 'sins,'" he wrote in his diary in 1950.[41] Even in his last months, when he was suffering excruciating pain from cancer, he told his wife, "Honey, when I pass, I want to go from the hospital to the crematory. I don't want you even to know where my ashes are because I don't want any moaning and groaning and visiting the grave and all that foolishness."[42]

Entering the uncertain world of the twentieth century, Frazier must have known exactly what it was like to experience, in the celebrated words of Du Bois, the "peculiar sensation" of a "double-consciousness, this sense of looking at one's self through the eyes of others, of measuring one's soul by the tape of a world that looks in amused contempt and pity. One ever feels his twoness—an American, a Negro; two souls, two thoughts, two unreconciled strivings; two warring ideals in one dark body, whose dogged strength alone keeps it from being torn asunder."[43]

But not only did Frazier battle to exist as both a Negro and an American. He also had to learn how to survive as a smart Negro, as a confirmed atheist, and as an activist interested in radical politics. He would need more than "dogged strength" to survive with his body and self-respect intact. His childhood, as Horace Cayton noted in a memoir, gave him a foundation of moral principles backed up by personal determination. "The matrix of social and personal relations into which he was born—one calculated to humiliate, crush and rob the Negro of his manhood—failed to limit the horizon of the young man. Rather it put iron in Franklin's blood and steel in his backbone."[44]

Several years after Frazier left Baltimore, he wrote a short autobiographical essay about the world of his childhood. It was never published, possibly not even submitted for publication. Written in 1926 or soon after, it is in contemporary language a self-criticism. It does not provide us with any facts or figures, but it reveals a great deal about the social pressures he faced as a promising member of the "talented tenth."[45] In this succinct piece, "In Defense of John Henry," Frazier leaves us a fitting race-and-class-conscious memoir of his youth:

When I was a child in Baltimore there was a saloon in our neighborhood conducted by an Irishman. Among his most noteworthy patrons was a shiftless Negro who was reputed to return his weekly wages each Saturday night to his Irish employer and consume them in drink during the ensuing week. After more than twenty years, memory images the familiar posture of this Negro, Tom F____, as he stood collarless with his trousers held up by one piece of a pair of suspenders or a rope, his left hand resting upon his hip while the other slowly stroked his black unshaven chin. He would generally end such moments of contemplation by suddenly darting into the saloon to resolve the perplexities that were taxing his mind in a glass of beer or whiskey. Not only did Tom become for me the object of all my prejudices against drinking which I have fortunately overcome, but he became the symbolic representative of the "lower elements" of the Negro race

who to my childish imagination were responsible for all the prescriptions
placed upon the Negro. For this wrong I did poor Tom because of my childish ignorance of the world, were it not for the Anti-Saloon League and
other such divine authorities, I would gladly offer a cold stein to cool his
soul in hell as compensation. But as it is, borrowing the words of Langston
Hughes:

If I ever cussed black old Tom
And wished he were in hell,
I am sorry for that evil wish
And now I wish him well.[46]

Keep Well Thy Tongue, 1912–1916

Prior to World War I Afro-American colleges were not hospitable to nonconformists. They were ruled by white boards of trustees who demanded obsequious faculty and docile students. Governance was autocratic and unilateral; the observance of religious conventions was required; and the rules of social life were based on a model of Victorian morality under which even unchaperoned dating might be grounds for expulsion.[1] When Edward Frazier arrived at Howard on a scholarship in 1912, the university had much in common with other black colleges: Its president, Stephen Newman, was a white Congregationalist; attendance at chapel and military training were mandatory; female professors who married after their appointment were automatically fired; and courses on Afro-American or African history were prohibited.[2] During Frazier's senior year of college (1915–16), the board of trustees turned down Alain Locke's request for a course on "interracial relations" and a faculty proposal for a course on "negro problems."[3]

Though northern and urban, Howard exhibited in many ways the same social provincialism and insularity as southern colleges. The *Howard University Journal,* a weekly student newspaper, devoted most of its pages to sports, social events, and gossip. Fraternities were large and active—though Edward was not a member because "he didn't measure up to the social standards"[4]—and the first sorority was organized in 1913, his sophomore year.

Like everybody else, Frazier sat in chapel for four years, though unlike most of his classmates he had no religious inclinations, and he attended "just enough not to be expelled from school." Here he spent hundreds of hours listening to pious and boring speakers who gave him "no intellectual stimulation. All I heard were people from the YMCA and you know there is nothing intellectual at the YMCA. I heard missionaries tell all sorts of tales. I will never forget my introduction to Livingstone in Africa. I heard nothing about the British Empire in Africa. I heard repeatedly about Livingstone's dying on his knees. So I had the impression that Livingstone spent all of his time on his knees. Everything tended to give a sentimental evaluation of life."[5]

However, Frazier was fortunate to be at Howard, the "capstone of Negro education,"[6] where he would discover several loopholes in the general rule that "the Negro intelligentsia was to be suppressed and hammered into conformity."[7] Unlike its southern counterparts, in which Booker T. Washington's model of vocational training had replaced the "higher education" introduced by missionaries during Reconstruction, Howard provided an eclectic curriculum based on classical education and liberal arts.[8] At Howard, social constraints were loosely enforced, allowing a degree of personal freedom that was not tolerated in the South. Moreover, two-thirds of the faculty and the most powerful deans were Afro-American, putting Howard in the vanguard of the black power movement that would sweep southern colleges in the 1920s.[9] Frazier also enjoyed the unique benefits of attending a college that was located in a black community in Washington, D.C., where he was exposed to the latest political and cultural developments. Here he could attend a classical play, a concert by Roland Hayes, or a political debate. He did not get into trouble at Howard, as he did later at Tuskegee, for being too intellectual or too bookish.

Political Maelstrom

When Frazier graduated from Howard in 1916, not only had he acquired the intellectual foundations of a classical education and been exposed to "high culture," he had also sharpened his political wits and developed commitments to socialism, women's suffrage, and racial equality. What was the milieu in which his rebelliousness and driving initiative flourished?

By 1912, when eighteen-year-old Edward arrived at Howard, the Socialist Party was an active force in American politics, with close to 120,000 members and some three hundred periodicals.[10] Though the party's racism prevented it from attracting a large black constituency and in some parts of the country its attitude to race mirrored all the prevailing prejudices of nativism, nevertheless it was able to attract a core of support within the Afro-American middle class. In 1907 Du Bois declared himself a "Socialist of the Path" who, while not advocating the "complete socialization of the means of production," supported "greater ownership of the public wealth for the public good. . . . Watch the Socialists," wrote Du Bois. "We may not follow them and agree with them in all things. I certainly do not. But in trend and ideal they are the salt of this present earth." [11] Du Bois joined the Socialist Party in 1911, resigned in 1912 to support Woodrow Wilson for the presidency, then expressed support again in 1914. [12]

During this same period the organized struggle against racism intensified, as did conflicts between opposing tendencies within the Afro-American movement. In 1909 the National Association for the Advancement of Colored People (NAACP) was initiated by white, liberal philanthropists and reformers concerned about the resurgence of racist attacks, the persistence of lynching, and the denial of civil and political freedom to blacks. Du Bois, the only Afro-American officer, was hired to publicize the organization and edit its journal, *Crisis*. Under his militant leadership, the NAACP "proved, between 1910 and the first World War, one of the most effective organizations of the liberal spirit and the fight for social progress which America has known." [13] In 1911 the National Urban League (NUL) was formed under similar auspices as the NAACP; its focus was on providing social services to newly arrived blacks in urban centers and on opening up job opportunities in segregated industries.

Du Bois and the political tendency that he represented not only eventually challenged the white, liberal leadership of civil rights organizations like the NAACP and NUL but also provided the first serious challenge to the leadership of Booker T. Washington, who, backed by the Tuskegee machine and white capital, preached accommodation to segregation, worked closely with the federal government and business leaders, and dispensed political and economic patronage throughout the United States. At one level, the Washington–Du Bois debate was about the appropriate education for blacks—with Washington advocating vocational training and Du Bois advocating higher education—but in reality it was a struggle between different generations, different political interests, and different visions about the future of American society. [14]

With Washington's death in 1915, during Frazier's senior year, the Du Bois position prevailed, and there was a general shift to the left in black politics. Marcus Garvey arrived in New York in 1917 and generated considerable support for his nationalist organization, the Universal Negro Improvement Association. In the same year two leading Afro-American socialists, A. Philip Randolph and Chandler Owen, formed the first black socialist political club in Harlem and made their magazine, the *Messenger,* a militant voice against racism and capitalism.[15] A few years after he left Howard, Frazier would devote most of his master's thesis to a favorable summary and interpretation of the *Messenger*'s Afro-American socialism. As we shall see, it certainly influenced his attitude to World War I and to the issue of black self-defense.[16]

For Frazier, going to college on the eve of World War I—a time of racial, cultural, and intellectual ferment and controversy—was comparable to the experience of students challenged by the politicized milieu of colleges in the 1930s and 1960s. At Howard, students were not simply vicarious participants in movements for social change who reacted and responded to the world around them, but also a critical part of these movements, direct participants who helped to shape their vision and militancy.

Political events and debates representing a full spectrum of views were quite common at Howard in the years preceding U.S. entry into World War I. For example, President William Howard Taft, running for reelection in 1912 after four years of concessions to southern segregationists,[17] opportunistically and belatedly courted black support in a campus speech advocating an end to lynching—"a disgraceful page in our social history"—and support for the university's effort to raise money for a gymnasium.[18] Representatives of the leading parties in the 1912 presidential race spoke at a "political mass meeting" on campus in November. As noted by a reporter for the campus newspaper, "the audience represented adherents to more political parties than were represented on the stage. There were Democrats, Republicans, Progressives, Socialists, Socialist Progressives, and Prohibitionists; in addition, many suffragettes were present."[19] Moreover, the feminist movement at Howard was sufficiently strong to be able to send the only college delegation to march in a huge suffrage parade in Washington, D.C., a few months later.[20]

Students at Howard who were interested in socialism tended to congregate around the Intercollegiate Socialist Society (ISS), the Social Science Club, and the NAACP. The ISS, organized by the Socialist Party in 1905, was essentially a debating club, created to develop an acceptance of socialist ideas among students and intellectuals. It was a means for recruiting socialists, but it also accepted a range of members, including nonsocialists. By 1915 there were ISS chapters in over sixty colleges and universities.[21] Howard's ISS was involved primarily in bringing speakers to campus, such as Harry Laidler, who spoke about how "the city of the future" would be planned, collectively owned, and democratically managed.[22] The chapter subscribed to a utopian, evolutionary vision of socialism that emphasized collective ownership and rational planning. "There are many obstacles to an adoption of all the socialist principles," noted Howard's ISS in an article for the campus newspaper, "yet they are gradually creeping into our national institutions. This is coming about not because we are adopting formal socialism but because the spirit of the age is socialistic."[23]

A NAACP chapter, established on campus in 1913, organized lectures by prominent speakers, collected funds for the national organization, and encouraged its members to be active in the struggle for the "full enjoyment of . . . rights as citizens, justice in all courts and equality of opportunity everywhere."[24] In its first public statement, it called upon "fellow collegians" to "consider how the Negro is deprived of respect as a human being" and to "not be misled by superficial and immediate gain, but stand on fundamental and universal principles. . . . Anything less than absolute unrestricted opportunity is not only unjust but detrimental to progress and prosperity."[25] The chapter was activist as well as educational. When the university administration refused to incorporate a course on race relations into the curriculum, the NAACP and Social Science Club cosponsored a series of lectures by Locke, "Race Contacts and Inter-racial Relations."[26] In October 1913 the Howard chapter was in "full attendance" at a mass meeting called by the NAACP to mobilize opposition to Jim Crow policies in Washington, D.C.[27] In 1915, following the release of *The Birth of a Nation,* the chapter circulated a petition signed by a majority of the student body that played an important role in making sure that the racist movie was not shown on campus.[28] A few years later, when the movie was revived, Frazier would find himself in a New York jail for marching on a NAACP-organized picket line.[29]

The Social Science Club also held regular meetings on campus, involving students in discussions about labor organizing, race relations, and economic conditions. In a typical event sponsored by the club, representatives of the Waiters' Union spoke "forcefully and without mincing their words" about exploitation in local hotels and called on students to support their strike.[30] At another event, a welfare worker talked about her personal experiences in a paper mill in Holyoke, Massachusetts, a "great manufacturing town owned and controlled by the mill owners" where "no relief of the present situation of nonsanitation, low wages and the like is possible except by organization of the laborers."[31] The leftist political inclinations of the Social Science Club were underscored when it decided in 1914 to affiliate with the ISS.[32]

Students at Howard were used to hearing informed speakers who addressed the burning issues of the day. Kelly Miller, who taught sociology at Howard, often gave public lectures, and his essays on politics, race relations and education were widely published in professional and popular journals.[33] Du Bois was also a regular speaker at Howard during Frazier's undergraduate years. He gave an "elegant and masterly" speech, "The Political Program of the Colored American," in the second month of Frazier's freshman year.[34] In March 1913 Du Bois delivered a series of lectures on "The History of the Negro," the basis of his 1915 book *The Negro*, which would be the first "readable history of the Negro race, written by a member of the race . . . , [to] reveal our history in the making of the world."[35]

A year later Du Bois was back on campus, lecturing on work and careers, the feminist movement, and socialism. He appealed to the students' idealism, urging them to pursue careers that would give them the joy of accomplishment and the esteem of their peers rather than only the "rolling up of wealth." Women were entitled to the same career opportunities as men, he noted, and "industries belong rightly to the community, and the community must own them, chiefly . . . through government ownership." Under socialism "merit would come into its own," and "the exclusiveness of the world which denies to the masses the right to exercise their fitness for the higher positions of life would be broken down, and genius would arise on every hand." The reporter for the campus newspaper, no doubt impressed by Du Bois's lectures, encouraged "all students to study Socialism, at least with the purpose of understanding its principles if not actually adopting its tenets."[36]

Du Bois's ideas at this time went far beyond the parochialism of even the most progressive views about race relations. He must have given

Frazier and other young students at Howard a powerful and positive sense of their historical roots and their potential for building a new world order. To Du Bois, then editor of *Crisis,* the struggles for racial equality and socialism were complementary, each one organically linked to the other. Negroes, noted Du Bois, "are today girding themselves to fight in the van of progress, not simply for their own rights as men, but for the ideals of the greater world in which they live: the emancipation of women, universal peace, democratic government, the socialization of wealth, and human brotherhood. . . . Already the more far-seeking Negroes sense the coming unities: a unity of the working classes everywhere, a unity of the colored races, a new unity of men. . . . A belief in humanity means a belief in colored men. The future world will, in all reasonable probability, be what colored men make it."[37]

Some Kind of Socialist

This, then, was the maelstrom that awaited Frazier at college. At Howard he found a new world that must have confirmed and given purpose to the rebellious experiences of his adolescence. He entered it with enthusiasm and pleasure, making the most of all that it offered. During his four undergraduate years, he was a member of the ISS and Drama Club, president of the Social Science, German, and Political Science clubs, vice-president of the NAACP, class critic, and president of his class in 1915.[38]

In addition, he worked a variety of jobs during the school year and summers—waiter, bellhop, stevedore, and so on—to augment his meager scholarship, and yet he still was able to graduate *cum laude* in four years. His peers voted him the second most "brilliant" member of his class.[39] Frazier "found the atmosphere [at Howard] very uncongenial for scholarly and idealistic tasks,"[40] but he nevertheless threw himself into the life of the campus and pursued a rigorous program of self-improvement. Coming "from a family that did not have a literary tradition," Frazier decided to take four years of English and "by writing a composition every day, I learned to write."[41]

Almost forty years after he graduated from Howard, Frazier's memories were vivid and positive: "During my college days at Howard University, when my curiosity to learn everything was at fever heat, my course of study embraced a wide range of courses, including mathematics and physical science, literature, Latin, Greek, French, German, as well as the social sciences with the exception of sociology because I heard that it was not presented in a serious fashion."[42] This was Frazier's polite way of saying that he avoided sociology because it was taught by Miller, whose politics were cautiously reformist and who was closely identified with Booker T. Washington's "Black Cabinet" in Washington, D.C.[43]

Of the professors at Howard, he was most impressed by those who, to use his words, were "firm" and "precise"—men like David Houston in English, George Lightfoot in Latin, E. P. Davis in Greek, and Carl Murphy in English.[44] His undergraduate courses included four years (or eight semesters) of English, three years of German, two years of Latin, two years of Greek, five semesters of history, plus economics, math, philosophy, and education. This broad, classical foundation would serve him well in his teaching jobs and future work in sociology.[45] One semester of French was enough to equip him to teach the subject in his first teaching jobs. His facility with languages enabled him in later years, as the stories go, to read aloud to his wife the Portugese version of *Gone with the Wind* during a trip to Brazil in 1940 and to write *Black Bourgeoisie* in French in Parisian cafés in the 1950s.[46]

This young, working-class Afro-American from Baltimore quickly found himself so steeped in classical culture and European languages that he was nicknamed Plato and chose a quotation from Chaucer for his yearbook statement: "The first virtue, son, if thou wilt learn, is to keep well thy tongue."[47] But Frazier did little to heed his own advice. His "wicked tongue," which would keep him on the edge of danger all his life, was fully exercised at Howard, where Frazier deepened his interest in race relations and began to explore socialist politics.[48] All politically minded black intellectuals of this era found it virtually impossible to separate their scholarly interests from the struggle for social equality. "One could not be a calm, cool, and detached scientist," observed Du Bois, "while Negroes were lynched, murdered and starved."[49] But choices could be made about the kind of activism one pursued, and Frazier chose the most militant wing of the student movement.

He was deeply involved in the ISS, the Social Science club, and the NAACP, all of which were the center of debates about social and racial equality, and the organizing impetus for student activism. Given that he was an officer of two of these organizations and was identified by his peers as one of the most daring members of his class,[50] it is clear that Edward's political identity was forged during his four years at Howard.

We know of at least one incident that indicates his activism. Howard was invited to send a delegation to participate in Wilson's inaugural parade during March of Frazier's freshman year. The parade was segregated, and Howard was asked to bring up the rear of the Afro-American section. Frazier joined a group of students who opposed this decision and took the position that all colleges should march in alphabetical order. The inaugural committee offered as a compromise that Howard could march at the end of the white college section.[51] Frazier "held out for his original request, but was deserted by the members of his committee." He refused to march in the parade and felt vindicated when he overheard a white woman who was watching the march say, "Look at those poor things bringing up the rear." This incident, Frazier told Davis, "crystallized in him a resentment against compromise which he never lost."[52]

Those who had some indirect knowledge about Frazier's formative years confirmed that he was an activist in college and subscribed to a vaguely radical political philosophy. "His approach was that of a socialist" (St. Clair Drake); he was an "avowed socialist" (G. Franklin Edwards); he had "a tendency towards giving socialist interpretations" (Randolph); he was "anti-capitalist. He was some kind of socialist. He didn't think that capitalist economic structures were good" (Marie Brown Frazier).[53] Frazier himself was not specific about his political ideas in the 1912–1916 period. Not until 1920, when he wrote his master's thesis, did he give a full statement about his personal views on the "New Currents of Thought among the Colored People of America."

But there is no doubt that by the time he left Howard in 1916 his ideological perspective had begun to crystallize, his youthful rebelliousness was still very much intact, and he had demonstrated that he was not afraid to act on his beliefs. "While in college," he recalled in 1950, "I had developed a keen interest in social problems."[54] An indication of the breadth of this interest can be found in his first publication, an article written for the campus newspaper in 1916. The topic was not race relations nor racism nor sociology. "Woman suffrage like Socialism," wrote Frazier, "marks the progress of the ages. It means a new interpretation of woman as Socialism means a new interpretation of capital. And consistent with man's attempt to rise above the material aspects of things, it raises woman from the plane of an objective beautiful creation for enjoyment to the realm of a subjective thinking creature to enjoy the fruits of existence." Frazier went on to criticize "extravagances" in the feminist movement and analogies to the "disenfranchised Negro" but concluded that woman suffrage was "a step taken by advancing humanity that cannot be diverted by those who fail to understand the sign of the times."[55]

With the United States on the brink of entering World War I, the "progress of the ages" would be severely tested, as would Frazier's beliefs and commitments as he left Howard in 1916—a smart, literate, self-confident, political Afro-American headed south for his first job at Booker T. Washington's Tuskegee, a bastion of patriotism, religion, and appeasement.

A Cruel and Devastating War, 1916–1918

"Will teach" was Edward Frazier's farewell prediction when he graduated from Howard University in 1916.[1] He had been exposed to worldy ideas, but he had seen little of the world outside of Baltimore and Washington, D.C. Life still had much to teach him.

In the next six years, before he moved to his first full-time teaching job at Morehouse College in Atlanta in 1922, he compensated for his provincial upbringing. He taught math at Tuskegee Institute in Alabama (1916–17), summer school at Fort Valley High and Industrial School in Georgia (1917), English and history at St. Paul's Normal and Industrial School in Virginia (1917–18), and math at Baltimore High School (1918). In 1918–19, he studied sociology at Clark University, a white liberal arts college in Worcester, Massachusetts, followed by another year of study and research (1920–21) at the New York School of Social Work. Finally, his last year (1921–22) of travels before settling in Atlanta was spent mostly in Denmark studying folk schools and rural cooperatives. During this stay in Europe, he also visited Germany, England, and France, where he attended the Second Pan-African Congress in Paris.

Cowardice and Sycophancy

Tuskegee must have been a sobering and clarifying experience for Frazier. Established in 1881 by Booker T. Washington in Alabama, not far from Selma and Birmingham, Tuskegee was the best known Negro

college in the United States. Part trade school, part education in self-
help, Tuskegee was much more than a third-class southern university.
It was the center of Washington's political base, from which he dispensed influence and patronage, and received visitors from banks,
boardrooms, and embassies.[2] The university was run with an iron hand,
with faculty and students alike subjected to a strictly enforced Victorian
code of prudery and discipline.[3]

To Frazier, "a landmark in Negro education, so far as the white man
was concerned, was reached when a type of education was discovered
that concerned itself with this world and at the same time did not disturb
the Negro as a worker. Tuskegee has stood in the white man's imagination as such a reconciliation."[4] Tuskegee's program accommodated
both the desire of southern whites for an educated black class that
would not challenge policies of segregation and the need of northern
capitalists for a "skilled, tractable, and hard-working . . . laboring
class."[5] Not surprisingly, the prosperity of Tuskegee was guaranteed in
1903 by a six-hundred-thousand-dollar gift from Andrew Carnegie,
who also helped to launch the National Negro Business League and
other black capitalist ventures. Other financial support came from John
D. Rockefeller, Julius Rosenwald, Andrew Mellon, H. H. Rogers, and
George Eastman. By the 1920s the combined endowment of Tuskegee
and the Hampton Institute, which was essentially a trade school, was
seven times that of Fisk and Howard.[6]

The year before Frazier went to Tuskegee, Washington assured his
benefactors that there was no danger of a New Negro emerging at his
college. "If education does not make the Negro humble, simple, and of
service to the community," said Washington in 1915, "then it will not
be encouraged."[7] With Washington's death the same year, perhaps Frazier thought that Tuskegee might be open to the winds of liberal change
that were sweeping through black colleges.

He was wrong. Robert Russa Moton, Washington's successor, who
had worked for twenty-five years as commandant of cadets at Hampton, was determined to turn back the clock, if that was possible. Frazier's future wife, Marie Brown, knew Moton well because her mother
was a classmate of Moton's and they used to visit him at Hampton. He
was "big and black enough to be a leader," but "I never thought of him
in any terms as an intellectual or thinker."[8] Major Moton, as he liked
to be called, worked hard to "keep the good will of the southern
white community, and all the old Booker T. traditions were carefully
abided by."[9]

These "traditions" made Tuskegee a combination of British boarding school and Marine Corps camp, where male students were organized into quasi-military regiments that drilled on campus; all students were required to have a Bible and attend daily religious services; tobacco and alcohol were prohibited; dating was chaperoned; and mail was opened and censored. Tuskegee even maintained a separate residence and dining hall for white guests. When Moton's wife was thrown out of a segregated Pullman coach in 1916, just before Frazier arrived at the college, Moton allowed the trustees to issue a humiliating statement announcing that he repudiated social equality.[10]

Frazier did not write much about his personal experiences at Tuskegee, but a few memorable anecdotes give us some indication of why he developed an antipathy to Moton and how he became much more militant than he had been in his attitude to race relations. According to the sociologist Horace Cayton, who worked for a few months at Tuskegee in the 1930s, Frazier refused to pay a voting tax to the city of Tuskegee on the grounds that Afro-Americans were not allowed to vote. The university administration smoothed over the controversy by paying the tax for him and taking it out of his salary.[11]

Frazier was also once "told by the Director of the Academic Department to stop walking across the campus with books under his arms because white people passed through the campus and would get the impression that Tuskegee Institute was training the Negro's intellect rather than his heart and hand."[12] Frazier in a candid moment, recalled another incident:

> In order not to act differently I placed in my room a bale of hay, some bricks on my desk, and some cotton. That was to conform—not to be radical. I was teaching mathematics—arithmetic and algebra. . . . Everything had to be concrete and this created some amusing situations. For instance I was teaching algebra which is purely symbolic if you understand what algebra is. A man said I ought to have a cube but I told him he didn't know what he was talking about and that he didn't know what algebra was all about. Then again one student asked me why I kept a bale of hay in the room since, he said a little embarrassed, "Prof., you never use it." I said that it was for the asses in here to eat and went on with the lecture.[13]

These experiences at Tuskegee left Frazier embittered about the politics of black education in the South but with a sharp awareness of the depths of racism as well as an increasing consciousness of his political commitments. Whatever respect he had felt for Booker T. Washington, with whose policies he profoundly disagreed, turned to disgust with the "reactionary policy" of Tuskegee under Moton's leadership:

> The position at Tuskegee carries with it the tacit assumption of the leadership of the Negro race in America. Moton has accepted this position and become the spokesman of the dwindling conservative school of thought. Washington, during his career, had broadened his program so that he had allowed a place for higher education for the more gifted members of his race; had denounced lynching, although emphasizing the harm it did the white man; and had advocated the admission of Negroes into politics after a period of schooling in the elements of civilization. But Moton, who has neither the vision nor the genius of his illustrious predecessor, has become, in his attempt to imitate the diplomacy and meekness of spirit of the former, a model of humiliating cowardice and sycophancy. Meekness in the master was noble but in the imitator has become grovelling. Moton condones the crimes of the whites against the Negro and declares that the average white man in the South treats the Negro with absolute fairness and the Negro has unreasonable ill-feeling against his white brother.[14]

Probably by mutual agreement, Frazier left Tuskegee in 1917. He later found himself in the illustrious company of Claude McKay, who had gone there to study agriculture but left within a year, complaining about its "machinelike existence."[15] In the 1930s Cayton survived less than a summer working at Tuskegee. "The experience left me shaken, and I was glad when I could start north again," wrote Cayton in his autobiography. "The ignorance of the South, its sudden violence, and the hopelessness of its people had thoroughly disheartened and discouraged me. I had felt like an alien in a strange country."[16]

By mid-1917 Frazier was considering his possibilities and choices. Though he was thinking for the first time of graduate study in sociology, the war and draft were on his mind. President Wilson had formally declared war against Germany on April 6th, and Frazier was scheduled to be drafted under the Selective Service Act.[17] During the summer he found a job teaching at Fort Valley High and Industrial School in central Georgia. A private school, supported primarily by northern philanthropists, Fort Valley did "all the public-school work for Negroes in the town." Unlike Tuskegee, Fort Valley was a place where Frazier enjoyed teaching; he especially appreciated the efforts of its principal and teachers to take educational programs out of the school and into rural areas, building a sense of community solidarity where none previously existed.[18]

If Frazier was still not clear about his career or future at this time, he was quite clear about his political beliefs and commitments. "After leaving college I continued my interest in socialism," recalled Frazier in 1951. "But after accepting my first teaching appointment at Tuskegee Institute, I began to take an intense interest in the Negro problem. I was militant in my opposition to the existing race relations and urged young Negroes to assume a militant attitude toward discrimination and oppression."[19]

God and War

As late as June, Frazier must have hoped to avoid military service. On the advice of Kelly Miller, who taught sociology at Howard, he wrote to the president of Clark University, applying for a scholarship "to pursue courses in Sociology." He told Clark's president, G. Stanley Hall, that he had spent the last year "not only in increasing my knowledge of sociology by reading but also in observing at close view social conditions afforded by Alabama and Georgia." Two days later Hall offered Frazier an appointment as a University Scholar in Sociology, which exempted him from any academic fees and made him eligible to apply for a fellowship. Not obtaining any response, Hall again wrote to Frazier on July 5th, the final day for all able-bodied men between the ages of twenty-one and thirty-one to register for the draft. By this time, the military had caught up with Frazier, and he was drafted. Frazier wrote to Clark University, asking them to postpone his scholarship "until a later date when released from requirements now made upon the manhood of the country."[20]

Frazier was "bitterly opposed" to the war and, according to Marie Brown Frazier, "tried to dodge the draft."[21] Years later, Frazier reminisced about his antiwar views. He was not a pacifist. "I resented being drafted in a war which, in my opinion, was essentially a conflict between imperialistic powers and in view of the treatment of the Negro in the United States, the avowed aim, to make the world safe for democracy, represented hypocrisy on the part of America."[22] But however much he opposed and resented the war, he registered for the draft on June 4th and did not pursue an exemption from military service. The fact that he was the major support of his mother helped to keep him from being sent to Europe.[23]

Aside from talking to his wife, Frazier did not discuss with his friends or write about his military service. He gave the impression to one colleague that he "never set foot in any army camp."[24] It was an impression that he no doubt cultivated, given his unambiguous opposition to the war. For example, when he filled out a government form in order to get a security clearance for a job with UNESCO in 1961, he completed every category except "military service," which he left blank.[25]

Whatever the circumstances surrounding Frazier's avoidance of military service until the summer of 1918—whether he traveled from job to job in 1917–18 in order to dodge service or whether his assignment was delayed because of bureaucratic incompetence or whether the local draft boards in the South refused to draft him simply because he was black—he finally ended up working for about two and a half months, from the end of June to early September 1918, as a business secretary at Camp Humphreys, Virginia.[26]

Though it was a paid job (eighty-five dollars per month) under the auspices of the YMCA, Frazier's employer was the War Work Council, U.S. War Department, and he was required to sign a contract that affirmed: "(1) That I have no conscientious objections to such a war as the one in which we are engaged. (2) That I heartily support the policy of the United States to fight the war to a victorious end. (3) That I am convinced that the cause of the allies is the cause of justice and freedom, and that I will use my official position to foster a similar conviction on the part of all with whom I come in contact." It must have been humiliating for Frazier to sign the oath, but he complied.[27] Furthermore, the camp was segregated, and Frazier was assigned to "colored work" as a secretary and purchasing agent.[28]

During World War I the YMCA provided close to ten thousand "war secretaries" who essentially performed welfare services in the camps. Though he later told his wife that he tried to undermine the war effort by informally "preaching" his antiwar views to recruits at the camp,[29] his service was uneventful, and he apparently accommodated himself to Camp Humphreys with its segregated religious services, its officers' training school "open to enlisted men, except colored troops," and its huge theater, where white audiences watched Afro-American entertainers demonstrate that "a talent for singing and dancing seems to be inherent in every colored man."[30]

Although the Socialist Party led a militant fight against U.S. involvement in the war—and many of its leaders were imprisoned under a

series of security measures adopted by the Wilson administration—and
the antiwar movement ranged from individual efforts to evade service
to organized demonstrations,[31] U.S. entry into the war had extensive
political and popular support. Frazier's position was certainly a minority viewpoint in the United States, and, among Afro-American intellectuals and professionals, his views on the war were quite heretical.
"There is no reason for the Negro to be an intense nationalist," he wrote
in 1924. "When his leaders boasted after the War that there was not one
Negro conscientious objector, they reflected the subservient and short-
sighted outlook of Negro leaders."[32]

This was a criticism not only of Moton, who worked closely with the
Wilson administration to generate black support for the war effort, but
also of progressive organizations and leading liberal figures, including
Du Bois, who urged his followers to "forget our special grievances and
close our ranks shoulder to shoulder with our white fellow citizens and
the allied nations that are fighting for democracy."[33] As one historian
has noted, "during World War I it would have been difficult to find a
more fully committed patriot than W.E.B. Du Bois."[34] Not only did Du
Bois lend his political and moral support to the war, but also, through
J. E. Spingarn's efforts, he was nearly given a captaincy in the War
Department's Intelligence Bureau. Du Bois was upset when the appointment was not made, the result of combined opposition from southern whites and a few powerful members of the NAACP's board who
wanted him to remain as full-time editor of *Crisis*.[35]

Under the leadership of Spingarn, the whole NAACP mobilized
Afro-American support for the war effort. The main concerns of the
NAACP were that southern blacks be allowed into the army and that
opportunities be made for them to become officers.[36] There was hardly
any discussion about opposition to the war, especially after Du Bois
issued his call to "close our ranks." Even the battle for integrated training of officers was quickly abandoned as Spingarn urged followers of
the NAACP to "show that the colored people of the country are loyal to
the flag, and to disprove the damnable charges of disloyalty that are
being made by the enemies of the race."[37] By May 1917 the NAACP
board of directors had voted its endorsement of a segregated officers'
facility.[38] Howard University assumed the forefront in rallying Afro-
American support for the war and in recruiting students to train as officers in Jim Crow camps. Miller, now dean of arts and sciences, played
a prominent role on campus in winning support for Spingarn's efforts

to recruit blacks into the war.[39] Before the war was over, two hundred thousand Afro-Americans would serve in army camps at home and another two hundred thousand would serve in France.[40]

Frazier's opposition to the war was the first of several disagreements of principle that he had with Du Bois. It was a mark of his growing political maturity and independence that only a year out of college he could break from the man whose lectures and books had so impressed him at Howard. On the issue of the war at least, Frazier had more in common with the black socialists A. Philip Randolph and Chandler Owen, who used their magazine, the *Messenger,* to rally opposition to the war. Addressing President Wilson, they wrote: "Lynching, Jim Crow, segregation, discrimination in the armed forces and out, disenfranchisement of millions of black souls in the South—all these things make your cry of making the world safe for democracy a sham, a mockery, a rape on decency and a travesty on common justice."[41]

It is not known exactly when Frazier became definitively resolved in his opposition to the war. The United States entered the war in April 1917; Frazier registered for the draft in June; and the first issue of the *Messenger* appeared in November. Some time in late 1917 or 1918 Frazier wrote *God and War,* a fifteen-page antiwar pamphlet he published himself and sold for fifteen cents per copy.[42] Though the style of writing in this pamphlet owes more to Du Bois than to Randolph and Owen, it is evident that he was influenced by the *Messenger*'s antiwar stand and that its existence gave credibility and courage to Frazier's decision, especially when the NAACP and other black organizations began to beat the war drums.

God and War was Frazier's first publication, aside from the brief article he wrote for the campus newspaper. It was also one of the first public statements against the war by an Afro-American intellectual. Written in the literary and philosophical tradition of *The Souls of Black Folk,* it expresses a utopian belief in progress through "Truth." Frazier at that time shared Du Bois's view, quite popular among pre-World War I intellectuals, that ignorance was a root cause of social injustice. "The Negro problem was in my mind a matter of systematic investigation and intelligent understanding," recalled Du Bois. "The world was thinking wrong about race, because it did not know. The ultimate evil was stupidity. The cure for it was knowledge based on scientific investigation."[43]

God and War is often crude and rhetorical, which is to be expected from a recent undergraduate, but it is also a bold critique of prevailing views about nationalism and institutionalized religion. It is primarily, though, a statement against a "cruel and devastating war" and a call for a new humanism. To Frazier, war and religion were the two "nurses" of mankind who in the past were necessary in order to develop nation states and group morality. "But now Man can dismiss the nurse, War, by abolishing international commercial competition and 'Spheres of influence.' The infidel no longer threatens Europe, and Africa was not made for European exploitation." Frazier argued that organized religion had become more like the "attempts of a magician to inspire fear" and that "such a pernicious system . . . may be religion but it certainly is not morality."

"Allegiance to humanity is the true religion," wrote Frazier. "A moral life is a life of activity in society." There should be no place in religion for magic or superstition. "If people are to be moral they must be taught that evil and human suffering are the inexorable consequences of a bad act and that all the prayers in the world, the building of libraries and the reading of scripture can not stop the operation of these laws. Penance can not make the crooked back of the wage-slave straight nor can it give sight to the child born blind through the ignorance of the parent." Frazier concluded his polemic by calling on the reader to break the "sacred images" that "keep the unlettered in superstition and exempt the educated from moral responsibilities. . . . Man is the only divinity we know and need to know. . . . He has eaten of the Tree of Knowledge and some day may eat of the Tree of Life. Earth will become his only heaven and exile his only hell."[44]

Frazier's ideological development during World War I set a pattern that would characterize his political praxis throughout his life. First, he took an uncompromising and unpopular stand against "sacred images," challenging not only prevailing white sensibilities but also the liberal orthodoxy of progressive black leaders. Second, he chose public opinion as his arena of struggle, and his preferred weapon was the written word, especially the polemic. Occasionally an activist, he would generally express his dissent on the battleground of ideas rather than on the picket line. Third, although a supporter of causes and organizations, Frazier preferred to express his politics individually, even individualistically at times, and typically chose to act as the lone rebel, deliberately putting himself outside the discipline and constraints of any collectivity.

The following unpublished memoir, written by Frazier several years after the war, captures both his rebelliousness and the sense of satisfaction he felt when he challenged established authority. Here again, albeit in a new form, is the adolescent who spat on the walls of Johns Hopkins, the undergraduate who refused to march with his classmates at the back of the inaugural parade, and the young teacher who took a bale of hay into his classroom at Tuskegee:

This happened during the war when I was a youngster just out of college. A husky friend of mine, with whom I had played football, and I were walking down the street one day in Baltimore when we noticed an advertisement for educated men to join the Marine Corps. Knowing that Negroes were excluded from this branch of the military organization, I suggested to my friend that we go into the recruiting office and apply for admission to the Marine Corps. Since both of us were young and husky we felt equal to any emergency which might arise. When we presented ourselves, the officer in charge, very condescendingly, but smilingly told us that we had made a mistake and that we should apply down the street where they were enlisting sailors. But I insisted with apparent naivete, that I did not want to join that branch of the service but that since we were educated, we wanted to join the Marine Corps. The officer in charge went on to explain that colored recruits were only accepted as mess boys and attendants in the Navy. He went on to explain: "Don't you see that if colored people were in the Marine Corps they would have to eat with white people." I replied, "O, yes, I never thought of that, that would be terrible wouldn't it?" The man in charge seemed to be a little irritated but made no reply to my ironical remark. I turned away as if I were going to leave and then came back and said, "If I cannot become a full-fledged Marine, could I be taken on as a sub-marine?" The man became furious and blurted out inaudible remarks. I simply smiled and left with my friend.[45]

4

Learning Sociology, 1919–1920

When Frazier finally went to Clark University in 1919 to pursue a graduate degree in sociology, he was one of a select cohort of young Afro-American intellectuals who suddenly found themselves courted by graduate programs in northern and midwestern universities. Prior to World War I only fourteen blacks in the United States received Ph.D. degrees from recognized universities. This number increased to fifty-one by 1929, when Frazier was completing his coursework for his doctorate in sociology at the University of Chicago. He was one of seventy Afro-Americans awarded doctoral degrees between 1930 and 1934.[1]

Transformation of Race Relations

Frazier's individual experience reflected profound economic, social, and political changes that were taking place in race relations at the end of World War I. The decline of the plantation economy in the South and the drastic reduction in emigration from Europe because of the war triggered a massive migration of rural blacks to urban centers. By 1919 some four hundred thousand Afro-Americans had been drafted into the segregated armed forces, where they tasted a new life, both bitter and hopeful, during World War I. Northern communities created by the migration of another four hundred thousand southerners searching for jobs and freedom emerged from the war as permanent ghettoes. In 1900, ninety percent of the Afro-American population lived in the South; by

41

1936 twenty-one percent were in the North, the majority concentrated in the growing metropolitan centers.[2]

By the early 1920s not only were blacks living increasingly in urban areas outside the South, but they were also working increasingly in industry. In the period of labor shortage during and after World War I, labor agents employed by large corporations went into the South to recruit thousands of workers for the railroads, steel mills, and automobile plants. When the labor shortage of the war period was over, employers continued to draw on unskilled black workers as a means of lowering wages, combating a militant but racist union movement, and creating a diversified and therefore more manageable labor force.[3] Between 1910 and 1920 the number of black men employed in manufacturing and mechanical industries increased by forty percent, in transportation by twenty-two percent, and in the extraction of minerals by twenty percent. The same period saw a significant increase in the number of black women employed in commercial laundries, food industries, and clothing trades. By 1928 black employees constituted thirty percent of the work force in the largest packing houses in Chicago; in 1919, twelve percent of the workers at the United States Steel Corporation plant in Homestead, Pennsylvania; in 1923, twenty-one percent of the workers in twenty-three steel mills in and around Pittsburgh; and by 1929 Afro-Americans were regularly employed in Detroit automobile plants.[4]

Black labor, like previous waves of immigrant labor, was used to break strikes and depress wages in industries where, especially between 1919 and 1922, the labor movement had shown its strength through strikes and union organizing. The American Federation of Labor's policies facilitated this tactic by excluding black workers from craft unions. Also, as Sterling Spero and Abram Harris noted, the use of blacks as strikebreakers was often supported by "race leaders" who argued that "after all the employer is the black man's best friend" because Afro-American workers were able to get a footing in industries where the union movement was weak and "where the white worker's opposition to his employment has consequently carried little weight."[5] The NUL, for example, encouraged strikebreaking and, as Frazier recognized, "went into plants to discourage Negroes from organizing."[6]

As blacks moved northward and into industrial jobs, a wave of racist violence swept the country. Bloody race riots erupted in 1917 in East St. Louis, where some fifty people were killed; they spread to several cities, culminating in the "red summer" of 1919, when thirty-eight people were killed and hundreds injured in Chicago.[7] Du Bois and other civil rights leaders, who earlier had encouraged their constituencies to join the war effort in the hope of postwar concessions, recognized that ground was being lost, not won. "We are cowards and jackasses if, now that the war is over," wrote Du Bois in 1919, "we do not marshall every ounce of our brain and brawn to fight a sterner, longer, more unbending battle against the forces of hell in our own land. We *return*. We *return from fighting*. We *return fighting*."[8]

These economic and demographic changes had significant consequences for the social organization and class relations of black communities. There was rapid growth of a new and influential, albeit small, stratum of the middle class—intellectuals, political leaders, writers, civil rights activists, lawyers, and other professionals—who began to share and supplant the traditional power of preachers and teachers. With urbanization and proletarianization came what Frazier called the "black bourgeoisie," which, in reality, was a petty bourgeoisie.[9] Politically, it was a highly diversified group, ranging from advocates of Tuskegee's policies of appeasement, through the NAACP and NUL with their program of interracial liberalism, to socialist and nationalist organizations. This emergence of the New Negro was countered by the renewed effort of old-fashioned segregationists, who were backed up by eugenics and other "scientific" justifications for white supremacy.

Scientific Racism

The recruitment of prospective Afro-American intellectuals into higher education was achieved, but not motivated, by corporate philanthropy. Farsighted foundations, such as the Rockefeller Foundation, Rosenwald Fund, and the Russell Sage Foundation, began to provide scholarships for black graduate students and to finance research on Afro-American communities. "It seems that ever since the Negro has been free," noted Frazier in his typically sardonic manner, "some foundation has watched over his destiny. Right after Emancipation the Peabody Fund was giving him wrong advice. Then later on the Rosenwald Fund corrupted his leaders."[10]

Concerned by the volatility of race relations and the increasing militancy of the New Negro, some business and political leaders looked to higher education as a way of training future leaders who would steer an alternative course to the Afro-American socialism of the *Messenger* and the Pan-Africanism of Du Bois and the Garvey movement. As one sociologist warned, "There is a large and steadily increasing group of men, more or less related to the Negro by blood and wholly identified with him by American social usage, who refuse to accept quietly the white man's attitude toward race. . . . The white man is no wiser than the ostrich if he refuses to see the truth that in the possibilities of race friction the Negro's increasing consciousness of race is to play a part scarcely less important than the white man's racial antipathies, prejudices, or whatever we may elect to call them."[11]

Although many young Afro-American intellectuals like Frazier were eager to go to graduate schools so that they could be equipped to become fighters for the "spiritual and intellectual emancipation of the Negro,"[12] they quickly found themselves in an academic milieu that, though socially liberal compared with black colleges, was extremely paternalistic and demanded a high level of ideological conformity. Dissent was tolerated only within limited parameters. At the turn of the century, academics could not take progressive positions on controversial issues and expect to keep their jobs. During World War I an informal loyalty oath was administered, and dissidents were fired for any expression of an unpatriotic attitude.[13]

With the exception of Du Bois's work, which was not taken seriously by most intellectuals,[14] academic writing on race relations ranged from the moderate interracial diplomacy of the Chicago Commission on Race Relations[15] to the defense of white, Western civilization in the name of "scientific racism."[16] At least until the late 1920s, as Frazier pointed out in a 1946 paper, sociological writings on "the Negro problem" were merely rationalizations of the existing racial situation" and were based on "several fairly clear assumptions: that the Negro is an inferior race because of either biological or social heredity or both; that the Negro because of his physical character cannot be assimilated; and that physical amalgamation is bad and undesirable."[17]

After the war, even Frazier's moderate socialism was beyond the pale of the most liberal elements in academia. Franklin Giddings, a leading sociologist whose textbook had influenced Frazier to pursue a career in sociology,[18] regarded "the socialistic dream" to be "the most serious of all dangers, since it attempts to establish that illegitimate democracy, which consists in the absolute rule of the least competent part of the population, to the exclusion of all remaining portions of the people." [19] John Spargo, another influential academic, called attention to a "bolshevist nucleus in America composed of virile, red-blooded Americans, whose conditions of life and labor are such as to develop in them the psychology of reckless, despairing, revengeful bolshevism." Spargo compared these "bolshevists" to "over-emotionalized religious enthusiasts" with "marked hysterical characteristics." [20] Such was the irrational nature of academic discourse about socialism after World War I.

During this first red scare and in the wake of the red summer of 1919 Frazier left the South and on a scholarship went to Clark University in Massachusetts, where he received his introduction to the nascent discipline of sociology. "Under Professor Hankins," recalled Frazier, "I began seriously my career as a sociologist. I have a feeling that the intellectual discipline which I received during my year at Clark University had a marked influence on my development as a sociologist. It provided me with a broad intellectual outlook that was uncontaminated by such matters of expediency as interracial policies in the United States." [21]

From September 1919 to June 1920 Frazier was enrolled as a graduate student at Clark, where he took ten courses, primarily in the social sciences—history of sociological theories, problems of social reconstruction, principles of economics, principles of education—but also in statistics, philosophy, and neurology. He took a seminar from G. Stanley Hall and three courses from Frank Hankins, who was both his adviser and supervisor of his thesis. [22] Hankins had learned his sociology from Giddings at Columbia University and then spent the first half of his successful career at Clark before going on to Smith College in 1922. Trained by one of the pioneers in American sociology and active in professional sociology circles, Hankins was rewarded in 1938 with the presidency of the American Sociological Association, ten years before his student, Frazier, became its first Afro-American president. [23]

When Frazier arrived at Clark, the study of racial differences was just coming into vogue. While the Ku Klux Klan was revitalizing its chapters throughout the country (by 1923 the Klan's membership was estimated at between three and six million), social scientists were busily constructing elaborate theories of racial differentiation to justify policies of social inequality, such as immigrant quotas, sterilization, and intelligence testing. [24] Scientific racism in the 1920s was not the work of a few right-wing fanatics on the fringes of academic life. It was the dominant, most respectable perspective of the best and brightest academics at the most distinguished universities in the country. "We might misinterpret the strength of the racism of the period," writes Thomas Gossett in his comprehensive history of racist ideas in the United States, "if we imagine that its most formidable proponents were emotional bigots like the Klu-Kluxers. It is essential to understand that quite a large number of people eminent in the sciences and social sciences were then genuinely convinced that races vary greatly in innate intelligence and temperament. . . . It is natural that in the histories of the period the views of the extremists have been accorded more attention, but it was mainly the academic writers on racial differences who made racism respectable."[25]

The study of racial differences was by no means a monolithic discipline. On the right, advocates of "Nordic" superiority used pseudo-scientific studies to justify military adventurism abroad and nativist policies of exclusion and segregation at home. The left was hardly represented in academia, with the exception of Franz Boas, who from before World War I was a lone voice of reason on behalf of cultural pluralism.[26] The majority of scientific racists, however, were liberals who supported benevolent social reforms.

Liberalism, however, certainly did not mean a belief in racial equality. After World War I there was a "veritable avalanche" of intelligence testing to document innate differences between classes and races. E. L. Thorndike, a pioneer in mental testing, used his studies to support ideas of racial supremacy. Carl Brigham, a psychology professor at Princeton, conducted research that "proved" the superiority of Nordic intelligence. William MacDougal, the celebrated psychologist at Harvard, in 1921 warned of the dangers of "race intermixture" and defended theories of inherited intelligence against the claims of environmentalists. Scientists from a variety of disciplines elaborated on the subject of innate ability—measuring and weighing brains, studying bone and tooth structure, and comparing racial "disharmonies" with crossbreeding in plants and animals.[27] As Gossett concludes, "The early 1920's became the time when racist theories achieved an importance and respectability which they had not had in this country since before the Civil War."[28]

When Frazier went to Clark in 1919, he came into close contact with two of the leading advocates of scientific racism. Clark's president, G. Stanley Hall, was the founder of the psychology laboratory at Johns

Hopkins in 1883 and the *American Journal of Psychology* in 1887. One of the most distinguished psychologists in the United States, Hall had argued in 1905 that the demise of slavery, combined with "idleness, drink and a new sense of equality," had unleashed "imperious lust. . . . The number, boldness, and barbarity of rapists, and the frequency of the murder of their victims have increased till whites in many parts of the South have told me that no woman of their race is safe anywhere alone day or night."[29] The other was Hankins, Frazier's mentor at Clark. Recognized primarily for his contributions to teaching and to the profession of sociology, Hankins published only one major book, *The Racial Basis of Civilization,* in 1926, several years after Frazier left Clark.[30] This book was very much in the mainstream of the scientific racism that flourished in the 1920s, though Hankins himself later defended it as "the first direct attack on the Nordic doctrine and all its ramifications." He conveniently forgot to mention that it was also a direct attack on racial equality.[31]

Writing in a tradition that combined eugenics with social reform, Hankins was critical of both the "extravagant claims of the Nordicists" and the "equally perverse and doctrinaire contentions of the race egalitarians." He argued that racial differences "must be thought of in terms of relative frequencies, and not as absolute differences in kind." For Hankins "superior rank within a race [was] of more importance than race. . . . The progress of a people is so greatly dependent on the abilities of its few ablest men that the primary question which a theory of the racial basis of civilization must answer is, what are those conditions which produce the greatest supply of genius?"[32] The answer, wrote Hankins, is to be found in studying the intelligence and temperament of leaders, for "if one is considering relative achievements whether in intellectual or artistic eminence, political power or financial accumulation and prestige, he must give a large, and in fact a predominant, role to inborn differences among men." These inherited traits explain why, according to Hankins, ruling class families "have produced distinguished persons with notable frequency," while the poor and racially oppressed continue to "live in a state of backwardness and simplicity that makes them appear like aborigines, though they are surrounded by a high and complex culture."[33]

Perhaps based in part on his experience with Frazier, Hankins begrudgingly acknowledged that a few "negroes" are superior to most whites, but overall, he noted, "the negro . . . has generally lagged behind the general level of [advanced] cultures while his contributions to them have been few and of a secondary order." The "general backwardness of the negro" cannot be explained by "the lack of social opportunity," noted Hankins. Like the Jewish or Japanese immigrant, "had he been sufficiently gifted he would have made his opportunity somewhere in the midst of the existing cultural milieu. The cause is deeper and must be sought in the difference of body and brain structure."[34] Concluding that "the races are unequal in mental equipment with consequent differences in cultural powers," Hankins doubted that "there could be found any pure negroes who, if brought up under the most favorable circumstances, could develop the intellectual powers necessary to carry on the higher cultural activities of the country."[35]

Consistent with this view, Hankins's policy recommendations included public education about "positive eugenics," an "effective means of birth control" for the "less intelligent," intelligence tests for immigrants, as well as a "gradual extension of the present policies of segregation and sterilization." The salvation of the United States is possible, exhorted Hankins, if "the wisest statesmanship would begin at once the discovery of the gifted strains and seek to introduce social conditions favorable to their preservation and multiplication."[36]

Fighting Back

Whatever Frazier thought about Hall and Hankins, he must have kept his views to himself because he left Clark on good terms. Hall gave him a positive if cautious reference for a possible job at Iowa State University. Frazier, he wrote, has "impressed me as a man of unusual mentality. I think all colored men have had a new race consciousness as a result of the war and he may be no exception to the rule, although he has done nothing criticizable here. My impression is that you need have no fear of any difficulty, for he seems to me to be quite gentlemanly and mentally white."[37] Similarly, Hankins closely followed and encouraged Frazier's career. A few years later he solicited a book review from Frazier for *Social Forces* and published it even though it attacked some of Hankins's cherished views.[38] Hankins also advised Frazier about doctoral programs and wrote a reference for him when he was applying for a fellowship in 1927. He commended Frazier as "a young Negro of very outstanding quality" who "in intellectual level, will power, determination to succeed, ambition to prove the intellectual worthiness of his race and desire to be of service in the elevation of Negro culture . . . can scarcely be surpassed."[39]

Though Frazier disagreed with Hankins's attitude to race, he maintained a collegial relationship with him. Frazier had many such relationships throughout his life. According to Marie Brown Frazier, her husband had a "strange sense of honesty" and remained friends with people with whom he had profound disagreements.[40] Frazier's generation always had some respect for any white academics, irrespective of their motivation or politics, who went out of their way to try to create opportunities for young Afro-American intellectuals.[41]

Frazier's graduate study at Clark University had significant consequences for his career. It was his first contact with an influential white university and with a leading personality in American sociology. Here he broke into the network of professional contacts and patronage that would later lead him to the University of Chicago and a distinguished career in sociology.

But Frazier's fighting spirit and independent views were not suppressed at Clark. While convincing Hankins and Hall that he was "quite gentlemanly," he devoted a considerable amount of time to understanding the logic of "racialism," to surveying the programs and literature of progressive black organizations, to investigating the socialist ideas of Randolph and Owen, to studying the writings of Du Bois, and to developing a critique of the Tuskegee tradition of accommodation. He left a record of this work in his seventy-five-page master's thesis.

Though the thesis is written in the style of a survey, dispassionate and nonjudgmental, Frazier's ideological interests and viewpoints can be detected by paying careful attention to nuances of phrasing and his choice of quoted materials. The essay is important in Frazier's career because it was his first attempt to systematically summarize his worldview and provides important clues to understanding his later intellectual and political development. Perhaps Hankins did not read it carefully or did not understand its implications, even though Frazier made his intentions explicit from the first page. The preface includes Claude McKay's militant poem "If We Must Die," which begins, "If we must die, let it not be like hogs/Hunted and penned in an inglorious spot," and ends, "Like men we'll face the murderous pack,/Pressed to the wall, dying, but fighting back!" For good measure, Frazier added a cautionary Bantu proverb: "The African race is like an india-rubber ball. The harder you dash it to the ground the higher it will rise."[42]

The thesis begins by providing a brief historical background, noting the significant contributions of Frederick Douglass, who "lived to see a once idealistic and enthusiastic North in its emotionless and soulless rush for industrial supremacy abandon the Negro to the mercies of the South."[43] This introduction is followed by an overview of the Washington–Du Bois debate and an analysis of the conditions that accounted for the "triumph" of "radical opinion." Frazier is cautiously critical of Washington's program of industrial education and political accommodation, recognizing the historical necessity for black economic development and self-reliance, but agreeing with Du Bois that Washington's policies of appeasement were likely to strengthen white racism and encourage black submission. Although Frazier approaches Washington with a certain amount of respect and diplomacy, he dismisses Moton, his successor at Tuskegee, for his "humiliating cowardice."[44]

Frazier attributes the rise of the "new" Afro-American radicalism to four factors—the spread of education, the failure of religious leaders to keep "pace with the growth of the race," the "failure of the Republican Party to ameliorate the condition of the masses of Negroes," and the war. According to Frazier, the war "more than any other factor stirred the depths of the Negro race and awakened in them a new conception of their value in American life. It created in the masses a respect for individual worth."[45] As a result of the war, Afro-Americans moved in thousands to "northern industrial centers" where for the first time "the Negro. . . began to think in terms of labor in relation to capital." Also, the war sent thousands to Europe, where "they fought and killed white men, expanded under the realization of their new found manhood and returned to America endowed with a new spirit."[46]

The remainder of the thesis is devoted to a description and analysis of "the new radicalism" and its press. Although Frazier examines Du Bois and the NAACP, the Garvey movement, and other progressive labor and radical political organizations, he focuses primarily on the ideas of Randolph and Owen. He describes their political tendency and its magazine, the *Messenger,* as "the most fundamental and thorough movement ever initiated among Negroes":

> The uncompromising stand taken by Douglass and other post bellum leaders only asserted the right of Negroes to enjoy the rights of other American citizens and made their appeal to abstract principles of rights; while the later radicalism, guided by DuBois, relied on the conscience of the American people and the courts. But this new school begins its career by a scien-

tific analysis of the problem and relying on the force of the Negro as an economic factor, and ignoring abstract principles, concludes that only force, economic and otherwise, can secure recognition for the Negro. . . . The group represented by the *Messenger* . . . places race interest above the nation and identifies it with the world-wide interest of the working classes. They would destroy national lines as readily as racial barriers. The *Crisis* would make the country right, while the *Messenger* holds right above country.[47]

Elsewhere in his thesis, signs of Frazier's emerging internationalism appear. He approvingly reports on Du Bois's participation in the Pan-African Congress held in Paris in 1919. The Congress, notes Frazier, demonstrates that "the Negro is beginning to recognize that his problem is only one of the many problems of subject *races* and that racial solidarity is the only way to escape the fate of disappearing races."[48] Frazier's interest was not only academic. In 1921 he would have an opportunity to attend the Second Pan-African Congress in Paris.

Though cautious and evenhanded in his concluding evaluation of the new radicalism, Frazier ends his thesis on an uncompromising note: "The new spirit which has produced the New Negro bids fair to transform the whole race. America faces a new race that has awakened, and in the realization of its strength has girt its loins to run the race with other men."[49]

Frazier's subsequent ideological development was very much shaped by his study of the *Messenger*'s program. He basically shared their critique of the Tuskegee "conservatives," religious leaders, and the leading political parties. He agreed with their analysis of and opposition to the war, and applauded their militancy and advocacy of armed defense in the face of racist attacks. Not long after leaving Clark, Frazier developed an interest in cooperatives as a form of economic self-help for black businesses, no doubt stimulated by what he read in the *Messenger*.[50] Later, Frazier would demonstrate his support for Randolph and Owen's politics by writing for the *Messenger*.[51]

At Clark, Frazier not only had his first serious introduction to the literature and ideas of sociology but also learned a new language. The conventions of academic sociology required both a specialized vocabulary and at least an appearance of dispassionate objectivity. Writing a thesis gave Frazier his first opportunity to see whether it was possible to maintain the integrity of his viewpoint under these constraints. Frazier's facility with foreign languages must have served him well in this task, for he was able to retain the core of his radical ideas while observing the etiquette of disinterested neutrality. For the rest of his career, with few exceptions Frazier used two styles: a sociological language in his academic publications and in his other writings—essays, letters, and stories—the polemical language learned in political debates at Howard and in the pages of the *Messenger*.

This dichotomy was not limited to literary conventions. Frazier learned his sociology at a time when academia exhibited an explicit antagonism to leftist ideas about economics, race relations, and politics. Hankins's right-wing views, for example, were regarded as moderate within sociology, while Du Bois was dismissed as an extremist.[52] Frazier had to operate within narrow ideological and theoretical constraints if he wanted to get past the gatekeepers of professional sociology. Unlike Oliver Cox, who adopted a more explicit Marxist framework and paid the price,[53] Frazier chose to accept the established parameters of sociological theory, while trying to stretch or subvert its boundaries. He also maintained his parallel careers, so to speak, and sometimes this double writing would lead to different theoretical and stylistic treatments of the same topic.[54]

In the two years after Clark, Frazier left behind the confining walls and ideas of sociology for the docks in New York, rural cooperatives in Denmark, and Pan-African debates in Paris. This experience would make him realize, inter alia, that there was "no academic freedom in America."[55]

A Complete Existence, 1920–1922

During the next two years Frazier did research on longshoremen in New York, spent nine months in Denmark studing rural cooperatives, visited Germany, France, and England, worked as director of a summer school in North Carolina, drafted several articles, and got married. He would continue this furious pace of activity throughout the 1920s.

On the Waterfront

After Clark, Frazier competed with some forty other college graduates and won a research fellowship to the Department of Social Research, New York School of Social Work.[1] Here he took several courses, including "Causes of Industrial Unrest" and "Human Behavior," taught by Bernard Glueck, a leading psychologist.[2] Glueck had a lasting influence on Frazier, and the two stayed in contact for several years.[3] Frazier's main work in New York was an in-depth research project on black longshoremen in New York City. In his thesis at Clark, he had expressed an interest in how southern migrants were adapting to industrial work in the North and whether there was any possibility for an interracial alliance within the postwar labor movement. With the support of the Russell Sage Foundation and NUL, he began his exploration of these issues early in 1921 and completed the study by June, though it was not published until three years later.[4]

As one of the first empirical investigations of black industrial workers in the North, Frazier's study broke new ground. It was written ten years before Sterling Spero and Abram Harris published their definitive study, *The Black Worker,* and eighteen years before the publication of Horace Cayton and George Mitchell's research on *Black Workers and the New Unions.*[5] Frazier's study describes working conditions on the docks and presents a demographic profile of eighty-two Afro-American longshoremen. Unlike most labor studies, then and even now, Frazier's study examines a group of workers both on the job and within their homes and communities.[6]

It took Frazier several months to gain the confidence of his interviewees, and he spent a great deal of time talking to the men and their families in bars, on street corners, in union halls, and in their homes. He found them filled with "suspicion" and a "stubborn indifference" to his research. "What white man do you want to sell me out to now?" he was asked by one worker who expressed a typical attitude.[7] Slowly but surely he gained the confidence of enough workers and union officials so that he could construct a profile of Afro-American longshoremen. He found that most of the men, although born in the South, had been living and working in New York or other cities for several years. Most were married, and almost half of their wives had to work because longshore work was casual and uncertain. "Several of the men said that without the assistance of their wives they would not like to contemplate their fate."[8]

Frazier reported that all the longshoremen in his study were poorly educated. The most education they had received in the South was "about equivalent to the education a child receives in the second grade in the North." He thought their conversations were filled with "ridiculous and childish conceptions," but they were well "schooled" in identifying "American race prejudice."[9]

Although Frazier found the men excessively distrusting of their union and not well informed about the purposes of the labor movement, he felt that white-led unions were largely responsible for the "mutual suspicion and fear" of white and Afro-American workers. Black workers need "equal treatment in fact as well as in theory," and white workers require educating that they will not lose their jobs to black workers. "The majority of labor leaders who are sincere and possess vision will do well to reflect upon the foregoing considerations," concluded Frazier, "for they alone can nullify the efforts of some unscrupulous leaders who exploit race antipathies for their own advantage."[10]

Overall, Frazier was discouraged by his finding that the "men as a whole live under the domination of fear and hopelessnesss." These longshoremen did not meet his expectations of a united proletariat but rather gave him the sense that "labor is helpless in its contest with capital," thus making them "resigned to their pursuit of a precarious livelihood." Furthermore, racism had implanted such a legacy of "diffidence and self-abasement" that "colored longshoremen expressed the opinion on every side that their fate is adverse because they are colored, and colored people in America are impotent and cannot stike back at their oppressors except at the price of annihilation."[11] This discouraging conclusion, based on a case study of a small sample of workers in one union, was confirmed a few years later in Spero and Harris's systematic study of black workers and the labor movement.

In his first research project, as in his master's thesis, Frazier tries to fit his political interests and ideas within the existing theoretical framework of sociology and the liberal policies of social work. This attempt leads to a certain amount of analytical confusion, as well as concessions to prevailing assumptions and prejudices. For example, Frazier refers to the "inherently sunny nature of the Negro sustain[ing] him in adversity" and even argues, his own atheism notwithstanding, that the "maladjustment" of many longshoremen may be related to their lack of church attendance.[12] Similarly, Frazier's policy recommendations are couched in the language and are based on the perspective of the "Americanization" campaigns—improved housing, lessons in "model housekeeping," provision of social services to families, education to reduce racial antagonisms within unions, and other conventional measures of uplift.[13]

Frazier's idealistic expectations for Afro-American workers in the North quickly turned to disillusionment. Black longshoremen in New York, unionized or not, were forced to live in Harlem's crowded, grimy, expensive, and "cheerless quarters," owned by "exploiting landlords" who "watched the general decay without any effort at rehabilitation, while gleaning rents from their tenants." He even reconsidered the possibility that the South might offer some benefits not found in the promised land. At least social life in the South, argued Frazier, was not so impersonal and alienated. "When we reflect, as these men also must, upon their former homes where their early years were spent in a genial climate and rural congeniality, the scenes of their present habitation become even more oppressive and dreary. Yet," observed Frazier with typical overstated irony, "they bear their fate without complaining because, as many say, they are free! . . . Although the average rural colored community is not ideal, its life possesses a degree of integrity and stability that is far superior to the disintegrating and demoralized atmosphere of segregated quarters in cities."[14]

A few years later, after Frazier had an opportunity to work in the South, where he confronted the impenetrable barriers of segregation and experienced firsthand the constant threat of racist violence, he would have second thoughts about southern "congeniality." Also, when he returned north to Chicago at the end of the 1920s, he would discover a vital cultural life within the "cheerless quarters" of the ghetto.

A Social Conception of Wealth

In the 1920s many young Afro-American intellectuals, writers, and artists made a pilgrimage to Europe or Africa, and some found it hard to return home. Langston Hughes crossed the "big sea" for the first time in 1923; Josephine Baker headed to Paris to make her fame and fortune in 1925; Countee Cullen took his first of many trips to Paris in 1926; and Du Bois, who had studied in Germany in the 1890s, visited the Soviet Union in 1926. From the 1930s at least through the 1960s, this form of voluntary exile was a common way for talented Afro-Americans, such as Richard Wright, James Baldwin, Sidney Bechet, Wallace Thurman, and Paul Robeson, to attempt to escape the color line.[15]

Edward Frazier was no exception. In May 1921 he was awarded a stipend of one thousand dollars by the American-Scandinavian Foundation to study "cooperative agriculture" and rural folk high schools in Denmark from September through June 1922.[16] Since 1913 this foundation had offered a small group of students the opportunity to participate in an exchange program between the United States and various Scandinavian countries. Frazier was the first Afro-American applicant, and it took an all-night session before the selection committee decided to make the controversial award. Even after he was chosen, his name and photograph were not included in the foundation's announcement of fellows for 1921–22.[17]

By the time Frazier left New York, he doubted whether the labor movement would serve as a vehicle in the fight for social equality. He was also concerned that urban life was destroying the social fabric of Afro-American communities, and he wanted to use his time in Denmark to see what might be applicable to rural blacks in the United States. But before he left, he made clear that he had not surrendered his militant spirit. In May he joined a small group of former servicemen and YMCA war secretaries on a NAACP-organized picket line protesting the re-release of *The Birth of a Nation,* which, in Frazier's words, was a "vicious anti-Negro film" [18] or, as Du Bois put it, was a "cruel and indefensible libel of the Negro and glorification of the mob in the Ku Klux Klan." [19] Frazier was among those arrested for disorderly conduct, and though he received a suspended sentence, he spent a few hours in jail. He later told his wife that the police "put him in a cell with a crazy man who kept hitting his head against the wall, trying to commit suicide." [20]

Frazier's decision to travel to Europe was motivated not only by a desire to see the world and escape the racist constraints that enveloped Afro-American intellectuals in the United States but also by his genuine interest in economic development and rural education, a concern that had been sparked during his study of the *Messenger* at Clark. He seriously prepared himself for the project. The language apparently was not a barrier. He had studied French, German, Latin, and Greek at Howard. On the ship to Europe, he studied Danish and then lived with a family in Denmark so that he developed, in his own words, a "fairly good speaking knowledge of Danish." It was good enough that Du Bois, as editor of *Crisis,* later asked Frazier to translate a newspaper story from Danish. [21]

Frazier wrote favorably about his experience in Denmark. He was impressed by the folk high schools, which were set up in the countryside to give agricultural workers a broad cultural education so that "their view of life is broadened and its meaning deepened." He particularly welcomed the focus on cultural values, the assumption that "each generation of mankind is linked to the great communion of the people, and those who would live a complete existence must see themselves in the stream of countless generations of mankind." [22]

Frazier's receptivity to folk schools was influenced more by Booker T. Washington's self-help programs than by the *Messenger*'s radicalism. [23] Frazier made a point of visiting the folk high school in Roskilde, where a few years earlier Washington had met its principal, "a fellow-worker in the advancement of mankind." [24] To Washington, the success of Denmark's rural schools, as well as its cooperative enterprises, "demonstrated that it pays to educate the man farthest down." [25]

When Frazier wrote about folk schools in a series of articles for the

Hampton Institute's conservative *Southern Workman,* he even sounded like Booker T. Washington. "The mind that has no cultural world to roam in soon pursues the call of the lower passions," noted Frazier. "So, into the lives of young men on the farms, who have neither the requisites nor the inclinations for cultural goals, creep vicious habits." In Denmark the folk schools offered "healthful association" and opportunities for "cultural enjoyment and self-expression."[26]

Frazier thought that the rural South could benefit greatly from a similar kind of educational program, but to make it effective would first require a program of compulsory education and a competent elementary education, both of which existed in Denmark but not in the United States. He envisioned "people's high schools" in the South helping to develop "broad and intelligent leadership," to "stem the tide of artificial migration to cities," and to "raise the general culture of the rural community." Such schools, concluded Frazier diplomatically, would also benefit rural whites because the "solution of the so-called Negro Problem involves a modification of the white man's attitude as well as raising the Negro to a higher level of culture and civilization."[27]

Frazier was similarly impressed with the cooperative movement in Denmark and thought that southern blacks could learn from an economic system that combined the best of individual thrift and collective methods of production and distribution.[28] In 1922 he was identified in the *Crisis* social column as an up and coming intellectual who "plans to teach sociology and inaugurate cooperative farming among Negro farmers."[29] When he went to teach in Atlanta after he returned from Denmark, he was hopeful that credit unions, cooperative marketing, and other forms of collective enterprises would develop in the South. "A great step towards economic emancipation," he wrote in his first article for *Crisis,* "could be achieved through the development of cooperative enterprises in many centers of Negro population."[30]

Cooperatives, he argued, offered "safe investment opportunities for small quantities of capital" and were "in harmony with the present tendency towards the democratization of wealth. It is needless for us to go through the cruder stages of individualistic enterprise before we reach a social conception of the nature of wealth."[31] Frazier urged black businesses to strive toward "true industrial democracy" and to establish cooperatives that would facilitate a "wide distribution of the economic surplus of the group."[32]

Frazier's brief experience with cooperatives in Denmark in 1921–1922 guided his political and economic views for several years. In 1925 he was still trying to convince an old friend that cooperatives were the "best means" to "amass capital through the mobilization of small amounts."[33] By 1928, however, he realized with some bitterness that cooperatives were no longer possible or viable. "A group isolated to the extent of the Negro in America could have developed cooperative enterprises. There has been no attempt in schools or otherwise to teach or organize this type of economic organization. The ideal of the rich man has been held up to him. More than one Negro business has been wrecked because of this predatory view of economic activity." Frazier criticized "black radicals" for failing to "enter the South and teach the landless peasants any type of self-help."[34]

Although Frazier returned to the United States with renewed optimism about the revitalization of educational and economic programs in the South, he also developed a realistic and sophisticated appreciation of how the rest of the world viewed his country. On his way home, he made a special trip to Paris to attend the Second Pan-African Congress, where he met "the leaders of the colonial peoples," supported a resolution condemning the U.S. occupation of Haiti, and participated in a debate about Garvey's back-to-Africa program.[35]

He also acquired an increased understanding of the limits of academic freedom in the United States. Studying and traveling in Europe made him realize, as he wrote in a letter to *The Nation,* the ideological blinders that had been imposed on his education. At the University of Copenhagen he was exposed to a breadth of viewpoints that made him rethink what he had experienced at Clark. The comparison was a revelation to Frazier. He wrote from Denmark:

> Here the university is certainly no "nursery" where babes are fed adulterated truth. A socialist lectures at the university. The students—no older than ours—can listen to any speaker they choose for their clubs—anarchist, atheist, bolshevist, nihilist, communist, or cannibalist. But, perhaps, we American students are weak-minded and must be taught Santa Claus' religion, Ray Stannard Baker's history, Gompers's labor policies, and Gary's economics lest thinking within university walls will disable the ship of state.[36]

Infidel without a Nickel

When Frazier returned from Europe in June 1922, he had little money and needed to find a job right away. A friend who worked in the state education department in North Carolina offered him a job as director of the summer school at Livingstone College in Salisbury, North Carolina.[37] Close by in Raleigh at a conference for summer-school teachers during this summer he met Marie Brown. She had heard from her society friends about his trip to Scandinavia, and he was considered an eligible young bachelor, though one with "strange ideas." He visited her at her home in Winton, North Carolina, stayed two weeks, proposed immediately, and they were married on September 14th. Her friends predicted disaster. "He's an infidel without a nickel," they told her. But they were married nearly forty years, and, from all accounts, it was a compatible and enjoyable, if conventional, relationship. When they got married, recalled Marie Brown Frazier, they made a deal: "You're from the black bourgeoisie," he said, "and I'm from the wrong side of the tracks. You do your thing and I'll do mine."[38]

Marie Brown came from a well-established family in Winton. She introduced Edward to her society friends and to the life of the black bourgeoisie in nearby Durham, "a city of fine homes, exquisite churches, and middle class respectability, . . . a place where black men calculate and work."[39] Marie's father, Calvin Scott Brown, was an educator and Baptist leader who was active in missionary work and founder of the Waters Normal Training School. She grew up with servants and enjoyed an "English" upbringing in a conventionally pious milieu. Her home was a center of social and political activity, and it was not unusual for distinguished leaders, including Washington and Du Bois, to come by when they were visiting North Carolina. She moved comfortably in Afro-American society but also was sufficiently light-skinned to pass for white. Years later, when she and Edward visited Europe together, people asked whether she was called a "Negro" because she was married to him. "No," he replied, "she's a sociological Negro."[40]

The match initially worked well because Marie Brown was a rebel in her own right, and they shared many of the same views. Despite her extremely religious upbringing, "none of it rubbed off" on her. She used to argue with her father for "preaching to those poor Negroes and telling them not to lay up things for themselves on earth because they'll get it all in heaven." Frazier "tried to find out what in my environment molded me because I didn't fit the pattern at all," she recalled. She grew up reading *Crisis,* which "was just like a Bible to me." While an undergraduate at Shaw University, she caused a stir on campus and at home when she refused to salute the flag. After her father intervened, she was allowed to stay in college but was restricted from public meetings.[41] She was more comfortable talking to poets than preachers. She knew and corresponded with Cullen, James Weldon Johnson, Locke, and other leaders of the black literati.[42]

She was encouraged to write poetry by Cullen, whose "pleasant lyricism" she preferred to Hughes's "propaganda," and though she did not think much of her own talents, some of her more sentimental poems were good enough to be published in *Opportunity* in the late 1920s, when Cullen was an assistant editor and in *Survey Graphic* in 1942, when Locke was guest editor of a special issue, "Color: Unfinished Business of Democracy."[43] But with marriage Marie followed the course of most middle-class women. She gave up the idea of going to law school, stopped writing her poetry, and devoted herself to taking care of her husband's personal needs and social life, as well as promoting his career in the "black bourgeoisie" that would serve as both his refuge and prison.

6

Practically an Outcast, 1922–1927

At the end of summer 1922 Frazier crossed the "Styxian Potomac" into "that land [which] rests upon principles as truly out of harmony with civilization as slavery itself." He went to Atlanta—a city that was being transformed into a "cosmopolitan center" by a "militant capitalism" [1]— for what he thought would be a short-term job as professor of sociology at Morehouse College and acting director of the Atlanta School of Social Work, filling in for Garry Moore, who had gone to Columbia University to complete his doctorate. Frazier did not plan on staying there long. But Moore died unexpectedly, and Frazier suddenly found himself director of the Atlanta School of Social Work, where he stayed for five years before moving on to Chicago to complete his doctorate in sociology. [2]

The Nether Region

Though Frazier expressed a political commitment to working in the South, he was often tempted to move north, where there were many more opportunities for bright young intellectuals. His ambivalence and divided loyalties were always close to the surface. In May 1923, after only nine months in Atlanta, he accepted an offer to teach sociology at Howard and was disappointed when the offer was withdrawn, presumably for budgetary reasons. [3] That summer he took his first graduate classes in sociology at the University of Chicago. In 1924, considering the possibility of entering the doctoral program at Columbia University, he started negotiations with James Hubert, executive secretary of the New York Urban League, about taking a job as director of the office's industrial department.[4] Early in 1925 Charles Johnson was encouraging him to apply for an award at the University of Chicago, but he stayed in Atlanta.[5] Even in 1927, when Du Bois offered him a job at *Crisis* and he was a likely candidate for a fellowship at the University of Chicago, Frazier applied for a sociology position at Fisk University in Nashville. "This would give me the opportunity to remain in the South," he wrote Du Bois, "and do the research I have wanted to do."[6]

During these five years (1922–1927), he built his reputation as a leading Afro-American intellectual and activist. By the time he left the South, he was widely known for his scholarly writings, polemics, controversial politics, and battles against racism. Frazier hated working in the South, with its material restrictions and relentless, daily round of petty humiliations, but he was also stimulated as never before. Probably at no other time in his life was he so productive, so challenged, so motivated to stretch his abilities and talents. Almost single-handed, he transformed the fledgling Atlanta School of Social Work into a professional program that attracted black students from all over the country. To effect this transformation, he worked tirelessly as an administrator, traveling through the South to recruit students and to raise funds for his program, speaking everywhere from national conferences to local church clubs. The school was so poor that he had to double as administrator and professor, which enabled him also to reshape the curriculum.[7]

During these same five years, he was an extraordinarily prolific writer, publishing thirty-three articles, plus several book reviews, in leading academic, professional, and civil rights journals (including *Crisis, Opportunity, Journal of Social Forces, Southern Workman, Messenger, Howard Review, The Nation,* and *Forum*). In 1925 he won first prize in the essay division of NUL's prestigious literary contest, joining a select group of winners that included Langston Hughes and Countee Cullen (poetry), Sterling Brown (essay), and Zora Neale Hurston (short story and play).[8] His essays appeared in two prominent anthologies—Alain Locke's *The New Negro* (1925) and Charles Johnson's *Ebony and Topaz* (1927)—and in 1928 he received the Van Vechten prize, awarded for the best contribution published that year in *Opportunity.*[9]

Before leaving Atlanta, Frazier also began his research on the history and development of the Afro-American family, a project that would form the basis of his doctoral dissertation at the University of Chicago (completed in 1931) and of his first three books—*The Negro Family in Chicago* (1932), *The Free Negro Family* (1932), and *The Negro Family in the United States* (1939). In addition, at Du Bois's request he somehow managed to complete a research project on black education in Georgia, Alabama, and South Carolina, part of which was published anonymously in *Crisis*.[10]

During this period Frazier's prodigious output was not restricted to academic writing. He wrote several short stories and essays, only one of which was published, and even submitted a play to *Opportunity*'s 1925 contest.[11] Moreover, Frazier maintained a variety of other interests that he pursued with passion and skill. He started a French club for students; he was a voracious reader, keeping up with the latest textbooks, political pamphlets, and novels; and his photographs were good enough to appear in *Crisis*.[12] A better-than-average artist—he specialized in watercolor portraits—he found time to submit cover designs to *Opportunity* and to sketch his father-in-law and other family members.[13] "Once in a while," Frazier told a colleague in 1925, "I 'dabble' in art. Most of my 'dabbling' is used to decorate the walls of my dwelling place, or a friend relieves me of a piece."[14]

Up north, the 1920s were the heyday of the Negro Renaissance, a time for literary gatherings, stylish banquets, and interracial experiments in the arts.[15] In Harlem the New Negroes were "intoxicated with optimism"[16] and regarded themselves, in Locke's words, as the "advance-guard of the African peoples in their contact with Twentieth Century civilization."[17] But down south, it was business as usual. "Dwelling in this nether-region," Frazier told Johnson, "I am somewhat isolated" and do not have any "contact with those movements that are giving opportunity for expression."[18] Frazier tried to compensate for his isolation by doing all he could to stay involved in what was happening in New York and other centers of Afro-American activism. He subscribed to the *Crisis, Messenger,* and *New Masses.* He took every opportunity to travel north, where he would inform anybody who would listen about southern atrocities while he learned about the latest political debates and controversies.

He was always on the road, speaking to small clubs and doing field research in the South, heading north for conferences and guest lectures. "I am traveling constantly," he wrote his friend "Dock" Steward in

1925, "spending only a day at a time in the office."[19] For example, in December 1923, Frazier was in Washington, D.C., for a social work conference.[20] In June 1924, he attended the annual social work conference in Toronto.[21] In May 1925 he attended *Opportunity*'s awards dinner in New York to recognize the winners of its literary contest.[22] In February 1926, he was a keynote speaker in New York City at NUL's conference, "Present Day Problems of Social Life: How They Affect the Negro." A month later he visited the Boston Urban League.[23] In May he was in Cleveland to present a paper at the National Conference of Social Work.[24] In May 1927 he joined labor activists and socialists at a conference on "Negro labor problems" at Brockwood Labor College in New York.[25] During the same month he presided over a session and presented a paper at the National Conference of Social Work in Des Moines.[26] This is a typical sample of his schedule during his five years in Atlanta.

Although he was continually looking north for information and stimulation, he threw himself into his work in Georgia and used his five years there to deepen his understanding of the South and its specific racial dynamics. Assuming responsibility to inform and educate northern liberals about southern racism, he quickly became an expert on all aspects of race relations in the South, especially demography, social services, economic trends, family life, education, and religion.

Negro Scientist

Working as an Afro-American intellectual in the South during the 1920s, Frazier had to overcome a variety of everyday obstacles in order merely to do his job. The fact that he was also a militant race man added considerably to his problems. Although he continually looked for job opportunities in the North, he chose to remain in the South for several years and even returned after completing his doctorate at Chicago. Cullen, for one, was impressed by Frazier's decision and determination. "I would rather be anything, no matter how menial, in New York," he wrote to Marie Brown Frazier from Paris, "than to be anything, no matter how elevated, in the South where neither mental nor material elevation is a protection against insult and assault. Perhaps I am not altruistic enough."[27]

But Frazier's decision to work in the South was not simply a matter of personal choice or altruism. If he wanted to teach in a university, the doors of the best (and the worst) colleges in the North were barred to him. Institutionalized racism in education operated at several interconnected levels. Segregated schooling and unequal distribution of personnel and resources tracked most bright black students out of higher education. For those few who, like Frazier, somehow made it through an undergraduate degree and into a graduate program, racism operated to restrict both employment opportunities and areas of specialization. As late as 1936, for example, more than eighty percent of all Afro-American Ph.D.'s were employed by Atlanta, Fisk, and Howard universities.[28]

"Until relatively recent years," wrote Michael Winston in 1971, "a virtually impermeable racial barrier excluded Negroes from white universities and their superior facilities for teaching and research."[29] Not until 1942 did a major university hire a full-time, tenure-track Afro-American professor; and even through the mid-1950s most black social scientists, like Frazier, could find jobs only in southern colleges.[30] "Whenever the door was opened," noted John Hope Franklin on the basis of his own experience, "it was done grudgingly and the opening was so slight that it was almost impossible to enter."[31]

Working as an intellectual in the South meant coping with inadequate resources, impoverished libraries, and ubiquitous humiliations. When Frazier sent an article on "King Cotton" to *Opportunity,* he apologized to Johnson for its shoddy quality. "If you do not find it suitable for your purposes I will not be offended. . . . You know we have scarcely any library facilities here."[32] In fact, his large personal library, which he kept in a classroom at Morehouse and made available to his students, was better in many respects than the university's library.[33]

In the 1920s black intellectuals had few opportunities to distinguish themselves as scholars. Most had attended or were then teaching at colleges where the emphasis was on industrial education, character development, and preparation of students for a "Christian life."[34] Frazier observed at the end of his life that aspiring Afro-American intellectuals probably had more encouragement to become scholars in the nineteenth century than they did after World War I. Unlike professional educators, the northern missionaries who went south after the Civil War had "a faith both in education and in the Negroes' capacity for the highest intellectual training."[35] In the 1920s, as Richard Bardolph observed, "trustees, donors, and visitors expected to hear Negro spirituals, not conjugations." Moreover, "graduate scholarships and fellowships were as yet rare, and the prospect of teaching graduate students hopelessly remote. When they entered college teaching, exhausted from the struggle to win an adequate training, they found microscopic salaries, crushing teaching loads, undergraduates with little interest in scholarship and no scholarly tradition."[36]

At least through the 1950s Afro-American scholars found themselves not only legally or practically barred from many conferences and research resources but also pressured to specialize in "Negro studies," which in turn were regarded by the academic profession as an inferior form of scholarship. Frazier found "a rather widespread opinion among social scientists that studies of the Negro had an inferior value scientifically to the studies of other people and subjects." This opinion was based on the "unconscious reasoning" that Negroes are not important and are not to be taken seriously.[37] The prime victim of this prejudice was Du Bois, whose pioneering studies of community life in the South prior to World War I were systematically unrecognized by the growing profession of sociology while scientific racists were applauded for their defense of slavery and studies of racial differentiation.[38]

An Afro-American scholar was regarded first as black, secondarily as a scholar. It was impossible for an Afro-American to be "an artist, writer, or scientist," as Frazier pointed out after a trip to Brazil in 1941. "In the United States he is always a 'Negro artist' or 'Negro scientist.'"[39] Franklin argued further: "When his work is recognized it is usually pointed to as the work of a Negro. He is a competent *Negro* sociologist, and able *Negro* economist, and outstanding *Negro* historian. Such recognition is as much the product of the racist mentality as the Negro rest rooms in the Montgomery airport are."[40] Any young black intellectual who aspired to be a scholar prior to World War II, observed Franklin, experienced "the most shattering and disturbing sensations as he looked about him in an attempt to discover one indication of confidence, one expression of faith in him and his abilities. If he doubted himself, it would be understandable."[41]

Not surprisingly, most Afro-American intellectuals of the 1920s looked for ways to get themselves or at least their children out of the South. In numerous small towns, commented Frazier, the pitifully small stratum of black professionals and entrepreneurs lived "in almost absolute isolation" and were forced to send their children away to school. They in turn, unwilling to live in an atmosphere of "unbending" racial intolerance, rarely returned home, not even during vacations, because they were likely to be insulted or threatened with violence.[42] "I do not know one intelligent young Negro who intends to stay in the South longer than to accumulate and get a start in life," observed Frazier in 1925.[43] "I see the South being drained of intelligent Negro leadership," he wrote in a letter to Frank Hankins, his former professor at Clark.[44] In one of his short stories, clearly based on his own experience, Frazier described the dilemma facing a young black doctor in the South: "After graduating from a northern college, he had settled in this southern town. Such a man is practically an outcast. Separated from the masses of the colored people by a large cultural gap and rejected by the whites who think he should be with 'his own people,' he finds himself living in comparative isolation."[45]

7

Publish and Perish, 1927

For five years (1922–1927) while he was in Atlanta, Frazier devoted himself as an administrator, researcher, and activist to making the educational program at the Atlanta School of Social Work viable. To build the program he gave up the possibility of jobs with the NAACP and NUL up north and postponed his long-held desire to obtain a doctoral degree. It is not particularly surprising that Frazier the sociologist-to-be found himself educating social workers in the 1920s. At this time the professional boundaries between the social sciences and social work were not yet clearly defined, and in its formative years sociology encompassed a commitment to dealing with policy issues. Frazier had studied at the New York School of Social Work and was interested in social work's activist perspective. Moreover, corporate philanthropists, notably through their financial control of NUL, were busily recruiting and attempting to coopt young black intellectuals like Frazier into the lower ranks of government service.

Racism in Social Work

This chapter in Frazier's life has been ignored by the official historians of social work. Aside from a useful anthology edited by Edyth Ross, leading social work texts are generally silent on the contributions of Afro-American professionals in the 1920s.[1] Standard histories of social welfare contain few references to the efforts of black organizations, intellectuals, and social workers to secure minimal social services for their communities and training for black social workers prior to World War II.[2] In *Seedtime of Reform*, Clarke Chambers recounts the efforts of reform-minded settlement workers such as Florence Kelly, Jane Addams, and Bruno Lasker to promote "good neighborship" and awareness of racial problems in the profession but neglects the legacies of black self-help organizations and social workers who battled against racism and segregation.[3] Similarly, John Ehrenreich's and Michael Katz's social histories of social work include perceptive chapters about the dynamics of racism in the United States during the 1920s but nothing about the activities or contributions of Afro-American social workers.[4]

Although many Afro-American veterans and college graduates had trouble finding work in the 1920s, there was a demand for black social workers. The focal point for this demand was NUL, which from its inception in 1911 considered itself a social work organization. Funded by white philanthropists, NUL lobbied for the creation of social service programs in black communities and for the training of social workers to staff these programs. *Opportunity*, NUL's journal, carried accounts of social work conferences and included information about social work in Afro-American communities that was not available in professional journals or the proceedings of conferences.[5] As Frazier noted in 1928, "the National Urban League is chiefly responsible for the beginning of professional education of Negro social workers on a large scale . . . [and] has been of indispensable assistance in producing the group of professionally educated social workers which we have today."[6]

Official social work publications, whether in the North or South, carried few references to black communities in the 1920s. Between 1920 and 1928 *The Family* carried only three articles that addressed the specific problems of Afro-American families.[7] The National Conference of Social Work regularly devoted a whole section to the problems of European immigrants but rarely included panels on Afro-Americans. Even the liberal *Survey*, the unofficial organ of social work, either minimized the significance of racism or portrayed the residents of Afro-American communities as helpless victims.[8]

The little coverage in social work journals was typically patronizing or racist or both. "Can real case work be accomplished with a negro family?" asked the general secretary of Memphis Associated Charities in 1921. Although the answer was a gracious yes—"He is teachable, though his reaction to moral and ethical influence is as yet not as stable or constant as it may eventually become"—Mary Russell then alerted her fellow social workers to the special needs of the "negro" client:

His inherited physical traits account for a sluggish temperament and a great susceptibility to climatic conditions, characteristics which are often misinterpreted as indifference. . . . The negroes as a race have great depth of feeling; they are very demonstrative and deeply religious. Superstition plays a large part in their lives, often working, contrary to the usual belief, to their betterment. The average negro is exceptionally fond of music, has a keen sense of the ridiculous and is of a cheerful disposition. Though he is often cruel to his enemies and prisoners he is naturally kindhearted and most hospitable to strangers.[9]

Homer Borst, general secretary of Jacksonville Associated Charities, similarly warned that it was difficult "to train [the Negro] for efficient civic capacity" because "we are asking the Negro to appreciate substance and neglect form, when as a matter of fact one of his chief racial characteristics lies directly across the path. It is form rather than substance which is likely to appeal to the black man. As a race he is a creature of ceremony."[10]

For all its liberalism, social work in the 1920s generally shared the prevailing world-view of scientific racism. In fact, liberalism and racism were quite compatible. For example, in a study of "Racial Factors in Desertion," Corinne Sherman argued that social workers had the responsibility to civilize "a race that has done little of itself at home" in Africa, "where there are no real homes." Slave owners "somewhat raised the standards of these easy-going savages [but] the present day negro in rural districts, brought up without the plantation discipline of his grandfather, seeing less and less of white men as the latter are drawn to the cities, and finding few and meager opportunities for education in his own neighborhood, often slips back into primitive ways."[11]

When Helen Pendleton, a white colleague of Frazier's at the Atlanta School of Social Work, criticized Sherman for her "somewhat stereotyped or pre-formed opinion about Negro life,"[12] Sherman reiterated the importance of inherited "racial" characteristics. "Economic conditions, of course," she conceded, "are largely responsible for the Negro's choices in work, but if Negroes are naturally as good as or better than Italians and Slavs in factory work, why did the manufacturers stimulate immigration from Europe rather than migration from the South before the World War?"[13]

If this was the prevailing attitude of progressive-minded social workers in the North, Frazier probably was not too surprised by what he found in Atlanta.

The Greatest Promise

In 1922, when Frazier was hired as acting director, the Atlanta School of Social Work had fourteen students, all black. The School was founded in 1920 in response to the growing demand in urban centers for Afro-American social workers and to the efforts of NUL and its supporters. According to Jesse Thomas, the field secretary of the Atlanta Urban League, by 1920 there was not one "colored person who had received training at an accredited school of social work south of Washington, D.C., or east of St. Louis."[14] Within social work, even in the South, there was a "consensus of opinion of those who have been pioneers in this field that only the well-rounded, colored family visitor who so well understands the handicaps and possibilities of her race can bring about the desired results in the negro family."[15]

Following the National Conference of Social Work's annual meeting in New Orleans in 1920, leaders of Atlanta's Associated Charities called a meeting of local welfare organizations and the presidents of Atlanta's black colleges to organize the initial political and financial support for the Atlanta School of Social Work.[16] But when Frazier arrived in Atlanta in 1922, the social work program hardly existed. Morehouse College provided classrooms and office space, and a part-time position for one professor; the Red Cross paid the salary of Helen Pendleton as field instructor; and students contributed about $150 in tuition fees. The educational level of the students ranged from fourth grade to the first year of college. Frazier found that "those possessing the social experience were lacking in academic preparation while those with the required academic background lack the acquaintance with life which social workers should have."[17]

Despite a lack of administrative experience, Frazier worked diligently to have the program accredited and "to make it a first class school of professional social work."[18] As with everything he did, he threw himself totally into the job, enjoying its demands and challenge. To Frazier, it was much more than a job; it was an "experiment."[19] He built the School from its foundations, working as administrator, teacher, recruiter, and fund-raiser, writing articles and giving speeches to promote the program, and infusing the School with his personal convictions and relentless energy. He raised admissions requirements, introduced student records, systematized the curriculum, recruited field workers from local agencies to teach at the School, and still found time to teach courses.[20] As Arthur Davis, Frazier's later colleague at Howard, wrote of this period, "Frazier did yeoman and pioneer work in building up the institution and making it standard. The matter of standards had not been important prior to his directorship. It was thought that a Negro social worker needed the 'right attitude' much more than he needed academic preparation."[21]

Although Frazier worked to bring the program into the mainstream of professional social work, he also tried to preserve or introduce some aspects that were at odds with dominant trends in the field. He allowed, for example, for some flexibility in admissions standards so that students "who have more valuable assets" than a college degree could be eligible to enter the program.[22] Also, at a time when social work was moving away from activism and striving to certify its competence in psychology, Frazier was interested in expanding cooperative enterprises and self-help organizations. He made sure that the curriculum included courses on economics, social problems, and rural sociology, as well as conventional courses on casework and human behavior.[23] He emphasized the importance of community-based institutions and urged social workers to become involved in indigenous organizations, such as Atlanta's Neighborhood Union, and to "devote full time to the organization of the neighborhoods."[24]

The Atlanta School of Social Work was incorporated as an independent program in 1924, when Frazier obtained fifteen thousand dollars from the Laura Spelman Rockefeller Foundation, followed soon after by contributions from the Russell Sage Foundation and Atlanta Community Chest. Frazier also traveled throughout the South and persuaded forty-nine contributors to match the foundation grants. The program was moved to its own buildings, a board of trustees and an advisory board were established, and the School became responsible for Helen Pendleton's and all other employees' salaries.[25] From Frazier's viewpoint, the program was a successful, growing enterprise that "had come to hold a very definite place in the South."[26] His efforts to promote the program, educationally as well as financially, produced results. National Afro-American periodicals carried advertisements for the School; Frazier's contributions were recognized by the National Conference of Social Work, and he was invited to present a paper at the 1926 annual conference and to preside over a round-table session at the 1927 conference; he was also asked to speak throughout the South on the "new scientific approach to the social problems of the Negro."[27]

Publicly at least, Frazier became an ardent advocate of social work, promoting it as a "new force, feeble . . . at present," that held "the greatest promise for improving race relations." He had lost hope long before in the possibility of any activism by southern black churches. To Frazier, institutionalized religion was "primarily a conservative social force," and religious leaders, he wrote in 1924, "are still more interested in getting Negroes into heaven than in getting them out of the hell they live in on earth." He was more optimistic about social work, which, he hoped, could use its secular methods and "scientific attitude" to diminish racial antagonism. "Good will is not sufficient. . . . Only the properly trained colored social worker can impress upon the community the value of the scientific approach and interpret social work in terms of personality."[28]

But even when he was writing in his public-relations capacity as director of the Atlanta School of Social Work, Frazier was careful not to feed illusions that social workers could "perform any miracles in the South." He pointed out, for example, that progress in race relations was going to be a long, hard road as long as national organizations like the YMCA and Boy Scouts practiced segregation as a "concession to Southern prejudice."[29] Privately too, Frazier was frustrated by the lack of support from community leaders in Atlanta. "I am working like the devil to build up a school of professional social work here," he wrote "Dock" Steward. "I find the apathy of colored people the chief obstacle. You know we are always looking for alibis."[30]

Nevertheless, Frazier was satisfied with the progress of the School and in 1926 was planning to establish a one-year program for college graduates and to raise money for a dormitory.[31] But Frazier's enemies were also busy, planning his removal. He fought hard to defend himself, but it was a losing battle from the start.

Under Fire

Frazier's problems were personified in his struggle with Helen Pendleton, a white social worker who had been with the Red Cross until she was put in charge of field work at the School.[32] Prior to 1924, when the program was incorporated, Frazier and Pendleton had equal rank and were equally responsible to the board of trustees. This system of dual control was nominally ended when Frazier was made the sole executive authority and was empowered to run the School. Pendleton, however, retained her seat on the board of trustees, where she colluded with other white trustees to discredit Frazier's leadership. Beneath the apparent personality conflict was a struggle over both politics and methods of leadership. On both counts, Frazier refused to make concessions to the etiquette of southern race relations, which, even in its most liberal manifestations, required black subordination to white benevolence. Pendleton in fact was unusually liberal regarding race relations but still could not accept Frazier's having any authority over her.[33]

The conflict came to a head in 1926 but had been endemic from the day Frazier arrived in Atlanta in 1922. A series of forays and skirmishes paved the way for the ultimate showdown. Pendleton typically took a four-month summer vacation, far longer than authorized by the School; Frazier complained to the board of trustees. Frazier was appointed treasurer by the board; Pendleton lobbied the board for his removal so she could get the job. Pendleton hired a white secretrary who refused to "come into a colored school to work or get her money"; Frazier insisted that as treasurer only he could disburse salaries. Pendleton asked Frazier to write a "favorable review" of *The Basis of Racial Adjustment*, written by Thomas Woofter, a member of the School's board of trustees; Frazier's review, which appeared in *Social Forces*, scathingly denounced Woofter's book as a "rationalization of the southern position."[34] And so the battles between Pendleton and Frazier escalated into a full-scale war.

Meanwhile, Frazier was developing a reputation for being outspoken and militant outside as well as inside the School of Social Work. In the 1920s he published several articles that located him within the left wing of the civil rights movement. Because of his outspoken opposition to segregation in any form, he quickly made enemies within the local white establishment and among those southern black leaders who "in the name of Christian humility," observed Frazier in 1924, encourage us to "entertain in our bosoms the tenderest sentiments toward our oppressors."[35]

Frazier had no patience for the niceties of interracial diplomacy. He walked out of a social work meeting held at the Atlanta Chamber of Commerce when he discovered that seating was segregated. "I have told you white people," he announced as he was leaving, "not to invite me to any meeting where you are going to place the Negroes to themselves as if they were roaches or fleas and unfit for human association."

On another occasion, while attending a meeting of the state Interracial Commission in Atlanta in 1925, he talked at length about "the usual [police] brutality of which Negroes are so often the victims. . . . Afterwards it was stated by some white people present that I had brought disharmony in a meeting that was going very well until I injected such unpleasant occurrences."[36]

Frazier's publications and activism added to his troubles in the School of Social Work. Pendleton and her allies began to circulate Frazier's writings at board meetings and to discuss his "position on the Race Problem." Pendleton told the board that it "seemed a pity" that Frazier's publications "were almost entirely on the subject of the race problem . . . when the school needed so much attention." She hoped that "with practice he would learn to express himself less crudely." Rhoda Kaufman, a board member and head of the state department of welfare, also took Frazier "to task for [his] attitude towards the South," and others were angry with him because he had asked the National Conference of Social Work to refuse to hold its annual meetings in the South until segregation was outlawed.

The attack on Frazier was successful, and in the fall 1926 the board of trustees asked for his resignation on the grounds that he "did not have the proper temperament for an executive." True to form, Frazier refused to resign and launched a counteroffensive. The board, surprised by Frazier's unwillingness to leave quietly, established a subcommittee to search for a new director and conceded that Frazier could be considered among the eligible pool. Frazier put up a strong fight and tried to hold on to his job. At the December meeting of the board, he submitted a long, documented memo calling for the resignation of Pendleton. He sent word to his friends in the hope that a lobbying effort might save him.[37]

W. A. Robinson, supervisor of high schools in North Carolina and an old friend, informed the president of Atlanta University that Frazier was "in danger of being victimized by circumstances." Robinson pointed out that the university had put Frazier in "a very difficult position" of supervising a "southern white woman," yet he had actually accomplished an "impossible task."[38] M. W. Adams, president of Atlanta University, responded politely but firmly, noting that Frazier "himself made it quite difficult for us to defend him. . . . He is an able man and in general it is unfortunate for a man to give up such a position 'under fire.'. . . But Mr. Frazier has himself made it very difficult for us."[39] Du Bois, who taught for years in Atlanta long before Frazier arrived there, was not surprised that Frazier was wearing out his welcome. "I knew that sooner or later you would have to give up work in Atlanta," he wrote Frazier. "Yours was a very difficult field and you have had unusual success."[40]

By mid-January 1927 Frazier was actively looking for another job, while still putting up a fight in Atlanta. Despite the obstacles, he hoped to remain in the South. Hearing that Fisk University in Nashville was looking for somebody to head the department of sociology and to develop a graduate program in social work, he told Du Bois that he was interested in the position because he could continue his research on the black family and build another much-needed program to train Afro-American social workers.[41] Du Bois agreed to "say a strong word" for Frazier and wrote a brief reference to Thomas Jones, president of Fisk, commending Frazier as a "man of unusual ability" who would be an "acquisition" for the southern university.[42]

Frazier was interviewed by President Jones in Nashville at the end of January. Frazier thought the meeting went well and returned to Atlanta with the false impression that the president regarded him as "most fitted for the position."[43] Jones, however, checked out Frazier's experience in Atlanta and although not questioning his "scholarship and experience," had grave doubts about his ability to work closely with southern whites and the Methodist Church. "I am not certain that Mr. Frazier is just the man we need," Jones wrote to Du Bois. "We need a man of pretty careful judgement, diplomatic temperament and with an appreciation of the spiritual and moral value in social work." "On this matter of personality and tact" Jones had questions about Frazier.[44] Du Bois, quickly replying in Frazier's defense, went sharply to the point. "I hope before you close your mind on the Frazier matter you will make a little investigation. One of the classic ways of getting rid of well-educated and efficient colored men in the South," wrote Du Bois, no doubt reflecting on his own experiences in Atlanta, "is the more or less vague accusation that they cannot get on with the white South." Du Bois pointed out that Frazier had managed to get on "extremely well with the white South" until Pendleton "used her position to insult and hinder him in every way possible" because she could not accept that she was Frazier's "subordinate."[45]

Jones, unmoved by Du Bois's arguments, repeated his concern that Frazier would have trouble fitting in at Fisk, where "we are trying to develop a community of truth seekers" and to restore "the old friendly spirit which has made this place famous." Jones was worried that "peculiarities about his personality which I have learned from his instructors" made Frazier too much of a risky proposition. "Until we have the department a little more firmly established and Fisk on a little firmer ground," admitted Jones with revealing honesty, "I think I cannot afford to take risks in the bringing of scholars and men of outstanding ability on our staff."[46]

Frazier also asked Frank Hankins, his adviser during his days at Clark University, to write a reference for him. Hankins obliged and sent "a very strong letter" to Fisk University. But Frazier's opponents were actively spreading the rumor that he had a reputation as a troublemaker and could not be counted on as a team player in academia. A couple of weeks later, Hankins confided to Frazier that President Jones "is looking very carefully into your capacity to get on with others. I judge someone has written him that you have a tendency to seek to dominate rather than to cooperate."[47]

During the first week of March, as Frazier was getting the message that his chance of a job at Fisk was bleak, he heard from the board of trustees at Atlanta that "in view of the entire situation in which the School finds itself, we think it best to nominate a new director." Or, in the words of Pendleton, "Did you think you could start anything with me on the Board and win out?"[48]

With this decision, Frazier finally concluded that he was *persona non grata* in the South and started looking north for a job with the NAACP or NUL, or a fellowship that would see him through graduate school. Before the end of January, he had submitted a research proposal to the Laura Spelman Rockefeller Foundation, sent word to his contacts in New York that he was interested in a job with NUL, and renewed his interest in completing his doctorate at the University of Chicago.[49] Frazier was especially interested in going to Chicago because he had already taken some graduate classes there during the summer session in 1923.[50] He wrote to Ernest Burgess and Robert Park, two of the most influential sociologists in the country, asking for their help and advice in getting financial support for completing his doctorate. Both were encouraging, but Park, who had a special interest in race relations and had worked closely with Booker T. Washington, went out of his way to recruit Frazier to Chicago. "We are hoping to have you with us next year," Park wrote Frazier in April, "and are looking forward to your work here as a preparation for a thoroughgoing study of the Negro family. There is no study connected with the Negro that is so important, in my opinion."[51]

Frazier's aggressive lobbying of his professional and academic contacts eventually paid off. By June he had been offered an eighteen-hundred-dollar social science scholarship by the Rockefeller Foundation and there was a potential job as research secretary for the Chicago Urban League.[52] With no possibility of staying in Atlanta or getting hired at Fisk, Frazier accepted both offers and informed his friends and colleagues that he planned to move to Chicago during the summer. "Dock" Steward for one was relieved that Frazier was leaving the South because he was worried about his safety. "I am glad that you are out of it." Steward felt that the real reason behind Frazier's troubles was that "deep down in Atlanta has always been the thought that you were an 'uppish' nigger, wanting to associate with white women—'associate with' meaning . . . 'go to bed with.' "[53]

Frazier's firing quickly became a cause célèbre in civil rights circles. Walter White, then assistant secretary of the NAACP, wrote to Frazier in April, saying that he had heard that Frazier "had been asked to resign because of your attitude on the race problem. I hope this is not true," continued White, "because I have been watching with great admiration your courageous and intelligent work there where it is so much needed." White asked Frazier whether he or the NAACP could do anything to help Frazier fight the decision,[54] but by this time it was too late and Frazier knew the battle was lost. Though Frazier had refused to resign and made the board fire him, he now preferred to get on with his life without making his dismissal a public issue. The board tried unsuccessfully to control any damage to its reputation by letting it be known that Frazier had resigned from Atlanta to complete his doctoral degree at the University of Chicago. "I laughed when I read you had 'resigned' to study at Chicago," Steward wrote Frazier. 'Resigned' was a word that held a worldful for me."[55]

Initially, Frazier did nothing to contradict the resignation story. He was busy getting ready for the move to Chicago. But before he could leave he was viciously attacked by the local press for an article in *Forum* in which he analyzed racism as a form of mental illness.[56] It was a total coincidence that this controversial article appeared in June because Frazier had been trying to get it published for several years. As we shall see, the Fraziers wasted little time in getting out of Atlanta when the publicity generated death threats. The Afro-American press had already been interested in the story about Frazier's firing. Now, with the Klan hot on his heels, the two stories were merged, and several papers reported that Frazier had been forced to resign because of the *Forum* article.

Atlanta's board of trustees accused Frazier of promoting this misinformation and sent out a press release proclaiming that Frazier "has been allowed perfect freedom of speech in press and on the platform and his personal views have never been under discussion by the Board during his entire five years as Director of the Atlanta School. As a matter of fact," the chairman of the board continued, "Mr. Frazier was asked to resign because he did not prove as effective an executive and administrator as was needed."[57]

Frazier, now safe in Chicago and preparing to resume his graduate studies, was furious with the board for circulating a statement that discredited his work in Atlanta. He sent off two letters of protest to the board of trustees, warning them that he was about to publish the "real reason for my dismissal."[58] Then he wrote a detailed and frank five-page account, "My Relation with the Atlanta School of Social Work," which he sent out as a press release. Finally, in a parting shot against southern social work, Frazier published an article about the industrial South in *The Nation* in late July in which he concluded that "neither the sentimental philanthropy which still lingers in the South nor the growth of scientific social work can eradicate the effects of [the] economic subordination of the Negro."[59]

Frazier's career in social work was largely over by 1927. Not only had he lost the battle to integrate social services in the South, but his vision of social work education also was increasingly at odds with that of professional leaders up north. As Frazier looked more and more to community and workplace organizing as the potential solution to personal and family problems, the field of social work was rapidly embracing Freudianism and attributing social problems to individual psychopathology.[60] Moreover, racism in social work was not simply a Southern problem. Even in Chicago, where the left wing of social work advocated economic and political equality, progressive social workers accepted segregation as inevitable or desirable and refused to integrate their settlement houses.[61]

By 1927 Frazier felt that political struggle and interracial organizing in the industrial working class offered the best hope for challenging "white supremacy."[62] No longer did he hold out any hope, as he had in 1924, that social work might be "the force that will remold Southern institutions and customs so that the Negro will occupy a place in Society affording his personality maximum development."[63] After all, social work had effectively blunted the maximum development of his own personality.

8

Becoming a Sociologist,
1927–1929

Frazier left Atlanta earlier than he planned, under the threat of "mob violence," as he put it,[1] not for something he had done but for ideas expressed in a short article published in a specialized periodical.

Farewell to the South

Of all Frazier's writings in the 1920s, "The Pathology of Race Prejudice" was the most controversial and evoked the most discussion and debate. Writing in what he later admitted was a "partly satirical vein,"[2] Frazier set out to make a case that "the behavior motivated by race prejudice shows precisely the same characteristics as that ascribed to insanity." Using the familiar categories of Freudian psychology, Frazier argued that racism was a form of "abnormal behavior," characterized by dissociation, delusional thinking, rationalization, projection, and paranoia. White people in the South, he argued, were literally driven mad by the "Negro-complex," which made "otherwise kind and law-abiding [people] indulge in the most revolting forms of cruelty towards black people."[3]

Frazier completed the article in 1924 but, not surprisingly, could not get it published for almost three years. He sent an early draft to the psychologist Bernard Glueck, a former professor at the New York School of Social Work, who read it "with a great deal of interest" and encouraged him to get it "published as soon as possible."[4] With this endorsement, Frazier sent the article off to various publications. The

Atlantic Monthly turned it down as a "careful and reasoned paper" better suited to an "academic review."[5] The *Survey Graphic* considered it, then rejected it. Alain Locke found it too abrasive for his glorification of *The New Negro,* settling instead for Frazier's subdued and relatively conventional portrait of the black middle class in Durham, North Carolina.[6]

Failing to get it published in a popular forum, which was his preference, Frazier then turned to academic journals. Here he met similar opposition and again was exposed to the double standards of academia, disguised in the language of scientific neutrality. The article was rejected by Emory Bogardus, the distinguished editor of the *Journal of Applied Sociology,* who notified Frazier that the journal "has a policy of avoiding as far as possible the publication of what might be called argumentative articles. It is our experience that these easily become 'controversial' and tend to separate scientifically minded persons rather than to build up science."[7]

Articles written within the framework of scientific racism, however, were not considered "argumentative" or "controversial." Robert Park, for example, could write the following passage without fear of censure or censorship in the leading sociological textbook of the 1920s:

> The temperament of the Negro, as I conceive it, consists in a few elementary but distinctive characterstics, determined by physical organization and transmitted biologically. These characteristics manifest themselves in a genial, sunny, and social disposition, in an interest and attachment to external, physical things rather than to subjective states and objects of introspection, in a disposition for expression rather than enterprise and action. . . . He is primarily an artist, loving life for its own sake. His *metier* is expression rather than action. He is, so to speak, the lady among races.[8]

Finally, almost three years after Frazier wrote it, "The Pathology of Race Prejudice" appeared in the June 1927 issue of *Forum,* a liberal periodical that addressed social policy issues. By this time, Frazier had been fired from his position as director of the Atlanta School of Social Work and intended to leave Atlanta at the end of the summer to resume his doctoral studies at the University of Chicago. But he was forced to leave town in a hurry in June when somebody sent a copy of his article to the Atlanta press.

Within a week of his article's appearing in *Forum,* Atlanta's *Constitution* carried an editorial condemning "this psychopathologician" as "more insane by reason of his anti-white complex than any southerner obsessed by his anti-negro repulsions." Sam Small, editor of the newspaper, was particularly incensed by Frazier's "revolting" suggestion— "the vilest this writer has ever encountered in a lifetime"—that "the white woman desires the negro."[9] Another newspaper editorialized that "it is generally accepted that he, Frazier, was suffering from some mental trouble and was as insane as those he alleged were insane. . . . The professor happens to be one of those highly educated Negroes who has disassociated himself from his people in pursuit of social equality," continued the *Atlanta Independent.* "He is over-educated."[10]

When Frazier went to Atlanta in 1922, he had taken some modest precautions to protect himself. "I knew that if I wrote truthfully about the situation, that is, wrote truthfully about what I observed and expressed frankly my thoughts and reaction, it would be dangerous for me to remain in the South." When he arrived in Atlanta, he was known as Edward F. Frazier. He decided to write under the pen name of E. Franklin Frazier in the hope that some people would think Franklin was not the same person as Edward. Unfortunately, in his article for the *Forum* he was identified as Edward Franklin Frazier. Soon after the article was published, "some white person called my house and asked my wife if E. Franklin Frazier was the same person as Edward F. Frazier. When she innocently answered in the affirmative, that was the signal for whites to force me to leave the city for safety."[11]

As a result of this phone call and the publicity in the Atlanta press, the Fraziers were threatened with lynching and friends urged them to leave town as quickly as possible.[12] "Things got so hot down there," recalled Marie Brown Frazier, "that he finally decided we had to leave. He put a .45 in his belt and said, 'Honey, I'm getting on this train. Now I don't want you to go with me because if I get in trouble, what's the importance of you being there?' And I said, 'When you leave, I'm leaving with you.' And I did."[13]

Their departure from Atlanta in June 1927 quickly assumed legendary status with Frazier portrayed as a "combative hero, fighting a rearguard action against the Ku Klux Klan."[14] "Everywhere I went," Charles Johnson wrote Frazier after a trip to the South in his capacity as editor of *Opportunity,* "the colored populace was asking, 'Have you read Frazier's farewell to the South?' I understand that the newstands have been exhausted of the issue. . . . Have you an extra copy or can you loan me your own?"[15]

Gustavus Steward, Frazier's friend and confidant, read the article as soon as it was available in Columbus, Ohio. He liked it but wondered whether it was wise to "cover white people with a blanket of insanity" and thereby "remove from them all responsibility." The "projection stuff," wrote Steward, was "pretty raw" for "a cracker of Georgia to swallow, particularly if he failed to understand you were talking of the unconscious, as the psychologists have it. For my part I enjoyed it." Still, concluded Steward, he was not sure it was such a good idea "letting southerners off so easily with their mind-sickness."[16]

Despite its notoriety, "The Pathology of Race Prejudice" was not reprinted for several years until Nancy Cunard, the aristocratic British leftist, included it in her celebrated anthology, *Negro,* originally published in 1934.[17] Cunard took Frazier's psychology more seriously than he did. "So many thanks for your good addition to the book," wrote Cunard to Frazier from Paris, "—more pathological reactions will ensue from its reading I know. . . . What has Freud said on this whole subject I wonder? . . . I will ask Havelock Ellis what his theory of this white-trash Negro-complex is. For they are nothing else."[18]

After Frazier was safely out of Atlanta, Steward made fun of his failure to be perform like a "good nigger" who knows how to do the "proper amount of bootlicking" and keeps "the good white folks believing that they are heaven-sent guardians of creation." If only he observed these rules, Steward advised Frazier, he would be in the "good graces of the philanthropic trust" and find his path "blooming with roses, and free trips to Europe thrown in occasionally."[19]

The Chicago School

Frazier arrived in Chicago in June 1927 with an eighteen-hundred-dollar scholarship from the Rockefeller Foundation, supplemented a few months later by a part-time job with the Chicago Urban League.[20] Unknown to Frazier, his scholarship was in doubt until late in May.[21] Leonard Outhwaite, executive director of the Rockefeller Foundation, had serious reservations about Frazier, especially given his notorious record in Atlanta. "I am . . . frankly puzzled about Frazier's case," Outhwaite wrote to the president of Morehouse. "The facts advanced in his behalf indicate that he may be useful as a research worker. On the other hand, his experiences indicate that he has found difficulty in working with people and that it may be difficult for him, even when his training is over, to find suitable employment."[22]

Will Alexander and John Hope came to Frazier's defense, albeit with reservations. "Encouraging him to apply his talents in the constructive field of research has a value, I think," wrote Alexander, "in that he will be less likely to become simply an agitator." Alexander, who had worked closely with Frazier at the Atlanta School of Social Work, encouraged Outhwaite to take a chance on Frazier. "I view the whole matter as an experiment. The training of any man for this work is an experiment. I feel there are many good things in Frazier's favor. If he does not make good it will, of course, be his own responsibility."[23]

Hope also did "not regard his case as hopeless." His experience in Atlanta "has had a sobering and, I may say, chastening effect on him. . . . I would be glad if he could have another good opportunity to get himself well set up." It was also a mark in Frazier's favor, noted Hope, that "his wife is a young lady of culture, unselfishness, and much good judgment. I believe that he is going to find her more and more helpful to him, and I am counting on her to do much in rounding out this man."[24] These references tipped the scales in Frazier's favor, and he was granted a two-year scholarship.

This was not his first time at the University of Chicago. He had taken three classes in sociology and passed his doctoral language exams in French and German during the 1923 summer quarter. In this first quarter he received an A in "General Sociology," a B in the "History of Sociological Theory," and a B minus, the lowest grade in his graduate career, from Park who felt that his final paper for a course on "The Crowd and the Public" lacked sufficient detail.[25] With credit from his previous studies at Clark University and the New York School of Social Work, Frazier quickly moved through his required courses in eight quarters, including summer sessions in 1927 and 1928. By 1927 the grading system had been changed, and graduate students were given grades of pass, pass with distinction, or fail. Frazier passed all his courses, including three—two on "The Negro in America" and one on "The Family"—with distinction. He left Chicago in summer 1929 to teach at Fisk University, then returned briefly in May 1931 to take and pass his preliminary examinations. In the same year he completed his doctoral thesis, "The Negro Family in Chicago," and formally received his Ph.D. on August 28th.

At Chicago Frazier found the kind of academic challenge he admired.[26] By the time he arrived in 1927 the university's second generation of sociologists had established the preeminence of the Chicago School. The department was built around the nucleus of Park and Ernest Burgess, who arrived in 1916, and Ellsworth Faris, who was appointed chairman in 1923 when Albion Small retired.[27] Park and Burgess's 1921 textbook, *Introduction to the Science of Sociology,* established the "direction and content of American sociology" for at least the next decade.[28]

Frazier, recalled Herbert Blumer, wanted to be identified as a "genuine sociologist," and he worked hard to understand and appreciate the territory and boundaries of this emerging field of knowledge.[29] "It was at the University of Chicago," observed Frazier, "that I developed a clearly defined conception of the field of sociology and acquired the technical knowledge and skill to carry on sociological research."[30] The program was rigorous and demanding. Everett Hughes said it was quite common for students to read German and French texts in their original languages.[31] Frazier studied statistics with William Ogburn, social psychology with Faris, sociological theory with Burgess, research methods with Blumer, and race relations with Park.

There was a lively and encouraging intellectual atmosphere in the department, a close relationship between professors and students, who knew that they were the pioneers of a new kind of research and scholarship in sociology. Blumer was one of Frazier's classmates in Park's collective behavior course in 1923, and the two formed an intellectual bond that endured beyond graduate school.[32] In the 1928 winter semester Frazier took a course on modern German sociology—"one of the most intellectually stimulating experiences in my university life"— where he met and developed a friendship with Louis Wirth, a fellow graduate student. According to Frazier, Wirth later suggested that he write *The Negro in the United States.*[33]

Frazier's other instructors and classmates included Hughes, Robert Redfield, John Dollard, Andrew Lind, and Paul Cressey. Though William I. Thomas had left the department long before Frazier arrived, his ideas and research were a long-lasting influence on the Chicago School.[34] In the 1920s ecological studies of the city and participant-observation research generated master's theses and doctoral dissertations that would shape sociology for several decades; Nels Anderson's *The Hobo,* Wirth's *The Ghetto,* Frederic Thrasher's *The Gang,* Harvey Zorbaugh's *The Gold Coast and the Slum,* and Ruth Cavan's *Suicide*

were a few of the classic studies that emerged from the second generation of Chicago sociologists.

Although Frazier was one of only a handful of Afro-American graduate students (including Charles Johnson, William Brown, and Bertram
Doyle) at Chicago in the 1920s, the racial atmosphere was certainly
different from what he had experienced in Atlanta. The department had
been actively involved in race-relations research since its involvement
in studying the causes and consequences of the 1919 riot.[35] Two of the
core faculty had special interests in race relations. Faris, who was a
missionary in Africa before he became a sociologist, was a well-known
critic of the leading exponents of scientific racism. Preferring the melting pot to genetic breeding, he ridiculed efforts to estimate the "ability
of races" by measuring animal characteristics or weighing brains.
"Those who make arguments upon inherited race characteristics,"
wrote Faris in 1927, "are not conversant with the known facts, for human nature is not a racial characteristic—it is a cultural or civilizational
phenomenon. . . . Civilization . . . is transmitted by means of contacts, sometimes formally in schools, at times informally by means of
apprenticeships or family contacts. But transmitted it is; it is not inherited, and seems to be quite independent of the biological differences
that divide races."[36] In another article published in 1929 Faris noted
that "there are no pure races. Strictly speaking, we are all mongrels."
He hoped that "if assimilation ever occurs anywhere, then surely America is a melting-pot."[37]

In addition to Faris, Park had a great deal of experience in and
knowledge about race relations. Park had worked for nine years (1905–
1914) as Booker T. Washington's personal secretary, aide, and speech-
writer. During this time, Park researched, drafted, or revised most of
Washington's writings, including magazine articles and important letters.[38] He spent several years with Washington, partly at Tuskegee,
partly "roaming about the South, getting acquainted with the life, the
customs, and the condition of the Negro people. . . . I think I probably
learned more about human nature and society, in the South under
Booker Washington," recalled Park, "than I had learned in all my previous studies."[39] Frazier studied race relations with Park and was encouraged by him to develop his interest in the Afro-American family.

Park, Faris, and others created an atmosphere in the department that
enabled Frazier to fully and seriously pursue his research interests.
Also, he must have found it encouraging that social workers in the uni-

versity's School of Social Service Administration were now open to liberal views about race relations, as exemplified in the kinds of articles being published in the new *Social Service Review.*[40] Moreover, Frazier was no longer subjected to the detailed code of etiquette that guided race relations in the South. He attended interracial dances and social events. Hughes could joke with him that "the issue of race supremacy was settled in such an unsatisfactory manner" when Frazier beat him at tennis.[41] Frazier could even make some of his more provocative comments without risking his life, such as when he warned the surprised participants at an interracial meeting that "if you remove the barriers between the two races, you might as well prepare to lose some sisters and daughters and even some wives."[42]

The Most Complete Student?

In general, the tendency has been to regard the Chicago School, especially Park, as having *the* determinative influence on Frazier's intellectual life. "It was at Chicago," wrote Grace Harris, "that Frazier became thoroughly socialized into what later came to be called the 'Chicago School of Sociology.' "[43] To Hughes, Frazier was Park's "most complete student," the disciple who went on to become the new master.[44] Similarly, according to Dale Vlasek, "Frazier's interest in race relations and concern for Afro-American social development led him almost inevitably into the race relations school of Robert Park. . . . In fact, given Frazier's earlier thinking and ideology, it is difficult to imagine his choosing a more ideologically compatible or academically prestigious mentor."[45] Elsewhere, Vlasek goes even further, arguing that at the University of Chicago "under the direction of the nation's leading sociologists and social theorists [Frazier] came to see the problems of the Afro-American as part of a larger social and cultural phenomenon."[46]

Frazier was certainly influenced by the Chicago School, but it was not as determinative as has been suggested. By 1927, when he went to Chicago, Frazier was not a young, impressionable graduate student. He was thirty-three years old; he had been teaching for at least part of the past eleven years; he had traveled to Europe and throughout the United States; and he had published widely in academic and other journals.[47]

Graduate study was not new to him; Chicago was his third graduate program, after Clark University and the New York School of Social Work. He certainly was not intimidated by powerful personalities: he had already studied or worked with people like Hankins, Du Bois, Moton, and Hall, and he had shown that he was quite prepared to argue with them and challenge their ideas when he had disagreements.

Throughout his life—and his years in Chicago were not an exception—Frazier was both fiercely independent and open to new ideas. He was not an original theorist, and he willingly drew on analytical constructs from an eclectic group of theorists. This flexibility was both a strength and a weakness in Frazier's intellectual development. On the one hand, he was not a dogmatist; he found and used ideas from several disciplines (especially sociology, history, psychology, and social work), even learning from people with whom he had profound political disagreements. On the other hand, he had difficulty speaking with a unique theoretical voice and, unlike Du Bois and Oliver Cox, did not leave his distinctive mark on sociological theory.

Thus, Frazier came to Chicago willing to learn from Park and others, but he did not arrive as a tabula rasa. He came with well-formed, strong views about racism; a wealth of personal and practical experience in the South; a compelling political interest in race relations and socialism; and a commitment to activism. He had also already absorbed ideas about theory from a variety of sources and had definite views about the functions and obligations of intellectuals. As we shall see later, Frazier's studies of the Afro-American family drew on several intellectual traditions, not only on the Chicago School.

Nevertheless, the Chicago School was an important influence, and Frazier absorbed the ideas of his mentors. He especially appreciated Park's intellectual rigor, his knowledge of race relations, and his interest in theoretical issues. He learned a great deal from Park, but he also had profound differences with him about politics, race relations, and sociology, and he was not reluctant to express them.[48] He thought, for example, that Park's early emphasis on the role of "racial temperament" in determining character was pseudoscientific nonsense, as well as an example of Park's political romanticism.[49] "Whenever I want a damn good fight," Park used to tell Frazier, "I know right where to come."[50]

Moreover, Frazier was influenced not only by his mentors in the Chicago School but equally by his peers in graduate school, by cultural and social events in Chicago, and by the growing political ferment that shook Chicago and the nation on the eve of the Depression.

Black and Red

The world outside the university competed for and engaged his intellectual and political attention. His work with NUL, for example, pulled him into the milieu of interracial diplomacy and the politics of the Black Belt. His scholarship at the university did not pay enough, and NUL had been trying to recruit him for several years, so it was mutually convenient when Frazier accepted a part-time job as director of research for the Chicago Urban League. Alfred Stern, Julius Rosenwald's son-in-law and an influential member of the League's board of directors, opposed the hiring of Frazier—probably more for reasons of organizational control than for political reasons—but the board ignored Stern's "ultimatum" and hired Frazier.[51]

The League essentially made Frazier into a public-relations functionary, not a researcher. It capitalized on Frazier's reputation and his ties to the University of Chicago. He made speeches to local clubs, attended interracial dinners, made his way into the gossipy news pages of the *Chicago Defender,* and even went on a radio program to exaggerate the effectiveness of the League's various programs.[52] By the late 1920s, the League's program had degenerated into publicity campaigns—"an interracial dinner, organization of an interracial committee, speeches attacking an evil, or League representation on a board or commission"[53]—as its patrons in business made sure that it was not radicalized by the deepening economic crisis.[54]

Meanwhile, beyond the constraints of the university and NUL, Frazier maintained his political identity and activism. Although he wrote some articles in the cautious language of professional sociology—receiving the prestigious Van Vechten award for a dispassionate essay, "The Mind of the American Negro," in *Opportunity* and contributing a conventional essay, "The Negro Family," to *The Annals*'s special issue on "The American Negro"[55]—he also wrote polemics that addressed controversial political issues. In an article for Johnson's anthology, *Ebony and Topaz,* Frazier raised critical questions about the nationalism of the New Negro movement.[56] In another notorious essay, written for V. F. Calverton's leftist *Modern Quarterly,* he exposed the class and political interests of "La Bourgeoisie Noire."[57]

He was also not afraid to support and be seen at events organized by socialists and communists. Taking a break from the respectable inter-racial dinners organized by NUL, he attended social events organized by the Communist Party's American Negro Labor Congress, where he watched with amusement as white European immigrants and southern Afro-Americans attempted to negotiate their cultural differences on the dance floor.[58] On another occasion, he attended a celebration of the tenth anniversary of the Russian Revolution and was impressed by the cultural performance of a group of immigrant workers who were "attempting to substitute proletarian for what they called bour-geois art."[59]

The vital cultural climate in the black community and the presence of leftist organizations in Chicago gave Frazier space in which to nour-ish his ideological commitments outside the university. There is no evi-dence that Frazier made any political concessions while he was at the University of Chicago. Although he learned a great deal from and greatly respected the intellectual abilities of his mentors in the Chicago School, he did not leave Chicago converted to Faris's missionary lib-eralism or, via Park, to Booker T. Washington's policies of appease-ment. He headed back to the South as militant as ever.

The Plantation, 1929–1934

Frazier was in Chicago for only two years, long enough to complete the required courses for his doctoral degree. Then, it was back to the South, this time to Fisk University in Nashville. He had little choice about where to go after Chicago, and of the available choices Fisk was the best one. Without a job offer from Howard, he had to go south if he wanted to teach in a college. Even though Fisk would be an improvement on Tuskegee, it was still the South and a long way, geographically and politically, from Chicago, where Frazier had been able to express his intellectual and ideological views without the daily risk of violence.

Aside from the limits on Frazier's choices, he also wanted to go back to the South. This upset his mother, who just before she died "hopped on" him about "returning to Crackerland," but he was committed to his decision.[1] Fisk was becoming the most prominent liberal arts college for Afro-Americans in the country, and its department of social science under Charles Johnson's leadership was actually hospitable to research. Here Frazier would be able to carry out significant field research on the Afro-American family, complete his dissertation, and publish his first books.

Personal-Relationships Man

Frazier was not happy being exhibited as anybody's protégé but if he wanted to be at least close to the mainstream of academic life and have access to the resources for developing and practicing his craft, then he had to play the role of "personal-relationships man," even though he hated it.[2] Looking back on his life in 1961, Frazier felt that he had done

most of his research at home and at night "in an uncogenial environment and without financial support."[3] This perception was mostly true.
After he became an established "Negro sociologist" at Howard, he
would get support from outside the U.S.—Gunnar Myrdal, a Swede,
hired him as a consultant for *An American Dilemma* in 1939, and in the
1950s his research abilities were recognized by UNESCO—but for the
most part he was not effective at glad-handing foundations, and they in
turn did not lionize him. An important exception was the funding of his
research in the late 1920s.

As soon as he arrived in Chicago in 1927, Frazier was advised by
Robert Park and Ernest Burgess to apply to the Social Science Research
Council for a grant to carry out field research on the Afro-American
family. The Council had as one of its priorities the funding of race-
relations research, and it had set up an Advisory Committee on Interracial Relations that included Will Alexander (with whom Frazier had
worked in Atlanta), Charles Johnson (who Frazier knew as the editor
of *Opportunity* and who was now at Fisk), and Harold Gosnell and
Edward Sapir (both at the University of Chicago). Frazier was well
connected to get his grant, but by the summer of 1929 it was still not
clear whether he would.

He submitted his first prospectus in August 1927.[4] In February 1929
he was told that his proposal had been "held in abeyance" until he completed more of his doctoral studies. In April Johnson wrote to him from
Fisk, saying that he was trying to get him a salary from the university
and encouraging him to be patient and persistent with the Council. "I
think I have never seen quite such a jinx on a project," Johnson wrote
Frazier.[5] There was some further delay, but finally, with the concerted
help of Park and Burgess, he heard in August 1929 that he been
awarded twelve thousand dollars for a three-year study of the "Negro
family."[6]

Without the support of the Chicago School, Frazier would not have
got the grant, and without the grant it is unlikely that Johnson would
have been so eager to have him use Fisk University "as a base from
which to carry on most of the field work in the plantation region."[7]
Frazier recognized his debt to Park especially for giving him this entrée
into research, financial support, and an academic career. "In a generation when nobody was opening doors for blacks who wanted to be
scholars, Park opened doors for Frazier."[8]

Fisk

Looking back with some bitterness at his career, Frazier once said that he had "never taught at any school in my life where I can say it was a . . . completely congenial place for carrying on research." Then, as a cryptic afterthought, he added, "Perhaps I might make an exception of Fisk University for reasons I won't state."[9]

Established in Nashville just after the Civil War, Fisk was generally recognized as the country's leading liberal arts college for Afro-Americans.[10] In the 1920s, under the leadership of Fayette McKenzie, Fisk's trustees sold the idea of an academic program to the Rockefeller General Education Board, the Carnegie Corporation, the John F. Slater Fund, the J. C. Penney Foundation, and even southern philanthropists. In return for their generous funding, McKenzie imposed a code of student conduct that rivaled Tuskegee's in puritanical severity. The student-government association was disbanded; its newspaper was suspended; and a request for recognition of an NAACP chapter on campus was denied.[11]

Near the end of 1924, after Fisk had met its goal of raising a million-dollar endowment, Du Bois and several alumni (including his daughter Yolande) began to support a growing student protest movement at Fisk. When McKenzie and the board of trustees responded with further disciplinary measures, the students organized demonstrations and an effective boycott of classes that lasted some ten weeks in the spring of 1925. As a result of this militant and well-organized struggle, McKenzie resigned in April, to be replaced a few months later by Thomas Jones, a Quaker missionary and pacifist who had spent several years working in Japan.[12]

As we have seen, in 1927, when Frazier was losing the battle to keep his job at Atlanta and looking for another job in the South, Jones had not felt sufficiently secure in his presidency to hire somebody as outspoken and undiplomatic as Frazier.[13] By 1929, however, Jones was receptive to Frazier, especially given his association with the University of Chicago and Park, and the fact that he would bring a sizable research grant with him to Fisk. From Frazier's viewpoint, Fisk was the best he could hope for in a southern Afro-American college. Jones had encouraged the addition of courses on black history and literature; he had sponsored conferences attended by prominent Afro-American scholars from around the country; and he had hired Johnson to build up a social science department and research program.[14]

Faculty support at Fisk was something of an exception among Afro-American colleges, which through the 1930s were characterized by low salaries, massive teaching loads, minimal libraries, negligible research support, and no travel funds.[15] In the five years (1929–1934) that Frazier was in Nashville, Fisk was one of only four black colleges that offered a serious graduate program.[16] But there was a huge gap between what Frazier found at Fisk and what he had left in Chicago. In the winter quarter of 1932–33, of thirty-four students enrolled for graduate courses at Fisk, only six were in sociology. In the absence of a specific graduate curriculum, students worked as apprentices to faculty who were involved in research projects. As of 1933 no graduate degrees in sociology had been granted.[17] According to Frazier, only Howard had the resources to develop a comprehensive graduate program. The other three colleges were required to concentrate their efforts in specific areas—Fisk in education, Hampton in home economics, and Atlanta in history and economics.[18]

Despite the meager resources, Frazier made the most of his five years at Fisk. For the first three years, subsidized by his grant, he was able to focus on research and writing—a luxurious situation indeed for an Afro-American academic prior to World War II. Between 1929 and 1934 he published his first two books on the family, *The Negro Family in Chicago* (1932) and *The Free Negro Family* (1932), as well as twelve articles in leading journals, including *Current History, Southern Workman, Opportunity, The Annals, Social Forces, American Journal of Sociology,* and *Journal of Negro History.* Two of his more controversial articles written in the 1920s were reprinted in anthologies that presented the views of the left wing of the New Negro movement. His critique of the black bourgeoisie reappeared in a collection edited by V. F. Calverton,[19] and his controversial article on the psychology of racism was reprinted by the leftist aristocrat Nancy Cunard in an extraordinary anthology, *Negro,*[20] a documentation of the global nature of racism in which "the chord of oppression, struggle and protest rings, trumpet-like or muffled, but always insistent throughout."[21]

Whatever Frazier's political and personal problems at Fisk, he benefited from being at a southern university that had recruited some of the leading Afro-American intellectuals in the country and where he had peers and students who expressed an enthusiastic interest in research and intellectual debate. During the late 1920s and early 1930s Fisk's faculty and graduate students included such well-known intellectuals as Johnson, Horace Mann Bond, Bertram Doyle, Preston Valien, Arna Bontemps, James Weldon Johnson, Sterling Brown, and Lorenzo Turner.[22]

By the early 1930s Frazier had made a reputation for himself as a bright intellectual and was well known in civil rights circles. H. L. Mencken sought him out at the urging of Walter White to see whether he would write on "the present state of civilization in Mississippi" for the *American Mercury.*[23] Between the end of 1932 and early 1934 Abram Harris and Du Bois corresponded about the possibility of setting up a black lectureship bureau that would send speakers to college campuses to educate students about current economic and social issues. Though the idea was never implemented, they both agreed that Frazier would be an excellent candidate for the bureau.[24]

Frazier was sufficiently well known to make the list of thirty-two "young leaders or potential leaders of the race" who were invited by the NAACP to attend the second Amenia Conference, held at the estate of J. E. Spingarn in August 1933. The purpose, as Spingarn wrote Frazier, was to "discuss the present and future situation of the Negro." It was hoped by the conference organizers that "a new vision of the Negro's future, and a new programme, will arise out of this independent discussion."[25] Frazier attended and played a prominent role in discussions, as we shall see later, but nothing came of the effort to build a new NAACP-led coalition.[26]

Frazier and Johnson

Prior to coming to Fisk, Frazier not only had tried to avoid any dependence on white mentors and philanthropists but also had made a point of asserting his independence from Afro-American leaders, from Moton at one end of the political spectrum to Du Bois at the other. At Fisk he came into conflict with Johnson, a black sociologist who had been appointed director of Fisk's social science department in 1928. Before coming to Fisk, Johnson had been a leading figure in the Harlem Renaissance and, as editor of NUL's journal, *Opportunity,* had developed a broad range of professional and literary contacts, including an amicable relationship with Frazier. The two men had similar histories: Born in

1893, a year before Frazier, Johnson grew up close by in Virginia, also was encouraged by his father to pursue a career in education, and also worked closely with Robert Park at the University of Chicago (where he received a bachelor's degree in philosophy in 1917).[27]

By 1928 Johnson was the leading Afro-American social scientist in terms of access to money, prestige, and power. He had made his name and built his career as a shrewd entrepreneur, with a penchant for "patient manipulation" and "gloved ruthlessness," in the literary circles of Harlem. As editor of *Opportunity,* he had successfully cultivated relationships with wealthy white patrons who funded his projects and fed his "passion for dominion."[28] According to one interpretation, Johnson was "the new Booker T. Washington, exercizing suzerainty over a more limited and specialized territory but within it possessed of a freedom of action never accorded Washington." He was the "overseer" and "establishment nigger" in sociology, "chosen at Chicago for annointment."[29] Although this view may overstate Johnson's influence and power, he was without doubt the pivotal black figure in the entrepreneurial milieu of the social sciences. He was a confidant of Edwin Embree (director of the Rosenwald Fund), John Hay Whitney, and Will Alexander (the leader of interracial diplomacy in the South). He was also at various times hired as a consultant on race relations by all the leading philanthropic organizations.[30] He "had his hands in the pockets of all the foundations," observed Frazier's wife. "You couldn't even get to Rosenwald unless you went through Charles S. Johnson."[31]

At Fisk Frazier's celebrated rivalry with Johnson was fueled.[32] It is not clear how or why this conflict began. On Frazier's part, he was no doubt competitive with somebody who had been given the job he had wanted. In January 1927 Frazier had indicated to Du Bois that he "would welcome the opportunity to go to Fisk and take charge of the department of sociology there."[33] It must have annoyed him that the job went to Johnson, who did not have any graduate training in sociology and who now was his supervisor.[34]

Moreover, Frazier felt that Johnson overcontrolled the department and was too subservient to the president and board of trustees. It was also rumored that Johnson blocked Frazier's rapid rise to prominence in sociology.[35] "Everybody called Johnson's outfit down there at Fisk, 'the plantation,'" recalled St. Clair Drake, "and they called Johnson 'Massah Charlie.' I've heard Frazier say that he had to tell Johnson, 'I ain't working on no plantation any more.'"[36] Of the leading Afro-

American sociologists in the 1920s and 1930s, Frazier, in the words of Everett Hughes, "lived closest to the edge of danger." Johnson, however, was an administrator and therefore always compromising. "He was the kind of man who could become one of the first Negro presidents of a white controlled university." [37]

Whatever the personal and organizational disputes that generated this rivalry, it is important not to lose sight of the significant differences in politics and ideology. Frazier had been a vociferous critic of U.S. involvement in World War I and had tried to dodge the draft. Johnson enlisted, fought in France, and was promoted to sergeant major. [38] Frazier was active in the left wing of the civil rights movement and interested in socialism. Johnson was a bureaucrat in NUL, a liberal who moved in the circles of interracial diplomacy that Frazier despised. Johnson tended to emphasize how race relations were improving, while Frazier grew increasingly embittered about the intractability of racism. [39]

While he was still at Fisk, Frazier was restrained in his public criticism of Johnson. Once he was secure at Howard, however, Johnson was a fair target, especially given the political atmosphere of the mid-1930s, when the polemic was a popular instrument of debate. In a 1935 book review for *The Nation,* Frazier was merciless in his critique of *Race Relations: Adjustments of Whites and Negroes in the United States* by Johnson and Willis Weatherford, a white academic. To Frazier this book, written in "an atmosphere of optimism and good will," typified the mindless pablum of interracial do-gooders. "When one reads the book one finds," wrote Frazier, "that each of these two leaders . . . has written his chapters as if he had no knowledge of what the other had written but aimed only at saying nothing that would offend the feelings of the other. . . . As a result we have the Negro author using much labored learning to express the most obvious trivialities, while the white collaborator speaks sentimentally about the Negro and treads softly where fundamental issues are concerned." [40]

On another occasion Frazier denounced Johnson's call for "realism" in Afro-American education. "Professor Johnson feels that the Negro's education should be designed to make him understand his status and seek compensations within his cultural life in order that he may have a balanced personality," wrote Frazier in his critique of Johnson's contribution to a symposium on "The Reorganization and Redirection of Negro Education."

If it were possible to carry out such a proposal, the Negro might be made satisfied with his present status. But who desires to make the Negro satisfied with his present status except those who benefit by it? . . . What is the use of prating about using the schools to develop racial self-respect, when the very persons who talk about inculcating racial self-respect help to throw a brilliant student out of school because he leads the students in a protest against participating in an entertainment at a Jim-Crow theatre?[41]

"Nigger, Do You Know Where You Are?"

Even though he did not attack Johnson in print until 1935, Frazier made his ideological differences clear during his Fisk years. Frazier's research project, dissertation, and other writings did not undermine his political commitments; nor apparently did his experience with the Klan a few years earlier make him any more cautious than he had been in crossing the color line. Aside from submitting some stories anonymously to the *Afro-American*,[42] Frazier was no more prudent in Nashville than he had been in Atlanta.

On campus he could be counted on by students to speak out against racist policies, even though President Jones and Johnson urged him to maintain a low profile. He joined six other faculty members in opposing the expulsion of a student who had demonstrated against a segregated theater near the Fisk campus.[43] When Juliette Derricotte, Fisk's dean of women, and a student died after a car accident in Georgia because they were denied medical treatment at a local, whites-only hospital, Frazier mobilized campus and community protests, despite Jones's order to keep quiet about the incident.[44] Frazier and others publicized the fact that it took six hours to transport the two injured women to a hospital thirty-five miles away in Chattanooga. They were not taken to the nearest hospital because, as one doctor remarked, "We don't take them there. You see we don't have any ward for them there."[45]

On another occasion, Frazier and two students were quickly on the scene to investigate the lynching of a young black man, Cordie Creek, who was kidnapped from his uncle and aunt's house two doors away from the house of Fisk's dean of women, driven through the campus, and taken to Columbia, Tennessee, where he was shot, dragged through the streets on a rope attached to a car, and left to die hanging from a tree. The day after the lynching, Frazier was out interviewing witnesses to "one of the most high handed and diabolical kidnappings and murders that have taken place in the vicinity of Nashville."[46]

Though Frazier was constantly on the road, collecting data for his research on the family and speaking at colleges, high schools, YMCAs, and even Sunday school forums, he was never far from controversy. In 1932 James Ford, an alumnus of Fisk, ran for U.S. vice-president on the Communist Party ticket. When Ford came to speak at his alma mater, Frazier was the only member of the faculty who would agree to introduce him.[47] Frazier was never a member of the Communist Party and over the years had significant differences with its politics and strategy, but, unlike the majority of his academic colleagues, white and black, he did not bow to anticommunism. Moreover, when he agreed with the party's views and activities, he did not hesitate to give his support. While at Fisk, he endorsed communist-led organizations that were fighting against lynching and racist justice. In 1933, for example, he corresponded with William Patterson, national secretary of the International Labor Defense; donated five dollars for the defense of the Scottsboro nine and signed a petition circulated by the National Committee for the Defense of Political Prisoners; and became a member of the Writers League against Lynching.[48] On one occasion, speaking before a youth forum at Bethel Church in Nashville, he encouraged the audience to look for solutions beyond those offered by interracial diplomats. "We have had good will in Nashville for sixty years and for every dollar spent on colored children, one dollar and fifty-nine cents is spent on the white children." Maybe it was time, he told the audience, to see if communism "might be of benefit to colored people."[49]

Meanwhile, Frazier continued his personal crusade against racism, even taking time to document the more outrageous examples of his deliberate breaches of southern race-relations etiquette. Once, returning by car to Nashville, he stopped at a gas station in Calera, Alabama, a small town notorious for its hostility to Afro-Americans. Johnson, who was in another car, pulled in behind Frazier and got out of the car. Frazier turned to a passenger and said, "Watch me violate the etiquette of race relations and get a sociological document." Then he turned to the gas station employee and asked, "Where did the gentleman in the Hudson behind me go?" The attendant immediately responded, "That *nigger* in the Hudson went across the street." When Frazier's companion expressed his disgust, the gas station attendant poked his head in the car window and said, "Nigger, do you know where you are? You ain't up there in Tennessee. You are down here in Alabama and I am going to show you how we hang niggers like you in Alabama." As the attendant was rounding up a lynch mob, Frazier drove off, quickly accelerating to seventy miles per hour, determined not to become "a martyr to social research."[50]

Frazier's actions were offensive not only to the uneducated sensibilities of working-class bigots in an Alabama gas station but also to the educated sensibilities of Vanderbilt University's chancellor. When Frazier attended a luncheon for University of Chicago alumni in Vanderbilt's cafeteria, people stopped and watched as he joined the food line. "Some of the people at the tables appeared to be paralyzed. I saw some stare and drop their forks and spoons. The man who was apparently in charge of the cafeteria seemed panic stricken." Frazier surprisingly survived the lunch and left the campus without incident. He later found out that the chancellor, many students, and some professors were outraged that a "nigger" had been permitted to eat in the cafeteria. Kirkland "said that I must have been crazy," Frazier was told, "and that it was the most disgraceful thing that had ever happened on the Vanderbilt University campus and that I had polluted the cafeteria by my presence." When the president of Fisk heard about the incident, he told Frazier that he was surprised he had "managed to get all the way around the steam table."[51]

This time Frazier did not wait to get fired or chased out of town by a mob. By the end of May 1934, when he crossed the color line in Vanderbilt's cafeteria, he had already been offered a job as chair of the sociology department at Howard, and shortly after his integrated lunch he was off to Washington D.C., where he would remain until a few years before his death.

10

Capstone of Negro Education, 1934–1942

When Frazier left Fisk and the South, almost two-thirds through his life, he took with him a profound, often bitter, understanding of racism and a fierce determination to participate in the struggle for social equality. By the time he went to Howard University to direct its sociology department in 1934, he was almost forty years old and had already been teaching for eighteen years. He was an experienced researcher, and his ideological views were finely honed.

Promise and Disillusionment

Howard represented the pinnacle of Frazier's career, though he himself increasingly regarded it as symbolic of the failure of Afro-American education. He had many opportunities to leave Howard for research, short-term visiting appointments, and lecture tours, but he was apparently never offered a full-time position at a major university in the United States. He started and ended his career in a segregated educational system.

Frazier came to Howard, as many did, with great hopes. It was the leading black university in the country. Moreover, it was the only one in the North that provided tenure-track positions for black intellectuals prior to World War II. During the early 1920s faculty morale was extremely low, academic standards had declined severely, and the university's finances were quite precarious. But the appointment in 1926 of its first Afro-American president, Mordecai Johnson, gave a renewed sense of optimism. Ernest Just, Howard's most prominent scientist, felt that "something new and wonderful was afoot for Howard and, by extension, for the black community."[1]

At first, Frazier found Howard as lively and stimulating as he remembered it to have been in his undergraduate days. It was not only the "capstone of Negro education," but also a center of political motion, controversy, and debate. In the mid-1930s, it was the "headquarters for the most articulate group of the young radicals" in the civil rights movement. Frazier headed the sociology department, Abram Harris was in charge of the economics department, and Ralph Bunche was chairman of political science.[2] For a short while at least, Frazier was in the kind of milieu that he relished—intellectually vibrant and politicized, with a link between theory and practice, race and class. As always, the more demands and stimulation he received, the more he produced. During his first few years at Howard, he was as productive and active as ever. He reorganized the sociology department and helped to develop a program in social work; between 1935 and 1940 he published two books, ten articles, and several book reviews; in 1935 he directed a major study of Harlem for Mayor Fiorello LaGuardia's riot commission and wrote an in-depth monograph; and throughout these same years he kept up a furious pace of public speaking, attendance at conferences, and political activism.

Frazier's main contribution to Howard's sociology department was in the area of curriculum development and educational standards. "When I came to Howard University," he recalled in 1948, "I reconstructed the entire curriculum" and increased student enrollment from about two hundred in 1934 to about two thousand fourteen years later.[3] "Forceful Frazier," as he was sometimes known, had a reputation among students as a demanding, often abrasive, but inspiring and stimulating teacher.[4] "The Frazier style," observed a former student, "was to give the student the shock treatment to command his attention, for he wanted the student to understand that the objective of sociology was to provide a realistic analysis of the world about him. . . . The basic idea was to teach 'big ideas' which, once grasped, would help the student educate himself."[5]

Though Frazier was successful in upgrading Howard's sociology department, he was not an effective bureaucrat. He did not have the temperament or diplomatic skills necessary in academic politics.[6] He disliked administrative work, had little patience for departmental infighting, and was not skilled at fund-raising. To his disappointment, he was never able to turn sociology into a high-powered graduate department with a serious doctoral program and substantial research agenda.[7]

Within the university, sociology was not a priority; the available limited funds were invested in the schools of medicine and dentistry. Through his first decade at Howard, Frazier was sustained by his teaching and work on the curriculum, and his contact with a small circle of progressive colleagues, known as the "thinkers and drinkers," who met regularly to discuss informally the burning issues of the day. In the 1940s Frazier became increasingly alienated from Howard as the brain drain took away important members of his circle—Bunche and W. O. Brown to the State Department, Harris to the University of Chicago, and Hylan Lewis to complete his doctoral studies.[8] Just died in 1941 after a long battle with cancer sapped his strength and an even longer battle with Howard's administration completely broke his spirit.[9] Disillusioned with the university, Frazier retreated more and more into his own research and writing, while looking for opportunities for research and travel outside Howard.

Beyond Howard

Throughout his years at Howard, Frazier participated in research projects that were originated and supported by groups outside the university—the Harlem commission in 1935, the American Youth Commission in 1939, the Guggenheim Foundation in 1940, the Carnegie Corporation in 1942, and UNESCO in 1951. All these associations were intellectually stimulating, extricated him for a while from Howard's provincialism, and helped produce some of his best work.

In March 1935 a property riot spontaneously erupted in Harlem, causing Mayor LaGuardia to quickly appoint a distinguished, predominantly liberal commission to investigate the causes and to make policy recommendations to prevent further outbreaks.[10] The commission, which included Countee Cullen, Hubert Delany, Oswald Garrison Villard, Arthur Garfield Hays, Morris Ernst, and A. Philip Randolph, hired Frazier as research director. This appointment was no doubt facilitated by his previous contact with Cullen through *Opportunity*, with Delany through his wife's social circles, and with Randolph through the *Messenger*. It was an extraordinary opportunity for Frazier to direct a large-scale research project and to do an in-depth investigation of the most important Afro-American community in the United States. Thirty researchers, recruited from the Home Relief Bureau, worked under Frazier for eight months to complete *The Negro in Harlem: A Report on Social and Economic Conditions Responsible for the Outbreak of March 19, 1935.*[11]

As Randolph recalled, "Frazier was the brains of the group and everybody else, including me, was window dressing." Randolph was glad that Frazier was in charge of the research because "he was not just an ordinary sociologist, he was also a militant. We not only needed facts but we needed an interpretation of these facts from a sound racial and class point of view. In other words, we needed the complete picture, not only the fact that Negroes were suffering from illnesses and so forth, but why. And Frazier was competent to give that sort of interpretation."[12]

Frazier's interpretation, as it turned out, was too leftist for some of the commissioners and too controversial for LaGuardia. Even though Frazier's final report was modified by the commission, three commissioners refused to sign it, and the mayor, embarrassed by its criticism of institutionalized racism in city agencies, refused to endorse or implement its recommendations.[13] Frazier thought about using the report as the basis for a book but abandoned the idea and settled for one published article.[14] Thus, his first large-scale research project was undermined by local politics, and his innovative and original contribution to the literature on riots gathered dust on a shelf in City Hall.[15]

For his next two projects, he reverted to the solitary style that characterized most of his academic work. In 1940 he completed *Negro Youth at the Crossways* for the American Youth Commission, one of several studies that focused on Afro-American youth in different regions of the country.[16] Frazier's study, a richly empirical investigation based on in-depth interviews and life histories, focused on the upper southern cities of Louisville and Washington, D.C. Though he worked closely with the Commission's project director, Robert Sutherland, and collaborated in his research with the psychoanalyst Harry Stack Sullivan, the book was mostly an individual effort.[17]

Soon after he completed this study, he received a Guggenheim Fellowship to study the structure of family life in Brazil. With little background on Latin America, a beginner's grasp of Portuguese, and only a few months to complete his research, it is not surprising that Frazier returned home with an overly optimistic and superficial understanding of race relations in Brazil.[18] He published a few articles and reviews, all of which underestimated problems of racism in Brazil and drew hasty and idealist conclusions for the Afro-American struggle back home.[19]

Frazier's foray into Latin American studies was interrupted when he became actively involved in the Carnegie Corporation's "comprehensive study of the Negro in the United States." Gunnar Myrdal, a Swedish economist, was hired by Carnegie in 1938 to direct the largest ever research project on race relations; six years later it culminated in the publication of *An American Dilemma*. Originally, Frazier had a somewhat peripheral role in the project. In 1939 he was one of several scholars asked to comment on an initial research prospectus.[20] He was also asked to submit a memorandum on the "the Negro family," but Myrdal quickly realized that this was a waste of Frazier's time since he had just published *The Negro Family in the United States*. Instead, a staff member abstracted the book for Myrdal,[21] and Frazier was contracted to write a paper on "Recreation and Amusement among American Negroes" and to summarize his "Stories of Experiences with Whites."[22] Frazier's memorandum on recreation was an uninspired, empirical survey that concluded without analysis or recommendations. It was reduced to a few insignificant pages in the final report, while his stories ended up in the archives at the Schomburg Collection.[23]

The war interrupted the project, and Myrdal had to return to Sweden in 1940. He came back in March 1941 and a year later was able to start work on the final draft of the manuscript. In May 1942 Frazier began to play a critical role when he (along with Louis Wirth) was asked by Myrdal to "read through my entire manuscript," some thousand pages, and "give me your detailed criticism."[24] Frazier quickly accepted Myrdal's offer and read the whole manuscript in fifteen days. "To speak frankly," he told Myrdal, "when you began the study I had grave misgivings as to whether it would set the Negro's problem in a new perspective and bring to it new understanding and insight. . . . I have been very pleasantly surprised. . . . Your study contains a lot of dynamite and . . . I agree with you that the explosion should take place upon publication."[25]

Myrdal, who was genuinely grateful for Frazier and Wirth's critique, publicly acknowledged the "invaluable help" provided by his "two friends who are at the same time outstanding social scientists."[26]

Myrdal also sent Frazier a personal note. "My gratitude to you is very great. I would like to be counted among your personal friends even though I have left America and the Negro problem."[27]

Frazier, like most Afro-American leaders, defended *An American Dilemma* when it was published in 1944. It was of course attacked by most Southerners, liberals as well as conservatives, but several social scientists, Marxists, and Communist Party members were also critical, some on narrow methodological grounds, others because of its liberal framework.[28] Frazier, however, regarded Myrdal as a fellow *enfant terrible* who exposed "America's greatest failure" and "did not indulge in a lot of foolish talk about the peculiar 'contributions' of the Negro and his deep 'spirituality.'" *An American Dilemma* "should be read by every intelligent American," wrote Frazier, because it represented a "scientific Charter" for the "right to full participation in American democracy."[29]

It took at least another ten years before the civil rights movement began to make the "Charter" a potential reality and some twenty years before the Civil Rights Act was passed by Congress. Meanwhile, in the years following World War II, Frazier found himself more and more estranged from civil rights organizations that were succumbing to anti-communism and from a left wing that was increasingly out of touch with the Afro-American movement.

Ideas

11

Setting the Record Straight

Frazier is typically remembered either for the writings that he produced after he was settled at Howard—notably his 1939 book on the family, his 1949 textbook, and his 1957 book on race and culture—or for his influence on the Moynihan Report. Both memories underestimate and distort his legacy. By the mid-1930s Frazier had already published two books and a variety of articles that expressed the basic themes of his future work. For the most part, his subsequent writings were an affirmation of, not a rupture with, his past. His 1939 book, *The Negro Family in the United States,* was built on research begun in the early 1920s. His 1949 textbook, *The Negro in the United States,* was the result, as Frazier himself noted in its preface, of a quarter century's research and experience with race relations.[1] The one important exception was his book *Race and Culture Contacts in the Modern World,* which was qualitatively different from his earlier writings and resulted from his experience with UNESCO in Paris in the 1950s. But for the most part, as we shall see, the pre-1935 and post-1935 Frazier had much in common.

As for E. Franklin Frazier and Daniel P. Moynihan, the two men came from diametrically opposed backgrounds, pursued different careers, disagreed on fundamental political beliefs, never worked together, and apparently did not even correspond with each other. By the end of his life, Frazier was a confirmed academic, thoroughly disenchanted with New Deal liberalism and looking far beyond governmental intervention to global and structural solutions to the enduring problems of racism. Moynihan, however, was an academic who had successfully crossed over into the world of politics, had served as an assistant secretary of labor in the Johnson administration, later (after Frazier's death) as a policy adviser to President Richard Nixon, then as a U.S. senator from New York. How then did Frazier and Moynihan become so inextricably linked? It is important to answer this question and to set the record straight before we proceed to an assessment of Frazier's intellectual development and contributions.

The Moynihan Report

In June 1965, three years after the death of Frazier, President Lyndon Johnson in a memorable speech at a Howard University commencement expressed the view that racism and discrimination were barriers to the full incorporation of Afro-Americans into American society. His speech was based on Moynihan's *The Negro Family: The Case for National Action*. By the end of 1965, a major debate raged among civil rights organizations and intellectuals about the merits of what became known as the Moynihan Report. The study itself was not particularly original either in its analysis or in its policy recommendations. Following in the liberal tradition established by Gunnar Myrdal's *An American Dilemma* (1944), it was essentially a restatement of the findings of various empirical studies that documented the well-known consequences of racism for black family life—poverty, disorganization, divorce and separation, delinquency. Like many previous studies, it attributed the problems of the Afro-American family to the legacy of slavery and discrimination, compounded by urbanization, unemployment, and social disorganization.

What made the Report so controversial was its timing and its focus on the family as the root of the "tangle of pathology" that strangles inner-city communities. According to Moynihan:

> At the heart of the deterioration of the fabric of Negro society is the deterioration of the Negro family. It is the fundamental source of the weakness of the Negro community at the present time. . . . The family structure of lower class Negroes is highly unstable, and in many urban centers is approaching complete breakdown. . . . In essence, the Negro community has been forced into a matriarchal structure which, because it is so out of line with the rest of American society, seriously retards the progress of the group as a whole, and imposes a crushing burden on the Negro male and, in consequence, on a great many Negro women as well.[2]

The victimization model, explicit in Moynihan's analysis and framework, posits that the injustices of slavery and racism destroyed stable family life, disorganized patriarchal authority, and generated a matriarchal family that was inadequate for the tasks of socialization. This "pathological model of black behavior under the stresses of white racism," as August Meier and Elliott Rudwick pointed out, "appeared amid the cresting of the wave of guilt feelings that the nonviolent civil rights demonstrations were arousing among many whites."[3] This victimization perspective was further legitimated during the 1950s and early 1960s by leading academics who documented the social and psychological damage resulting from racism—for example, Abram Kardiner and Lionel Ovesey in *The Mark of Oppression* (1951), Stanley Elkins in *Slavery* (1959), Charles Silberman in *Crisis in Black and White* (1964), and Kenneth Clark in *Dark Ghetto* (1965).

At the height of its academic and political popularity, this viewpoint was challenged and reassessed in the context of ghetto revolts and the rise of the Black Power movement, with its emphasis on nationalist sentiment, pride in the distinctiveness of Afro-American culture, celebration of the uniqueness of black contributions to religion, music, and the arts, and the capacity of the family and community to endure against all odds.[4] The 1960s and 1970s witnessed the publication of several studies that in different ways affirmed the integrity, resilience, and vitality of Afro-American culture in the United States—to name a few, LeRoi Jones's *Blues People* (1963), Charles Keil's *Urban Blues* (1966), Harold Cruse's *Crisis of the Negro Intellectual* (1967), Ulf Hannerz's *Soulside* (1969), John Blassingame's *The Slave Community* (1972), Eugene Genovese's *Roll, Jordan, Roll* (1974), and Herbert Gutman's *The Black Family in Slavery and Freedom* (1976).

Released during the height of the civil rights movement and just before the Watts riot, the Moynihan Report met with a storm of protest and was widely criticized for its one-dimensional view of black community life, its tendency to blame the victims of racism for their own troubles, and its effort to detract attention from the economic, political, and structural roots of racism.[5]

Frazier Remembered

Because Moynihan acknowledged his intellectual debt to Frazier and the report quoted approvingly from Frazier's writings, the congruity of Moynihan's and Frazier's ideas about the black family became widely assumed and accepted in the media, and among academics and activists. In a more recent book, Moynihan even portrays himself as something of a heretic who followed an analytical tradition pioneered by Du Bois and Frazier.[6]

Critics of Moynihan were quick to find Frazier guilty by association. Despite a lifetime of original, complex, and varied scholarship, Frazier is typically remembered for his work on the black family and his posthumous association with the Moynihan Report. Although this topic clearly was of great concern and interest to Frazier, it was by no means his only specialization. He also, for example, took great pride in his textbook, *The Negro in the United States* (1949), and his comparative analysis, *Race and Culture Contacts in the Modern World* (1957), neither of which focused on the family.[7]

But Frazier's work on the family, especially its popularization by Moynihan, led a variety of progressive intellectuals to accuse Frazier (after his death) of creating a pejorative stereotype of Afro-American family life and of initiating a racist sociological tradition that culminated in the publication of the Moynihan Report. According to Lee Rainwater and William Yancey, for example, "the basic paradigm of Negro life that Moynihan's report reflected had been laid down by the great Negro sociologist, E. Franklin Frazier, over thirty years before."[8]

This conclusion, generally shared by experts on the sociology of the family, is no longer a matter of interpretation but rather has become a commonplace, established fact. References to Moynihan's thesis invariably cite Frazier to the point that the two names are interchangeably used as personifications of the pathology perspective.[9] "The Moynihan Report," noted a typical study of race relations, "echoed the words of E. Franklin Frazier."[10] This phrase aptly describes the relationship between the two men. Call out one of the two names and the other resonates: "Frazier? Moynihan." "Moynihan? Frazier."

Most critics of Frazier's work assume his endorsement of Moynihan's view that the roots of racism are to be found in the "internal deficiencies" of the black community and that the primary focus of reform efforts should be on the family itself. Charles Valentine, a sociologist, asserted that the Moynihan Report "contains very little more than another updated rehash of Frazier" and that Moynihan continued "the Frazerian tradition of moralistic denigration of the lower class":

> Frazier describes existence among the modern Negro poor as an immoral chaos brought about by disintegration of the black folk culture under the

impact of urbanization. . . . Frazier creates an image of the black poor as so abysmally disorganized and so hopelessly infected with social pathologies that they even lack public opinion, social control, or community institutions. . . . Any depiction of ongoing social existence in a human population is conspicuously missing from Frazier's work. The reader does not get the feeling that the author has observed the life of slum dwellers intensively at firsthand, much less participated in that life.[11]

This assessment of Frazier is generally shared by scholars from varying perspectives. To the black sociologist Abd-L Hakimu Ibn Alkalimat, Frazier was "a brother who was strong enough to collect a lot of important data but fell victim to theory based on the racist, white liberal ideology."[12] Similarly, the noted historian Herbert Gutman attributed to Frazier the deficit or pathology model of the black family and suggested that "Frazier's influential writings paradoxically fed the racist scholarship he attacked."[13] To another critic, Frazier stood for the view that "the Black Family was a broken, subdued social institution. Its matriarchal character and tolerance for illegitimacy led to a pathology which was replicated in modern Black life."[14] Similarly, Ulf Hannerz nominated Frazier as the "grand old man" of the "slavery school of interpretation" of the black family, characterizing his work as based on "the prejudices of early evolutionism and some romantic imagery about simple peasant folk."[15]

The prevalence and acceptance of these charges have distorted a balanced assessment of Frazier's work. Frazier's critics generally assume without investigation that Moynihan's presentation of Frazier's ideas is accurate and that Frazier's work on the family was based on a pathology model of analysis. Moynihan, however, inaccurately and opportunistically misused Frazier's early writings, which in fact were guided by Frazier's desire to refute monolithic and pathological interpretations of the Afro-American family. Whatever Moynihan's motivation for misusing Frazier's scholarship—to legitimate his own ideological viewpoint or to promote his own career or to cloak his analysis in Negro respectability—his technocratic report articulated a liberal-managerial view of politics that Frazier had repudiated. In the last few years of his life, Frazier was increasingly losing hope that racial equality could be achieved in the United States and was looking with some enthusiasm at the revolutionary stirrings in Africa.

Moynihan's Frazier

Given the debate that raged after his death, one would expect that Frazier, who died three years before President Johnson's Howard University address, played a dominant role in the Moynihan Report. In fact, he is cited only six times in the seventy-eight-page study. The first and fifth references repeat Frazier's point that there is considerable diversity within black communities and that middle-class Afro-Americans place a great deal of emphasis on conventional forms of family stability.[16] The second, third, and fourth references quote Frazier's 1939 book, *The Negro Family in the United States,* to support the argument that the migration of rural blacks to urban centers disorganized traditional family life;[17] and the sixth reference, quoting from an article written by Frazier in 1950, argues that family disorganization in the Afro-American community is responsible for the psychological and behavioral problems of its youth.[18]

Of the above references, the two that address the stability of the middle-class family were not controversial. The other four references supposedly made Frazier the father of the Moynihan Report and gave him a reputation for portraying urban black communities as "abysmally disorganized," reified victims of racism. This assessment of Frazier comes primarily from Moynihan's reliance on Frazier's book *The Negro Family in the United States,* written twenty-six years earlier, and on an article written by Frazier fifteen years earlier.[19] Significantly, Moynihan could not find usable quotations and references in Frazier's later work.

Frazier plays an important symbolic role in the Moynihan Report in that he is quoted extensively on one page and quoted again in a highly visible place in the conclusion. Aside from the fact that Moynihan was selective in his use of Frazier's writings and ignored his contemporary works, the specific quotes used in the report were also surgically abstracted from Frazier's writings and quoted totally out of context. Moynihan had to use a fundamentalist methodology to locate authoritative sources in Frazier's scriptures. For example, the following three quotations, which appear consecutively on one page in the Moynihan Report, are taken from three different places in *The Negro Family in the United States.* When they are read out of their original context and abstracted from their situated meanings, one might easily conclude that Frazier regarded most black family life as disorganized, chaotic, and pathological. But if we add materials that Moynihan conveniently omitted, it is clear that Frazier's view is by no means so simplistic or linear. The omitted sentences, which surround the ones used by Moynihan, are in italics.

First, Moynihan conveniently ignores Frazier's observations about the growing class consciousness of poor blacks in the 1930s, a development that Frazier regarded as a hopeful sign:

> *Although competition and conflict with whites have tended to stimulate race consciousness, other forces are bringing Negroes into cooperative relations with whites. This is especially true where liberal and radical labor organizations are attempting to create a solidarity between white and black workers. Such phrases as "class struggle" and "working class solidarity," once foreign to the ears of black workers, are the terms in which some Negroes are beginning to voice their discontent with their present status.*[20]

Instead, Moynihan quotes a fragment that mentions the disorganization of the Afro-American community but fails to quote the qualifications and complexities that Frazier adds:

> The impact of hundreds of thousands of rural southern Negroes upon northern metropolitan communities presents a bewildering spectacle. Striking contrasts in levels of civilization and economic well-being among these newcomers to modern civilization seem to baffle any attempt to discover order and direction in their mode of life. *On the one hand, one sees poverty and primitiveness and, on the other, comfort and civilization. In some quarters crime and viciousness are the characteristic forms of behavior, while in others a simple piety and industry seem unaffected by the currents of urban life. On the streets of Negro communities, painted and powdered women, resembling all the races of mankind, with lustful songs upon their lips, rub shoulders with pious old black charwomen on their way to "store-front" churches. Strutting young men, attired in gaudy clothes and flashing soft hands and manicured fingernails, jostle devout old men clasping Bibles in their gnarled hands as they trudge to "prayer meetings." On the subways, buses, and streetcars one sees men and women with tired black faces staring vacantly into a future lighted only by the hope of a future life, while beside them may sit a girl with her head buried in a book on homosexual love or a boy absorbed in the latest revolutionary pamphlet. Saunterers along the boulevards are interrupted by corner crowds being harangued by speakers on the achievements of the black race or the necessity of social revolution. The periodic screeching of police sirens reminds one of the score or more Negroes who daily run afoul of the law.*

Children of all ages, playing and fighting and stealing in the streets day and night, are an ever present indication of the widespread breakdown of family control. Finally, unseen but known to doctor and nurse and social worker are the thousands who lie stricken by disease or are carried off by death.[21]

Second, in the following quotation, Moynihan omits the first two sentences, which enrich and complicate what follows. Without these two sentences, Frazier's meaning is changed:

Despite these various forces in the urban environment, the sympathetic ties sometimes draw the deserters back to their families. The behavior of Negro deserters, who are likely to return to their families even after several years of absence, often taxes the patience of social workers whose plans for their families are constantly disrupted. In many cases, of course, the dissolution of the simple family organization has begun before the family reaches the northern city. But, if these families have managed to preserve their integrity until they reach the northern city, poverty, ignorance, and color force them to seek homes in deteriorated slum areas from which practically all institutional life has disappeared. Hence, at the same time that these simple rural families are losing their internal cohesion, they are being freed from the controlling force of public opinion and communal institutions. Family desertion among Negroes in cities appears, then, to be one of the inevitable consequences of the impact of urban life on the simple family organization and folk culture which the Negro has evolved in the rural South. The distribution of desertions in relation to the general economic and cultural organization of Negro communities that have grown up in our American cities shows in a striking manner the influence of selective factors in the process of adjustment to the urban environment.[22]

Third, the following comments about how proletarianization fundamentally changed the social composition of the Afro-American community—a central point in Frazier's book—are ignored by Moynihan:

The most significant element in the new social structure of Negro life is the black industrial proletariat that has been emerging since the Negro was introduced into Western civilization. . . . That the Negro has found within the patterns of the white man's culture a purpose in life and a significance for his strivings which have involved sacrifices for his children and the curbing of individual desires and impulses indicates that he has become assimilated to a new mode of life.[23]

Instead, Moynihan searches only for self-serving quotes:

First, it appears that the family which evolved within the isolated world of the Negro folk will become increasingly disorganized. Modern means of communication will break down the isolation of the world of the black folk, and, as long as the bankrupt system of southern agriculture exists, Negro families will continue to seek a living in the towns and cities of the country. They will crowd the slum areas of southern cities or make their way to northern cities where their family life will become disrupted and their poverty will force them to depend upon charity. *Those families that possess some heritage of family traditions and education will resist the destructive forces of urban life more successfully than the illiterate Negro folk. In either case their family life will adapt itself to the secular and rational organization of urban life.*[24]

Meanwhile, Frazier has a much more complex and dialectical understanding of the interplay between family and community relations: *"But, in the final analysis, the process of assimilation and acculturation will be limited by the extent to which the Negro becomes integrated into the economic organization and participates in the life of the community."*[25]

Moynihan was highly selective not only in his use of *The Negro Family in the United States* but also in his exclusion of any of Frazier's writings that repudiated the pathology model of family life. For example, Moynihan used a relatively obscure article by Frazier to make his point in the conclusion of the report that "as a result of family disorganization a large proportion of Negro children and youth have not undergone the socialization which only the family can provide. The disorganized families have failed to provide for their emotional needs and have not provided the discipline and habits which are necessary for personality development." Again, Moynihan fails to quote an important qualifying statement that, in Frazier's original article, appears right before the sentences above and in the same paragraph:

> *It appears that the first most important problem resulting from widespread family disorganization among Negroes is economic because about a fifth of the Negro children and youth must depend upon the earnings of the mother or female head of the family. This problem has been alleviated to some extent by the provision of aid to dependent children. However, the lightening of the burden of Negro mothers has not helped much the social problems of children and youth in disorganized Negro families.*[26]

Frazier in fact did think that social instabilities in family and community life generated enormous hardships and problems for black youth, but he did not share Moynihan's social-psychological framework of analysis. Moynihan fails, for example, to cite Frazier's important 1940 study on black youth, *Negro Youth at the Crossways,* no doubt because it offers a complex, subtle discussion of the interrelationship of racism, segregation, family life, and personality development.[27] Furthermore, if Moynihan had referred to Frazier's 1949 textbook, *The Negro in the United States,* he would have found that Frazier did not attribute responsibility for youth crime to the family.[28]

By the early 1950s Frazier was questioning quantitative studies based on positivist methodology, such as the Moynihan Report, on the grounds that they generally failed to "show any organic relationship among the elements which they utilize for analysis." In this article, readily available to Moynihan, Frazier, for example, rejected as simplistic the theory that lack of education is "the most important factor in the high crime rates among Negroes." He pointed to the increasing criminal behavior of college graduates, while "small semi-rural Negro communities with a high degree of illiteracy have remained relatively free of crime."[29] Similarly, he rejected the social-psychological approach as "too narrow" because "it does not reveal the important economic, political, and other cultural and institutional factors which are determinants of race relations."[30]

Unfortunately, most critics of Frazier's interpretation of the family either have accepted Moynihan's version of Frazier's ideas or, following Moynihan, have abstracted Frazier's early work from its social milieu and from the totality of his contributions. Most of Frazier's critics, with the notable exception of Gutman,[31] have failed to observe C. Wright Mills's advice that "the biographies of men and women, the kinds of individuals they variously become, cannot be understood without reference to the historical structures in which the milieux of their everyday life are organized."[32]

Saving the Negro's Self-Respect

In the aftermath of the Moynihan Report, Frazier was accused of either denying the authenticity, even existence, of a distinct Afro-American culture or viewing this culture as simply a reaction to the dominant culture. "Frazier," wrote one critic, "wanted to achieve the race's salvation through its eventual disappearance, culturally and biologically." [1] A review of Frazier's writings and speeches, especially from the 1920s and 1930s, suggests that he had a different and much more complex understanding of cultural issues.

The Greatest Crime

Frazier argued—and it was a debate that he carried on with Melville Herskovits until the day he died—that the institution of slavery destroyed the legacy of African traditions and made the African experience in the United States different from that of the European immigrant.[2] "The manner in which Negro slaves were collected in Africa and disposed of after their arrival in this country," wrote Frazier in his 1930 study of slave families, "would make it improbable that their African traditions were preserved." [3] Frazier felt that it was futile to explain the behavior and norms of black communities by reference to African traditions, whether this effort was undertaken by racists who wanted to prove that the "loose morality" of Afro-Americans was an indication of their "primitive" past or by cultural relativists who wanted to demonstrate that the culture of Afro-Americans was not inferior but just different or by nationalists who wanted to celebrate their African roots. "In spite of the efforts of those who would dig up his African past," asserted Frazier, "the Negro is a stranger to African culture." [4]

Frazier also held the view, later shared by Stanley Elkins and others, that slavery was a total institution that destroyed or deformed traditional forms of black family and community life. At the same time, Frazier did not see this destruction as uniform, nor did he see the Afro-American family as monolithic. As discussed later, he found tremendous variety, resilience, and strength in the slave household. Similarly, he did not take a mechanical view of culture but rather examined how black communities continually created and asserted the validity of indigenous institutions and social relations in the face of efforts to negate their existence. To Frazier, an essential aspect of the struggle against racism was the defense, assertion, and reproduction of cultural integrity in a society whose "greatest crime of the age" was the "denial of personality to the Negro."[5]

Frazier tirelessly chronicled community life and social customs, sketching portraits of human diversity and articulating contradictions that challenged the prevailing reification of Afro-Americans as "saints" or "stones."[6] "White Atanta," he wrote in a scathing piece for the *Messenger,* "knows nothing of black Atlanta, except through Negro servants and criminals." He despised the white press for reducing black people to "contented darkies, criminals and clowns."[7]

For Frazier, it was a political, as well as an intellectual, obligation to paint a full picture of the communities he knew, with all their nuances, social distinctions, traditions, and sorrows. Drawing on social work's case method, he went to the docks, union halls, and saloons in New York to document the lives of black longshoremen; using what he learned in his studies of cooperatives in Denmark, he explored neighborhood organizations and self-help enterprises in Atlanta and Durham; "tramping through the rural South," as he put it,[8] he talked with sharecroppers about their daily lives and mechanisms of survival; he visited the homes and businesses of the rising class of black entrepreneurs; an atheist, he sat for many hours in churches and talked to people about their religious and spiritual beliefs; and he walked the neighborhoods and back streets of Chicago in order to appreciate the rhythms of big-city life. Moreover, between 1916 and 1934 he taught in almost every kind of Afro-American school—private, state, church-related, and public—an experience that gave him an intimate and direct knowledge of the problems in black education.[9]

His work of this period is filled with ethnographic richness and complexity based on firsthand experience and appreciation of the subjective factor in social life. In many of his writings and speeches, Frazier illuminated the complexity of black communities and brought to life the strengths and traditions that were ignored or distorted in the press and academia. For example, he took the readers of *Opportunity* on a journey through Chicago's Black Belt, describing how its worlds of business, religion, education, and culture were characterized by "social distinctions and class divisions," and "reproduced all the stages of culture and various aspects of Negro life at large." [10]

In a radio talk delivered when he was working with the Urban League in Chicago around 1928, Frazier challenged the prevailing stereotypes concerning the Black Belt. Most people, he said, think of it as a "region of Black and Tan Cabarets, where mulatto women give vent to the voluptuousness of their African blood, and white men forget their troubles in the intoxication of passion and bootleg liquor . . . while the rest of the population when not in church singing spirituals is disporting itself in cabarets." In fact, noted Frazier, the truth was much more mundane. The majority of southern blacks who came to Chicago were just like any immigrants who "had to stop praying and singing and dancing long enough to work and make a living."

However, Frazier warned against overly pathetic and sentimental interpretations of Afro-American life. "The Black Belt is not a place of lost souls. It is more often the place where Negroes find their souls. . . . It is within the struggles and achievements of this communal life that Negro life expresses itself in all of its phases." Visit the Black Belt and really look around, he told the audience. You will see artists, "the well-to-do who don't take in roomers," people shouting the blues, others singing conventional hymns, the sophisticated and ignorant. In sum, "it is a cross-section of Negro life in America."

He told the audience that he was sorry to "destroy the exotic and romantic picture of the Black Belt" as a place of "wild abandon and unbridled passion." If his listeners visited their black neighbors in their homes, "I must confess that it would be disappointing," concluded Frazier, "for it would show them to be no more interesting and exotic than most human beings." [11]

Cultural Self-Determination

Frazier did not regard culture as an amalgam of symbols and attributes in need only of preservation. It also had to be "consciously built up" and constructed in the face of competing values. In this sense, culture was an arena of political combat. "A group situated as the Negroes," he wrote in 1924, "must avoid the danger of unconsciously assimilating values which either have no meaning for [them] or which the leaders of thought in the world are trying to replace with higher values. The Negro, rather advantageously situated, should be a pioneer in enunciating values that those overwhelmed by their own culture could never attain. For example, there is no reason for the Negro to be an intense nationalist."[12]

Frazier made a point of reporting on efforts at self-help that built community cohesion and challenged stereotypes about the disorganization of Afro-American community life. In 1923 he wrote favorably about the efforts of Atlanta's Neighborhood Union to combat "rampant individualism" and develop a "self-sufficient and respectable community."[13] Similarly, he was impressed by the Fort Valley High and Industrial School in Georgia, where he taught summer school in 1917, because its teachers went out of the school to build institutions of "community life" for rural blacks.[14] Refuting "critics among colored people" who argued that "the race has not learned to cooperate," he pointed to the widespread participation in religious and civic organizations.[15] His textbook, published in 1949, devoted considerable space to slave revolts and resistance, mutual aid and fraternal organizations, and social movements.[16]

This politicized view of culture propelled Frazier into one of his first controversies. Among his early articles for Du Bois's *Crisis* was a polemic against black critics of self-defense who, "in the name of Christian humility," condemn "so-called agitators" and "even go so far as to repudiate the use of force on the part of their brethren in defending their firesides." Frazier, outraged by "this sort of self-abasement," argued that hatred could serve as a "positive moral force" and called on activists to "fight for the observance of the established principles of democratic political society."[17]

Frazier's brief article caused a stir at *Crisis*. Ellen Winsor, a Quaker and supporter of the NAACP, sent a letter of protest, expressing her "shock" at Frazier's views and asking, "Has not the Negro learnt to his sorrow that violent methods never win the desired goal? The Civil War but transferred the Negro from one form of slavery to another. The world has had enough of death, hatred and destruction since 1914. Where has Mr. Frazier hidden himself that he has not breathed the poison of disease, poverty, famine and bitterness sown broadcast over the nations of the earth by the makers of war?"[18]

Du Bois replied in defense of Frazier and published Frazier's response to Winsor as an editorial in *Crisis*. It is worth quoting much of
Frazier's response here because it reveals a great deal both about his
militancy and about his critique of any program, cultural or otherwise,
that encouraged Afro-Americans to disengage from the struggle for full
equality:

> Let me just make it clear that I could not, in the face of patent facts,
> believe that wholesale violence on the part of Negroes would win for them
> the status they desire in this country. Yet, I am convinced that violent de-
> fense in local and specific instances has made white men hesitate to make
> wanton attacks upon Negroes.
>
> I too have beheld the harvest of disease, poverty, famine and bitterness
> reaped by those who trusted in war to achieve democracy and make an end
> of wars. And, living in the South as I do, I must breathe in daily the stench
> of race prejudice. Yet, however much we may lament war, it appears that a
> disillusioned, but stupid world must undergo another war before white men
> will learn to respect the darker races. . . .
>
> I am primarily interested in saving the Negro's self-respect. If the
> masses of Negroes can save their self-respect and remain free from hate, so
> much the better for their moral development. One's refusal to strike back is
> not always motivated by a belief in the superiority of moral force any more
> than retaliation is always inspired by courage. In the first case it is often
> pure cowardice while in the latter, the fear of the censure of the herd. I
> believe it would be better for the Negro's soul to be seared with hate than
> dwarfed by self-abasement. Therefore my essay was directed against those
> Negro leaders who through cowardice and for favors deny that the Negro
> desires the same treatment as other men. Moreover they are silent in the
> face of barbarous treatment of their people and would make us believe this
> is the Christian humility.
>
> I do not oppose the efforts of those who endeavor to instill into the Ne-
> gro a genuine belief in the brotherhood of man and the superiority of moral
> force. But suppose there should arise a Ghandi to lead Negroes without
> hate in their hearts to stop tilling the fields of the South under the peonage
> system; to cease paying taxes to States that keep their children in igno-
> rance; and to ignore the iniquitous disenfranchisement and Jim-Crow laws.
> I fear we would witness an unprecedented massacre of defenseless black
> men and women in the name of Law and Order and there would scarcely
> be enough Christian sentiment in America to stay the flood of blood.[19]

Frazier's primary interest in "saving the Negro's self-respect" was a
recurring theme in his writings during the 1920s. "Only education and
culture," he wrote in 1925, can generate "a sense of personal worth and

save them from reliance upon a group egotism whose only badge is color."[20] He initially hoped that Afro-American colleges, emerging from their longtime dependence on missionary and philanthropic control, might play a critical role in preparing students for a "deeper and more responsibile participation in our civilization." To Frazier this meant more than a "narrow and selfish individualism" or the "hypocritical and militant counterfeit Christianity of white civilization."[21]

Frazier had further ideas about what an Afro-American culture did not entail. He was opposed to any cultural program that hinted of moral uplift or interracial benevolence. For example, he was offended by the efforts of white reformers to clean up vice in Chicago's Black Belt. It did not surprise Frazier that people preferred "living in hell as equals than living in a Jim Crow heaven supervised by white folk."[22] He was often sceptical about what Western civilization had to offer Afro-Americans. On one occasion he recalled "the remark of an Alabama judge that there was as much difference between human nature and Negro nature as between chalk and cheese. Well," said Frazier, "let us hope that the Negro will never acquire such human nature as one finds in such barbarous parts of America as Alabama and Georgia."[23]

However, Frazier was also critical of middle-class projects, embodied in the New Negro movement, to build a self-contained, indigenous black culture. In the 1920s he readily agreed with his friend "Dock" Steward that the "New Negro hokum" was not particularly new nor particularly black.[24] Frazier also thought that an exclusive focus on culture undermined the struggle for social and economic equality. This new nationalist movement, wrote Frazier in 1928, "looks askance at the new rising class of black capitalism while it basks in the sun of white capitalism. It enjoys the congenial company of white radicals while shunning association with black radicals. The New Negro Movement functions in the third dimension of culture; but so far it knows nothing of the other two dimensions—Work and Wealth."[25]

Frazier worried too that the tendency to "build up an isolated and self-sufficient Negro culture," however much it was dictated by the necessities of enforced segregation, would further marginalize Afro-American communities. A narrow and precarious line had to be walked, noted Frazier in his 1927 essay "Racial Self-Expression," between "an attempt to efface Negroid characteristics" and "a glorification of things black." He thought that both these positions were extremist.

On the one hand, he advocated efforts to "turn within" Afro-American experience in order to generate "materials for artistic creation and group tradition." He thought it was quite possible that the "Negro artist working on the materials of the Negro's experience in America will create greater works than white artists" and make "a distinct contribution to the general fund of American culture." In fact, he thought it was undesirable for "the Negro to acquire uncritically all the traits of American culture," to be "smothered . . . into generally accepted molds."

On the other hand, he was opposed to the concept of a "unique cultural development for the Negro." He thought this idea was oversimplified and politically dangerous because it confirmed the prejudices of scientific racism and condemned Afro-Americans to a separate and inferior isolation. To Frazier, "any nationalistic program that made the Negro seek compensations in a barren racial tradition and thereby escape competition with the white man which was an inevitable accompaniment of full participation in American culture, would lead to intellectual, spiritual and material impoverishment such as one finds among the Southern mountain whites."[26]

In 1928, noting that the New Negro movement was heading "in the direction of cultural autonomy," Frazier raised his concerns. Given his view that Afro-Americans were severed from their "African past" and through slavery and other institutions were "forced to participate in the whole gamut of American life," he felt that culturally—as well as economically and politically—"the Negro . . . is tied up so intimately with the whole fabric of American life." This did not mean, however, that the Afro-American had to "fall in with every fad of American life."[27]

In a speech delivered at Bethel Church in Nashville in 1934, Frazier was critical of Afro-American leaders who encouraged people to aspire simply to white culture and fashions. Maintaining one's racial identity was more important, he said, than slavish imitation, which led to skin bleaching and hair straightening.[28] In another speech, he pointed out that "in this mad attempt to conform to the white man's ways and standards, the Negro's behavior ranged from attempts to change his physical features to an almost morbid fear of being ungrammatical in his speech. . . . This passion for identity and equality with the whites was a part of the naive faith on the part of the Negro that racial barriers would be broken down as soon as he proved himself the same as the dominant race. But he found that where greater participation was

gained in the culture of the whites he felt himself shut out more than
ever."[29]

Frazier was grappling to formulate a set of values that would develop
the notion of cultural self-determination in the context of American
life. At stake was the content of culture, which, Frazier argued, could
not be separated from issues of class and politics. Frazier's contributions were unique because of this effort to understand culture as a political and economic as well as an aesthetic phenomenon.

Racial Self-Expression

Frazier argued that there was a vital tradition of folk culture that needed
to be recognized and incorporated into modern life. Overall he appreciated the efforts of the New Negro movement to reconstitute "a sick
soul that is divided and is seeking to be made whole." And he did not
totally reject the significance of African cultural traditions. He argued,
however, that such traditions had to be "incorporated into the racial
tradition of the Negro group in America" through "artistic creations and
historical narratives." For Frazier, the past was a heritage for building
the future rather than a retreat from the present. African art and Afro-
American folk culture should not be "looked upon as something pathetic," observed Frazier, "but as a unique human experience which
adds to the fund of the world's spiritual values."[30]

He had concrete ideas about how to develop artistic expression in
everyday life. For example, he suggested that instead of holding annual
fashion shows—which promoted consumerism and illusions of
wealth—schools should take the "opportunity to create a real appreciation of the folk life of the Negro through dramatic expression." These
performances would develop acting skills in students and enable the
Afro-American school to play a strategic role in the cultural life of the
community. He was impressed by the efforts of socialist workers'
groups to develop a new form of proletarian culture and thought that
this goal could be adapted easily by "the Negro [who] has an experience
which is fertile with possibilities for creating a folk art." He welcomed
efforts to popularize and teach Afro-American history (as exemplified
in Negro History Week), the development of courses on Afro-
American history and children's history books, and the formation of
study clubs. He called on the New Negro leadership to "exploit a rich
source of racial experience for the enhancement of the lives of the

masses and at the same time bring the masses into communion with the creative spirits of the race. In this way the Negro will be creating a culture that will be unique but not in opposition to his growth and wider participation in American life as a whole."[31]

He was hopeful that "out of this struggle will come the Negro's soul—not sick and whining and torn with doubts—but sure of itself." In 1928 he thought it was a good sign that more and more Afro-Americans were boasting that they were descended from slaves who came to the United States on the last slave ship. This development demonstrated that people were coming to terms with their racial history and identity. "One may venture to prohesy," said Frazier anticipating the resurgence of cultural nationalism some forty years later, "that some day in the future the last slave ship will be as crowded as the Mayflower."[32]

Providing the Soul of a People

Perhaps Frazier's most definitive and straightforward statement about cultural issues appeared in his response to a survey conducted by the *Messenger* in 1927.[33] Writing with clarity and boldness, as he always did in nonacademic publications, Frazier succinctly expressed his views about racial consciousness.

> *Messenger:* 1. Is the development of Negro racial consciousness (a definite group psychology, stressing and laudation of things Negro) compatible with the ideal of Americanism (Nationalism) as expressed in the struggle of Aframericans for social and industrial equality with all other citizens?
>
> *Frazier:* The development of racial consciousness among Negroes may help the Negro to place a true valuation upon his personality; but it does not appear compatible with the ideal of the modern commonwealth. Much of the fanfare about racial consciousness has been forced upon the Negro by white people who are only interested in making the Negro a lower caste. The modern state may lose its present place in social development but new associations will hardly be formed strictly along racial lines except in the centers of homogeneous groups. The present problem of the Negro is to make white Americans recognize him as a citizen. *Civis Americanus sum* must mean more than shouldering a gun and dying.
>
> *Messenger:* 2. Will this ideal of equal rights and privileges be realized within the next century?

Frazier: I always hesitate to make any prophecy concerning the course of social evolution and events since over a million reputed freedom-loving Americans permitted themselves to be dragged across the ocean to insure the payments of allied debts to American capitalists. It appears to me, however, that before the American white man will voluntarily give equal rights and privileges to the Negro, the darker world, including China, India and Africa, will be militarized and industrialized enough to force the white world to throw off its mask of Christian missionary effort and the "white man's burden" ideal, with which it attempts to conceal its arrogant economic exploitation, and treat the darker races as equals. This will be bound to improve the black man's status in America, although I would not be surprised to find black fools fighting for their own enslavement.

Messenger: 3. If and when this ideal is realized, will it or will it not result in the disappearance of the Negro population through amalgamation?

Frazier: I believe that absolute equality will naturally lead (in how many centuries I dare not say) to amalgamation. I do not think it would proceed as fast as it has always done when the two populations are closer in physical appearance.

Messenger: 4. If the struggle for the attainment of full citizenship rights and privileges, including industrial equality, is to result in the disappearance of the Negro through amalgamation, do you consider the present efforts to inculcate and develop a race consciousness to be futile and confusing?

Frazier: As I said in answer to Question 1, the inculcation of racial consciousness can not be wholly futile, no matter what the outcome in America, if it makes the Negro place a true value upon his personality.

Messenger: 5. Do you consider complete amalgamation of the whites and blacks necessary to a solution of our problem?

Frazier: I do not consider complete amalgamation of the whites and blacks necessary to the solution of our problems. I often find white and black prostitutes, thieves and bootleggers living in harmony, without issue, while the smug inhabitants of Main Street, with yellow bastards hidden in the alleys, have stoned the homes of respectable Negroes.

Messenger: 6. Do you desire to see the Aframerican group maintain its identity and the trend toward amalgamation cease?

Frazier: I am not interested in the color of the future Americans; although I have some sentiment in regard to the continuation of civilization to which men of any color can be heirs.

Messenger: 7. Can a minority group like the Aframericans maintain separate identity and group consciousness, obtain industrial and social equality with the citizens of the majority group, and mingle freely with them?

Frazier: Social equality in its broadest interpretation will, I believe, gradually destroy both racial identity and group consciousness.

Messenger: 8. Do you or do not believe in segregation, and if so, in what form?

Frazier: I do not believe in any form of enforced segregation, except that of the insane and feeble-minded. The natural tendency for people of the same culture and interests to segregate themselves is not involved in the question of segregation as it affects Negroes.

Interest in the politics of culture diminished with the decline of the Negro Renaissance, which was replaced by a focus on economic issues in the 1930s and by the political and legal aspects of civil rights after World War II. But Frazier maintained his interest when the topic was no longer popular or fashionable. His 1940 study of Afro-American youth in Louisville and Washington, D.C., explored the self-identities and attitudes of young men and women living under forced segregation. He explored the "social and cultural world of the Negro" not from the viewpoint of "some peculiar racial endowment" but as a "more or less isolated social world, with its peculiar social definitions and meanings and with its own social evaluations and distinctions."[34]

His textbook, *The Negro in the United States,* begun in 1939 but not completed until ten years later, was essentially a cultural study. Unlike Gunnar Myrdal's *An American Dilemma,* which examined the nature and consequences of racism, Frazier's book focused on "the processes by which the Negro has acquired American culture and has emerged as a racial minority or ethnic group." Like his earlier writings that challenged the view of Afro-Americans as "saints or stones," *The Negro in the United States* challenged conventional "social problems" texts, which "usually treat Negroes as atomized individuals 'floating about' in American society."[35]

Until Frazier went to Paris to work with UNESCO in the early 1950s, his perspective on Afro-American culture was rooted in a national framework of analysis. Although his 1949 textbook ends on a provocative note, suggesting the necessity for global solutions to racism,[36] his overall analysis focuses on the social relations of Afro-Americans within U.S. society. In *Race and Culture Contacts in the Modern World,* published in 1957 after Frazier had the benefit of working with international scholars at UNESCO, Frazier examines racism from a global perspective. Here, for the first time, he explores the possibility of an "international society" based on "federated cultures" in a postimperialist world order where there is "racial and cultural differentiation without implications of superiority and inferiority." [37]

By the end of his life, armed with a new vision of the world, he returned once again to the cultural issues that had preoccupied him in the 1920s. In 1959 he was concerned that "the Negro intellectual and artist is sterilized by the dilemma in which he finds himself, by cutting himself off from his Negro or African background." With the exception of a few lone voices—such as those of Du Bois, Robeson, Langston Hughes, and Richard Wright—Frazier felt that most Afro-American intellectuals had become "parrots" and "opportunists," who "seek acceptance by white Americans at the price of losing all their racial and cultural identity and of being swallowed up in white America." [38]

In one of his last essays, published just before his death, Frazier reiterated his critique of his fellow intellectuals for failing to "place the fate of the Negro in the broad framework of man's experience in the world. . . . They have failed to dig down into the experiences of the Negro and provide the soul of a people." What little hope he felt for the possibility of racial equality in the United States was now inspired by revolutionary movements in Africa, which, one day, "would probably save the soul of the American Negro in providing him with a new identification, a new self-image, and a new sense of personal dignity." [39]

Scourges of the Negro Family

Frazier is variously celebrated and impugned for his pioneering studies of the Afro-American family. A close look suggests a more complex judgment about the originality of his scholarship, his innovative contributions, and problems in his analytical framework. It is necessary to get beyond a reductionist assessment—whether to idealize him as the "great man" of black sociology or to discredit him as the founder of the pathology perspective—and situate his ideas about the family in their historical and social context.

Origins

It has been argued that Frazier's work on the Afro-American family can be traced to the Chicago school. There is some truth to the claim, but, again, this one-dimensional interpretation underestimates both the variety of forces that influenced Frazier and also his own creativity and initiative. Frazier himself recalled that his first interest in the Afro-American family predated his studies in Chicago and was sparked by reading Du Bois's 1908 study, *The Negro American Family*, and working as a social worker in the South. "My feeling in regard to the work which some of us are doing," Frazier wrote Du Bois in 1939, "has been that we are building upon a tradition inaugurated by you in the Atlanta studies."[1] The tendency to ignore or underestimate Du Bois's influence on Frazier is echoed more generally by historians of sociology who typically do not take Du Bois seriously as a pioneer in the social sciences.[2]

Frazier's acknowledgment of Du Bois's influence was not just a polite gesture. His early work on the family was very much indebted to

Du Bois, whose 1908 report was essentially a prospectus for further research and analysis. Modern critics of Frazier who accuse him of being the father of the Moynihan Report generally omit the fact that Du Bois then must be its grandfather. There is little doubt that Frazier derived his world-view and initial research propositions about the family from Du Bois. Consider the following quotations from Du Bois and Frazier:

> For past American conditions the chief printed sources of information must be sought in the vast literature of slavery. It is difficult to get a clear picture of the family relations of slaves, between the Southern apologist and his picture of cabin life, with idyllic devotion and careless toil, and that of the abolitionist with his tale of family disruption and cruelty, adultery and illegitimate mulattoes. Between these pictures the student must steer carefully to find a reasonable statement of the average truth. (Du Bois)[3]

> Our information concerning the character of the slave family has been furnished chiefly by apologists for slavery, who have given us a picture of idyllic happiness under benevolent patriarchs; and by abolitionists whose literature abounded in stereotyped scenes of slave families being torn asunder by soulless masters. (Frazier)[4]

> Careful research would doubtless reveal many . . . traces of the African family in America. They would, however, be traces only, for the effectiveness of the slave system meant the practically complete crushing out of the African clan and family life. No more complete method of reducing a barbarous people to subjection can be devised. . . . On the whole it is fair to say that while to some extent European family morals were taught the small select body of house servants and artisans, both by precept and example, the great body of field hands were raped of their own sex customs and provided with no binding new ones. (Du Bois)[5]

> Probably never before in history has a people been so nearly completely stripped of its social heritage as the Negroes who were brought to America. Other conquered races have continued to worship their household gods within the intimate circle of their kinsmen. But American slavery destroyed household gods and dissolved the bonds of sympathy and affection between men of the same blood and household. Old men and women might have brooded over memories of their African homeland, but they could not change the world about them. Through force of circumstances, they had to acquire a new language, adopt new habits of labor, and take over, however imperfectly, the folkways of the American environment. (Frazier)[6]

The private home as a self-protective, independent unit did not exist. That powerful institution, the polygamous African home, was almost completely destroyed, and in its place in America arose sexual promiscuity, a weak community life, with common dwelling, meals, and child nurseries. . . . Broadly speaking, the greatest social effect of American slavery was to substitute for the polygamous Negro home a new polygamy less guarded, less effective, and less civilized. (Du Bois)[7]

In Africa the Negro lived under regulated sex relations which were adapted to his social and physical environment. It was through the destruction in America of these institutionalized sex relations that slavery was able to bring about complete subordination. (Frazier)[8]

The slaves on the plantations lived in the demoralized condition that naturally followed the destruction of the African tribal and family controls and the exigencies of the status of chattel property. (Frazier)[9]

Though Frazier relied on Du Bois for perspective and a research strategy, his writings went far beyond what Du Bois himself recognized as only a "sketch."[10] Between 1926 and 1933 Frazier wrote two books and published ten articles on the Afro-American family. His major and best-remembered book, *The Negro Family in the United States*, published in 1939, was a synthesis of his previous studies. Frazier's approach to studying the Afro-American family was quite eclectic; his theoretical framework drew on history, sociology, social psychology, and Afro-American studies. And, in addition to Du Bois, he relied on his mentors and colleagues in Chicago. From Robert Park he received confirmation of his views about the severance of African links and demoralization of the Afro-American family in slavery; from Ernest Burgess and Ernest Mowrer came the ecological approach and the impact of urban processes on family structure; from W. I. Thomas and Florian Znaniecki's classic study of *The Polish Peasant in Europe and America* (1927) came the methodology of "natural history" and the twin concepts of disorganization and reorganization.[11]

Frazier was first exposed to the ideas of the Chicago Shcool when he went to Atlanta in 1922. "My interest in the study of the Negro family," he recalled, "began while I was director of the Atlanta School of Social Work. Through the reading of the works of Burgess and Mowrer, I developed the idea that a more fundamental knowledge of the processes of disorganization and reorganization of Negro family life than was in existence at that time should be made available for social workers."[12]

When Frazier attended summer school at the University of Chicago in 1923, he took Park's class "The Crowd and the Public." During that summer, he and Park discussed the possibility of a dissertation on the Afro-American family. Frazier hoped to return to Chicago in the summer of 1924 but his work at the Atlanta School of Social Work prevented him from doing so. "This does not mean," he wrote Park in July 1924, "that I have abandoned my work on my doctorate, or that I have ceased to work on the thesis subject that you suggested to me. I feel now that I have a clearer conception than ever of just what you want me to work out."[13] "I am very glad to know," responded Park, "that you are still interested in the thesis subject which we agreed upon last summer."[14]

Park was one of several people who encouraged Frazier's interest in the Afro-American family. In the summer quarter of 1927 Frazier took a course on "The Family" from Earle Eubank, whose dissertation, "A Study of Family Desertion," was completed at Chicago in 1915.[15] In another class Frazier took that summer, "Social Origins," taught by Park, he studied the work of anthropologist Melville Herskovits and wrote a research paper entitled "The Family among Some Tribes in the East African Cattle Area."[16] When he was ready to begin research on his dissertation topic, the Negro family in Chicago, he was encouraged to apply an ecological framework, at that time the dominant paradigm of the Chicago School. "One day in 'The Temple,' as the old social research laboratory was called, I separated the data on Negro home-ownership from similar data for whites according to zones of urban expansion in order to find out if the rates for Negroes showed a gradient as did the figures for the total population." This exercise led Frazier "to discover zones in the Negro community which became a frame of reference for my other data on the family."[17]

Finally, it should be pointed out that Frazier had been teaching courses on the family since 1923 and doing research and interviews on the history and variety of the Afro-American family in the South for many years before he began seriously studying with the Chicago School. Thus he brought a wealth of experience, knowledge, and empirical data to the sociological theories that he absorbed in Chicago. In a sense, Frazier came to the formal study of the family as a historian. Sociology gave him analytical constructs for shaping his narratives into a new language.

1. Edward F. Frazier, c. 1906. Courtesy: E. Franklin Frazier Papers, Moorland-Spingarn Research Center, Howard University.

2. Frazier at Ullerod's Consumers' Cooperative in Denmark, 1922. Courtesy: Hampton University Archives.

3. Frazier, center, with Langston Hughes, Charles Johnson, Rudolph Fisher, and Hubert Delany in New York, May 1925. Courtesy: E. Franklin Frazier Papers, Moorland-Spingarn Research Center, Howard University.

4. Frazier speaking at May Day rally in Washington, D.C., 1937. Courtesy:
E. Franklin Frazier Papers, Moorland-Spingarn Research Center, Howard
University.

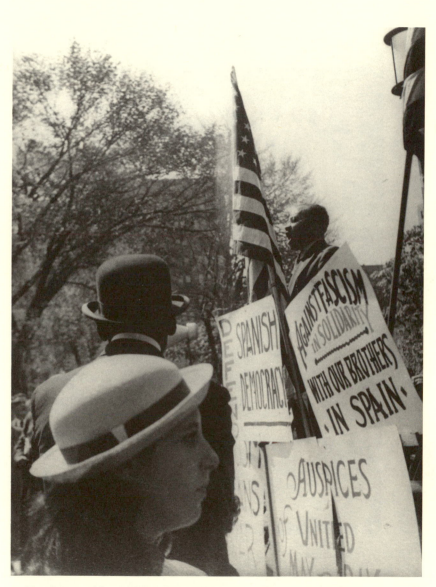

5. Frazier speaking at May Day rally in Washington, D.C., 1937. Courtesy: E. Franklin Frazier Papers, Moorland-Spingarn Research Center, Howard University.

6. Hilda Wilkinson Brown, "In the City of Destruction," linoleum cut from *The Negro Family in the United States,* by E. Franklin Frazier (Chicago: University of Chicago Press, 1939). Courtesy: University of Chicago Press.

7. Frazier, center, with W.E.B. DuBois and Horace Mann Bond; in fore-
ground, Julian Bond and Jane Bond, 1942. Courtesy of Julian Bond and Jane
Bond Moore.

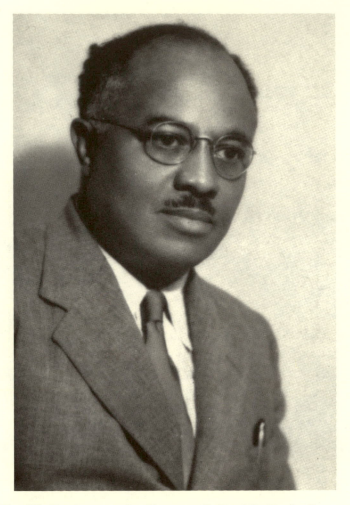

8. E. Franklin Frazier, c. 1961. Courtesy: E. Franklin Frazier Papers, Moorland-Spingarn Research Center, Howard University.

Criticisms

When Frazier began his research on Afro-American families, most of the available studies "presented a gloomy picture of widespread family disorganization and sexual immorality."[18] The prevailing literature assumed that Afro-Americans were either inherently or culturally incapable of being assimilated into "Western civilization." Frederick Hoffman (writing in 1896) noted that "neither religion nor education" had appreciably influenced "the moral progress of the race." William H. Thomas (1901) wrote about the "moral putridity" of Afro-Americans, and sociologist Howard Odum (1910) characterized "the Negro" as "destitute of morals as any of the lower animals." Joseph Tillinghast (1902) thought that the weaknesses of the Afro-American family was the result of the lack of parental affection and responsibility in the West African family structure, while Jerome Dowd (1926) argued that "the animistic and polytheistic religion of the African Negroes . . . promotes sexual incontinence, and exalts it to a virtue." Similarly, sociologist Edward Reuter (1927) suggested that an extrovert temperament and "strong sex appetite . . . dispose the Negroes to a degree of sex promiscuity not common to other groups."[19]

Frazier explicity set out to repudiate these racist interpretations and to demolish stereotypes about the monolithic nature of the black family. As Herbert Gutman noted, Frazier was the first intellectual to challenge seriously those who articulated racial theories of Afro-American culture and family life.[20] Frazier hoped his work would refute the predominant view that the "widespread demoralization of family life was a sign of the inability of the Negro to measure up to the sex standards of Western civilization."[21] In 1930 he recognized that "there does not exist a systematic study of the Negro family that gives authentic information on this important aspect of Negro life."[22] He wanted to correct the bias of existing studies, which "have most often dealt with the pathological side of family life and have become the basis of unwarranted generalizations concerning the character of the whole group."[23]

Although the storm of controversy about Frazier's portrait of the Afro-American family did not erupt until after his death, he was aware that his work was controversial. He noted in 1944 that he had been "attacked as a 'prejudiced Texas cracker'" because "instead of building a defense of the disorganization of Negro family life, I accepted it as a fact and documented it." Sometimes, he continued, "I was criticized by Negroes because I did not represent Negro women as martyrs in their relations with southern white men, and I was criticized by some whites for being 'too damned objective.' "[24]

Three major criticisms of Frazier's work on the family, commonly raised after his death and in the wake of the Moynihan Report, deserve serious attention here: that he regarded the black family, destroyed or permanently deformed by slavery, as culturally "deviant"; that he promoted the view, in the words of one his professors at the University of Chicago, that "*the chief handicap* from which the Negro suffers is perhaps not poverty, nor overcrowding, however serious and challenging these problems may be, but the persistence of an unorganized and disorganized family life";[25] and that he regarded most Afro-American families as matriarchal and therefore dysfunctional.[26]

Disorganization

Frazier focused extensively on the disorganized Afro-American family in all its historical forms—under slavery, after Reconstruction, in the countryside, and in the metropolis. For Frazier, even under the most favorable conditions of slavery, "the slave system made the family insecure in spite of the internal character of the family."[27] After slavery, the rural family, "with its dependence upon the exigencies of a capitalistic agriculture and the dominant white community," generally expressed "the degradation of the impoverished country Negro."[28] Later, after the great migration to urban centers, "the widespread disorganization of family life among Negroes has affected practically every phase of their community life and adjustments to the larger white world. Because of the absence of stability in family life, there is a lack of traditions. Life among a large proportion of the urban Negro population is casual, precarious, and fragmentary. It lacks continuity and its roots do not go deeper than the contingencies of daily living."[29]

As Herbert Gutman and others have pointed out, there are some serious problems with Frazier's use of disorganization as an analytical construct. He had a tendency to read the modern condition of the family after World War I back into the nineteenth-century slave experience.[30] At times, Frazier used *disorganization* in a normative sense, juxtaposed with *civilization*; occasionally he used it synonymously with *urbanization*.[31] With his continued reference to the chaos and disorganization in urban black family patterns, Frazier seriously underestimated the resources, ingenuity, and *organization* of "demoralized" families.[32] Moreover, he shared many of the prevailing assumptions of a Victorian-gendered morality, no doubt reinforced by his own conventional marriage and sexual division of household labor. His writings on the family are filled with prudish and class-biased allusions to "moral degradation" and "promiscuous sexual relations."[33]

However, we should not impose contemporary insights on Frazier's efforts from the 1920s onward. When he began writing about the Afro-American family, the prevailing interpretations were racial or biological, and in academic and professional circles the superiority of an idealized, middle-class, nuclear family was assumed. Frazier was innovative in demonstrating that the problems of the black family were socially constructed rather than culturally inherited, that the disorganization of the family was created within and by Western civilization, not by the failure of Africans to live up to American standards.

Another tendency has been to overstate Frazier's pathological perspective. He did not regard the Afro-American family as permanently and uniformly disorganized by slavery and its aftermath. Frazier's family is in fact a broad spectrum of families, constantly in a process of change and reorganization, depending on a complex interrelationship of economic, cultural, and social forces. He was interested in the varieties of the Afro-American family as an institution that, at different times and under different conditions, was sometimes disorganized and demoralized, sometimes tenacious and resourceful. On many occasions he was nonmoralistic and evenhanded on this issue. "In the Negro family we have two forces at work," he wrote in 1927, "those causing its integration, and those tending to disintegrate it."[34] In particular, Frazier did not find any relationship between "the racial or biological factor" and social disorganization in families. "I found mulatto and pure black families that were well organized and mulatto and pure black families that were completely disorganized."[35]

Although he was clearly alarmed about the demoralizing impact of racism on black family life, Frazier was also committed to investigating and describing the diversity of the family. "It is not surprising," he wrote in 1926, "that [Negro] family life without the support of custom and a venerated tradition, has tended towards instability, but rather that it has shown such vitality."[36] In his essay "The Negro Slave Family," Frazier pursued this theme, exploring how slave families compensated for their legal nonrecognition, which reduced them to "utilities with no will of their own," by creating "a little society of their own" and a "relatively autonomous social world," characterized by "distinctions of status and social functions. They had their own religious and moral leaders and in some communities a public opinion was powerful enough to restrain unapproved conduct."[37]

Frazier described how slave families developed "a family consciousness and a family organization" despite the economic imperatives of slavery, which necessitated the continous breaking up and reshaping of social relations. He reported that "in some slave families we find a high degree of organization and a deep sense of family responsibility. . . . That there developed within the circle of the slave family enduring sentiments that held the members of the family together is attested by numerous cases." Frazier noted that there was "a wide range of differences in the status of the Negro family under the institution of slavery."[38]

In *The Negro Family in the United States*, to which critics usually point as an example of Frazier's reductionist paradigm, again we find that Frazier is quite sensitive to how the various forms of the Afro-American family, from the earliest days of slavery through the rise of an industrial proletariat, were shaped both by impersonal socio-economic forces and by subjective initiative. It is true that Frazier emphasized the disorganized family—"the waste of human life, the immorality, delinquency, desertions, and broken homes"—but he also devoted a major portion of the book to documenting how the slave family endured despite its treatment as "human chattel," how mothers and grandmothers during slavery and after Reconstruction provided the family unit with untold stability and continuity, and how the newly urban family was strengthened by a "racial consciousness that they had never known" in the South.[39]

Many year later, in the aftermath of the Moynihan Report and in the context of a resurgent cultural nationalism, some objected to Frazier's emphasis on the damage done by racism to family and community. The same controversy was revived in the late 1980s with respect to the "underclass" debate.[40] But in the 1920s and 1930s, when Frazier was trying to document the pathology of race prejudice, such a view was still heretical. Richard Wright, for example, relied on Frazier's research to document the legacy and atrocities of racism within black communities. Wright was much more eloquent, but his framework was clearly derived from Frazier:

Perhaps never in history has a more utterly unprepared folk wanted to go to the city; we were barely born as a folk when we headed for the tall and sprawling centers of steel and stone. We, who were landless upon the land; we, who had barely managed to live in family groups; we, who needed the ritual and guidance of institutions to hold our atomized lives together in lines of purpose; we, who had known only relationships to people and not relationships to things; we who had never belonged to any organizations except the church and burial societies; we, who had had our personalities blasted with two hundred years of slavery and had been turned loose to shift for ourselves—we were such a folk as this when we moved into a world that was destined to test all we were, that threw us into the scales of competition to weigh our mettle. And how were we to know that, the moment we landless millions of the land—we men who were struggling to be born—set our awkward feet upon the pavements of the city, life would begin to exact of us a heavy toll in death?[41]

Disorganization as the Chief Handicap

There is no foundation for the second charge against Frazier. Although he regarded instabilities in family life as a tremendous impediment to social and racial equality, he found it almost impossible to separate the family from other institutions, and certainly he did not subscribe to the view that disorganized family life was the chief handicap of the black community, no matter how much Burgess, Moynihan, and others attributed this view to him.

Frazier's perspective on the family was genuinely interdisciplinary, and his solutions to family disorganization were similarly complex and multifaceted. Though he was more of an economic determinist than a social psychologist, he was opposed to one-dimensional approaches to social policy. In one of his earliest essays on the family, for example, he described the "three scourges of the Negro family" as disorganization, poverty, and lack of health services. He recognized that standing behind the problems of the family were "big economic forces which are to a large extent beyond our control" and "with people living on such a level [of subsistence] the slightest cessation of income brings a crisis in the family."[42] In another essay, Frazier similarly observed that the "fate and fortunes" of newly urbanized families "will depend upon both their economic and their cultural resources."[43]

By the mid-1930s, after Frazier had begun to express a more global and more developed socioeconomic perspective, his statements about the family regularly were couched in a broad framework. In his 1935 study of Harlem, prepared for Mayor LaGuardia's riot commission, he rooted the problems of everyday life and community relations in the "injustices of discrimination in employment, the aggressions of the police, and racial segregation." He was convinced that "the low economic status of the Negro in Harlem is basic to every other problem in the community."[44] A few years later, he noted that "the poverty and disorganization of Negro family life in the urban environment only become intelligible when they are studied in relation to the organization of Negro commuities and the social and economic forces which determine their development."[45] This remained his viewpoint throughout the rest of his life.

Matriarchy

The third major criticism of Frazier's work on the family asserts that he exaggerated the statistical significance of female-centered households and created a demeaning, sexist stereotype of the "black matriarchy."[46] Gutman and others have conducted a variety of sophisticated studies to demonstrate that Frazier overcounted the female-headed households among slave and antebellum black families.[47] On this point, there is little dispute.

Regarding Frazier's sexism, his influence on the Moyhihan Report is again the starting point for most critiques. "Ours is a society," noted Moynihan, "which presumes male leadership in private and public affairs. The arrangements of society facilitate such leadership and reward it. A subculture, such as that of the Negro American, in which this is not the pattern, is placed at a distinct disadvantage."[48] According to Paula Giddings, one of Frazier's fiercest critics, Moynihan derived his basic argument from Frazier—"Black family stability could be achieved only if Black men could 'strut,' even, if need be, at the expense of women." With Frazier "setting the tone," continues Giddings, "Black women were scolded for being too domineering and too insecure; too ambitious and too decadently idle, all in the same breath."[49]

Like Moynihan, Giddings reads more into Frazier's texts than the evidence warrants.[50] Many of Frazier's writings on the family assumed that the nuclear family and patriarchal authority represent an evolutionary development, that masculine and feminine gender roles are naturally constituted rather than the result of a socially constructed and negotiated process. However, he did not approve of masculine superiority within the family, nor did he regard assertive women as emasculators. Writing, for example, about middle-class families after World War II, he noted that where there was a "spirit of democracy" in households, it was "due partly to the tradition of independence among Negro women."[51]

In the last years of his life, Frazier witnessed the rise of the civil rights movement and recognized the central role played by women. One of his last essays was an unqualified defense and appreciation of women's leadership:

> The Negro woman in the United States has always played an important role both in race relations and in the social organization of Negro life in general. One might almost say that the Negro woman has occupied a strategic position from the standpoint of race relations. During the period of slavery the biological tie between the Negro mother and her offspring was the only human relationship among the slaves that could not be disregarded altogether. . . . Then, from the standpoint of the Negro's revolt against slavery, the Negro woman was a conspicuous figure in the Underground Railroad.
>
> After Emancipation when the whole social fabric of life crumbled and the very economic basis of Negro existence was destroyed, it was the Negro woman, often alone with her children but always aiding her husband when there was one, who made the survival of the Negro possible. . . . During the years of strife and struggle of Negroes for rights as citizens or even to be treated as mere human beings, when Negro men were lynched and not permitted to play the normal masculine role in an American culture, the Negro woman achieved a position of dominance and dignity.
>
> As Negro men have gained increased economic emancipation and security by becoming part of the army of industrial workers of the country and have entered professional and technical positions, Negro men have played a more important role in family life and their relation with the Negro woman has changed. Nevertheless, the traditional spirit of independence and self-assertion of the Negro woman has not been lost. *It has provided generally a pattern of equalitarian relationships between men and women for Americans.* . . . Today as the younger Negroes, especially the students, are revolting against the complacent and hesitant leadership of the respectable bourgeois leadership, the young Negro women, who are imbued with the spirit of self-assertion and self-reliance of their mothers and grandmothers, are fighting alongside their brothers and going to jail with their male classmates. Therefore, it appears that as the Negro women gains a real education and true sophistication, she will no longer be a mere

symbol of bourgeois sentimentality pleading a cause. For she is breaking down racial barriers by gaining true distinction as an artist, singer, dancer, actor, sculptor—and promises in the not too distant future to become an independent thinker as well. *Therefore, if she is true to her tradition of independence and self-assertion, she will not be satisfied with mere acceptance by white America but will join with the women of the world in the revolution which is creating a new world which will be free of colonialism, racial distinctions, and economic exploitation.*[52]

Black Bourgeoisie

Frazier's work on the middle class has generally been regarded as peripheral to his substantive contributions. His *Black Bourgeoisie* has been called variously a "polemic," "impressionistic . . . rather than scholarly," and "Menckenesque burlesque."[1] The issues raised in Frazier's 1955 book, however, were both a political concern and an object of study throughout his life, from his first polemic in 1918 to his last essay in 1962.

His antiwar pamphlet *God and War,* written during World War I, included a critique of the historical role of the "priestly class," who, although originally a creative social force, were soon "turning nations into stone and the past into sacredness" in order to "maintain their authority and inviolable position."[2] Some forty-four years later, Frazier launched a similar polemic at "Negro intellectuals" for their "abject conformity in thinking."[3] Even after his ashes had been scattered, Frazier aimed a final barb at the "petty tyrants in the Negro churches" and "their counterparts in practically all other Negro organizations."[4]

Although he may have first written *Black Bourgeoisie* sitting in cafés in Paris,[5] he treated the topic with the same seriousness and passion that he brought to his other work. Throughout his career Frazier struggled to capture the changing role of the Afro-American middle class, its complex character and interests, its role in shaping and restraining the politics of the Afro-American majority, its deprecation of folk culture, and its love-hate relationship with white society. He was particularly interested in demonstrating the socioeconomic diversity within Afro-American communities and exposing the collaborative and oppressive role played by a black bourgeoisie that "has exploited the Negro masses as ruthlessly as have whites."[6]

Dark-skinned and coming as he did from a working-class family with petty-bourgeois sensibilities, Frazier well understood the contradictions of the middle class he worked so hard to enter but from which he always felt a profound alienation. On the basis of his own experience, Frazier agreed with Benjamin Stolberg that a black intellectual was "less likely to be a shock trooper than a shock absorber."[7] The middle class, he noted in the 1950s, "placed an exaggerated importance upon academic degrees, especially if they were secured [like Frazier's] from white colleges in the North. If one secured the degree of doctor of philosophy in a northern university, he was regarded as a sort of genius. . . . Education was an indication of their 'superior culture' and a mark of 'refinement.' "[8]

Shock Absorbers

As Oliver Cox correctly pointed out, Frazier's class analysis was theoretically imprecise and stretched almost beyond recognition Marxist concepts of productive and economic relations.[9] Frazier's muddled middle class included the owners of small businesses, intellectuals, lawyers, doctors, preachers, service and clerical workers, plus skilled workers and foremen.[10] Frazier's concern and focus, however, were more political than economic. He knew that he was departing from traditional class analysis. "The term 'middle class' as used here," he wrote in his 1949 textbook, "refers to the class having an intermediate status between the upper and lower classes in the Negro community. Only a relatively small upper layer of this class is 'middle class' in the general American meaning of the term. Moreover 'middle class' as used here is essentially a social class though occupation and income play some part in determining its place in the class structure of the Negro community."[11]

In the same way that Frazier brought a class analysis to bear on cultural issues, so he also refused to accept a view of black communities as homogenous victims. What made Frazier controversial and subversive was his exploration of the dynamics of collusion and collaboration, notably the opportunism of "Negro leaders who through cowardice and for favors deny that the Negro desires the same treatment as other men."[12] This was hardly a popular endeavor given the prevailing efforts of organizations like the NAACP and NUL to focus on how all blacks were equally victimized by white racism. Moreover, the leaders of Afro-American organizations, the ones whom Frazier charged with cowardice, saw themselves as front-line activists in the struggle for racial equality. To Frazier, however, many were the descendants of the "faithful house-servants" and "waiting men" who took "presents of old coats, etc. from their masters" and betrayed Denmark Vesey.[13] Frazier regarded the rising, urban middle class as the new "waiting men," who on the basis of "a little education or turn of fortune" all too readily turned their backs on the "mass of Negroes." This stratum rejected Afro-American folk culture and was eager to "damn the black, greasy, boisterous Negro peasant in one breath and boast of their pride in Negro ancestry in the next."[14]

Frazier also had little patience for interracial ambassadors, well-meaning black and white liberals who encouraged cooperation without challenging the roots of segregation. To the New Negro crowd, in the words of historian David Lewis, "there was nothing wrong with American society that interracial elitism could not cure."[15] Frazier, however, had nothing but contempt for any program or attitude that hinted of paternalism, benevolence, or noblesse oblige. "The Negro does not want love. He wants justice," wrote Frazier in an essay written for *Crisis* in 1924. "Colored people who talk glibly of the white man's love forget that a man may love his dog. Love may make a man behave very unjustly towards those he loves. . . . Where love has appeared of such dubious value, as in the South, we take our stand under the banner, *Fiat Justitia, Ruat Amor.*"[16]

On another occasion, Frazier recalled the example of a white philanthropist who donated large sums of money for black education in the South. All went well until she attended a meeting where she met "Negroes as cultured and as intelligent as white people!" She left, "guilty and dismayed," determined never to support this cause again. "Her attitude towards Negroes," concluded Frazier, "was primarily that of a kindly lady who has sponsored a society for the prevention of cruelty to animals, but naturally resents rescued dogs, for example, assuming roles reserved for homo sapiens."[17]

Even on his speaking tours during the 1920s, important for fund raising and public relations, Frazier was neither reticent nor prudent. For example, at Oberlin he spoke out strongly against the Georgia Interracial Commission, an important sponsor of the social work program he directed; an irate member of the audience sent word back to Atlanta that Frazier had described the Commission as a "sentimental movement" that was "accomplishing little or nothing."[18]

Similarly, in a scathing critique of a book by Thomas Woofter, a white leader of the Committee on Interracial Cooperation and a trustee of the Atlanta School of Social Work, Frazier lectured the author on his myopia: "Mr. Woofter thinks the Negro objects to the Jim Crow car and segregation, because he receives unequal accommodation. Most Negroes whom I know object because it stigmatizes them as unfit for human association." As an evenhanded afterthough, Frazier berated Afro-American leaders who were willing to settle for Woofter's benevolence. "This book may offer consolation to a group willing to remain serfs because there are men who will protect them from the grosser forms of injustice and violence, but it offers no hope to that growing number of self-respecting and intelligent Negroes who want to be treated as other people."[19]

Frazier consistently spoke out against those he once called "professional good willers." Some advocated "separate but equal," some genuinely fought against segregation, but, "on the whole," reflected Frazier after he left the South, "the people who comprise the interracial committees are sentimental in their attitudes toward the Negro, and, what is more important, either do not possess power, or do not care to use it, in changing the status of the Negro in any fundamental sense."[20]

The Business of Culture

Frazier's critique of the black bourgeoisie—a topic he first tentatively explored in his master's thesis in 1920—was alluded to in various articles during the 1920s, hinted at in his essay for Alain Locke's *The New Negro,* and fully elaborated for the first time in 1928 in an article written for V. F. Calverton's *Modern Quarterly.* Frazier's controversial book on the same topic was first published in France in 1955,[21] but it was not until 1957, almost thirty years after he first forumulated his thesis, that the book was published in the United States.

Frazier's first serious article about the strengths and weaknesses of black business appeared in *Opportunity* in October 1924. Noting that the "ramifications of capitalist enterprise scarcely leave any phase of our economic life untouched," Frazier argued that it was time to clear away misconceptions about the possibilities for a self-sufficient economy. "Our zeal has often outrun our knowledge and experience. The failures along the road attest this disharmony." Frazier reviewed the leading examples of black-controlled enterprises—churches, real estate firms, insurance companies, banks, and retail stores—and concluded that their high mortality rate was due to lack of sufficient capital and credit, compounded by the tendency of business leaders to invest in extravagant consumption and "unproductive wealth."

Frazier was especially concerned that with the growth of Afro-American businesses "economic interests are going to divide Negro society into warring classes" and the rising petty bourgeoisie will "ape the manners and wasteful consumption of the liesure class in its days of unrestraint." Frazier initially hoped, albeit faintly, that the era of black business would "mean raising the general economic level of our group rather than the eruption of peaks of affluence to dazzle the mob." He called on business leaders to give up the false hope of launching corporate ventures and instead to develop cooperative enterprises.[22] Charles Johnson, at that time editor of *Opportunity,* thought that Frazier's article was "one of the best critiques of Negro business that has yet appeared in any publication," and it generated several appreciative comments from readers.[23]

This article led Alain Locke to ask Frazier to contribute an essay to an expanded anthology on *The New Negro.* Locke specifically wanted him to write about the "real Negro economic start" that was underway in Durham, North Carolina. Though Locke told Frazier, "you need not worry about liberal interpretation—the book is going to be full of that—and you need not be overlaudatory," he also made it clear that he wanted the book to "paint a vital phase of the race life."[24] Frazier agreed to Locke's request even though he had little information about Durham and had to complete the article within two weeks.[25]

In the Durham article Frazier attempts to straddle the fence. At first reading, it is a purely descriptive and appreciative discussion of how the "Negro is at last developing a middle class, and its main center is in Durham." The article describes the social origins of black businessmen, their efforts to acquire the "spirit of modern enterprise," and their successes in banking and insurance. "More and more," concluded Frazier in a tone of subdued neutrality, "certain elements of the race are absorbing the typical spirit and push of modern industrialism in America. . . . Through his effort and success, the Negro is becoming an integral part of the business life of America, and is sharing particularly in the economic development of the New South, which is perhaps the outstanding economic consequence of the World War on America."[26]

A close reading of "Durham," however, reveals nuances of irony and parody submerged within its celebratory ambiance. The new generation of black businessmen, noted Frazier, has "the same outlook on life as the middle class everywhere. They support the same theories of government and morality. . . . They are as typical of the New South as any white business man. Their outlook is the same. . . . White men have recognized these men as the supporters of property rights. They know these men would no more vote for Debs than they. Yet, there are still Jim Crow cars in North Carolina, and the Negro is denied civil and political rights."[27]

These subversive subtexts, however, constituted a fraction of the overall article, which, like the total contents of *The New Negro*, were designed, in Locke's words, to "celebrate the attainment of a significant and satisfying new phase of group development, and with it a spiritual Coming of Age."[28] Perhaps Frazier decided to be diplomatic and tactful for once; perhaps he settled for bland neutrality because it was flattering to be considered a leader of the New Negro movement. Whatever Frazier's motivation, the article, although not explicitly misrepresenting his views, did not accurately represent them. He did not believe that black economic progress would result from conventional capitalist enterprises. "I know, of course," he wrote in 1925 to his close friend, who worked for an insurance company, "that we need to amass capital through the mobilization of small amounts; but in my opinion the co-operatives appear the best means."[29] In 1927 he noted again that "the superstructure of Negro business which is being hailed as a significant economic development will rest upon an insecure basis in the absence of an industrial class."[30]

Even as he participated in and was recognized as a leader of the New Negro movement, Frazier regarded its development with scepticism and mistrust. Frazier and "Dock" Steward exchanged several letters in which they privately and candidly expressed their personal views. "I am losing patience with 'this new nigger' as typified by Locke, and the esoteric, esthetic Greekish crowd of his associates," wrote Steward in December 1927. He derided Locke as a "dilettante, . . . vain as a poppinjay" who finds it quite easy, given the "present fauning over Negroes the world offers," to "persuade himself" that he is "Jovian in significance. Alas!"[31] A few weeks later, Steward wrote Frazier that he was getting "weary of those fulsome self-adulations the Negro in America is so fond of dishing out to himself."[32]

Not long after, Steward found a journal that was willing to publish "The New Negro Hokum," an article that had been rejected by the Afro-American press and that he had revised several times to "appeal to some muddle-headed editor."[33] In this piece, Steward vented his critique of Locke's "crowd" without naming any names. The "New Negro legend," he wrote, is "unmitigated bunk." This "mythological figure" is being sold to the public like a publicity stunt. Whatever advances blacks had made in the struggle for social equality, Steward continued, could not be attributed to the "New Negro who, after the tumult and shouting dies, comes in for surveys and conferences and interracial backscratching and ponderous tomes." He pointed out that generations of activists and intellectuals preceded the New Negro, whose "renaissance" was exaggerated "hocus-pocus" and "not without profit to budding scribes, precariously financed Aframerican editors, and to even popular authors." Steward welcomed the fact that there were now more black writers, more black poets, more black artists. "But a New Negro? Hardly!"[34]

Meanwhile, Frazier was looking for an opportunity to express his views and to correct the favorable impressions of the New Negro that might have been communicated by his Durham article. He seized his chance when he was invited by Calverton, editor of the leftist *Modern Quarterly,* to submit "an article on the harmful influence of bourgeois psychology on the Negro movement, or something of the sort."[35] Some two weeks later, about the same time that "The New Negro Hokum" was published, Frazier completed his critique, which he titled in French, "no doubt to camouflage his Negro self-criticism," suggested Harold Cruse.[36] Frazier may have shown some prudence in his choice of title, but the contents matched Steward's in candor. Gone was the oblique innuendo of the Durham piece.

There are essentially two themes in "La Bourgeoisie Noire," in which Frazier attempted to explain why "the Negro, the man farthest down in the economic as well as social scale, steadily refuses to ally himself with radical groups in America." First, he contested the widely held notion that the black community was monolithic and homogenous, pointing out that it was "highly differentiated" and that industrial workers, who were more likely to have a revolutionary consciousness, constituted only a small percentage of black workers. Second, Frazier analyzed the conservative role played by the new, rising middle class and its cultural spokesperson, the New Negro, in ensuring that "bourgeois ideals are implanted in the Negro's mind." Consistent with his exchange with Steward, Frazier pointed out that the new black artists and writers were willing to settle for "Negro in Art Week" in return for agreeing "not to compete with the white man either politically or economically." Meanwhile, the New Negro businessman, who promoted middle-class ideals and conspicuous consumption, had absolutely no interest in creating a "society of equals."

Frazier sadly noted the demise of the postwar black radical movement, typified by the *Messenger,* which had degenerated from an "organ of the struggling working masses" to a "mouthpiece of Negro capitalists." The new Afro-American communists, however, were trying to recruit industrial workers in the North, "but none ever undertook to enter the South and teach the landless peasants any type of self-help." Frazier also was furious at the new nationalistic movement because, under the encouragement of its white patrons, it had retreated into a narrow and depoliticized concept of culture.[37]

Choosing Sides

Frazier's assessment of the black middle class in 1928 formed the basis of his later writings on this topic. He elaborated his views, deepened his analysis, added new evidence, and became more vitriolic in the 1950s, but at the core was the critique he formulated in the 1920s. Through the 1930s, he sustained his fierce attack on Afro-American leadership, accusing Du Bois of aspiring to be "king" of the "Black Ghetto" and exposing James Weldon Johnson and other "Negro *leaders*" for their opportunism and unwillingness to "risk their own security."[38] During the Depression there was a "disillusionment" within the middle class when they lost their ability to prosper "upon the earnings of the black masses" and the "hot-house growth of Negro business behind the walls of segregation shrivelled and died." As the hope of upward mobility dissipated, most businessmen embraced "racial chauvinism" and dreamed of a "Black Utopia where the black middle class could exploit the black workers without white competition."[39]

After World War II he found his critique confirmed by the rise of a new middle class in the urban ghettoes, as politicians, lawyers, realtors, and shop owners took their place alongside the preachers and teachers who had traditionally wielded power within black communities. This stratum, argued Frazier, had developed "vested interests" in the "system of segregation," from which they derived the "exclusive enjoyment of . . . social and material rewards."[40] His 1949 textbook summarized his previous views about stratification within black communities and, bolstered by Abram Harris's *The Negro as Capitalist* and other new studies, reiterated his critique of the "marginal position of Negro enterprises" and their "insignificant role in the economy of the nation."[41]

In the last years of his life, he returned to the issues that had preoccupied him during the 1920s. The publication of *Black Bourgeoisie*, first in France in 1955 and then in the United States in 1957, plus the resurgence of the civil rights movement in the South, reawakened his interest. *Black Bourgeoisie* caused a stir because it was widely reviewed and made Frazier a controversial celebrity who was in demand as a speaker and who provided good copy in the Afro-American press.[42] But the book contained nothing new in the way of analysis or interpretation, though his style was even more acerbic and polemical than before. Here was the familiar history of stratification within black communities, the exposé of the "myth of Negro business"—sustained, said Frazier with a new turn of phrase, by "Negro businessmen [who] can best be described as a 'lumpen-bourgeoisie' "—and a savage demystification of the "world of make-believe into which the black bourgeoisie has sought an escape from its inferiority and frustrations in American society."[43]

Frazier's analysis of the black bourgeoisie shifted from being exclusively domestic to being global after he spent two years (1951–1953) in Paris as chief of the Division of Applied Social Sciences in UNESCO. As a result of his contact with Third World intellectuals and leftists, he began to compare the Afro-American middle class with "colored middlemen" and "compradors" around the world.[44] He was struck by the similarities between the Afro-American middle class, "increasingly bewildered and frustrated in the white man's world," and the new native bourgeoisie of decolonized nations, who, in the words of one commentator, were "like derelicts, frantically seeking some foothold of security for body and mind."[45] For Frazier, it was not inevitable that the middle class play a conservative and coopted role. A choice had to be made, sides had to be taken. In Africa, Frazier was impressed by Kwame

Nkrumah, the leader of the Convention People's Party and later president of Ghana, because he had "a deep understanding and sympathy for the aspirations of the masses of Africans [and] wanted to make the nationalistic movement a mass movement."[46]

Meanwhile, with the resurgence of an Afro-American student movement back home, Frazier began to apply lessons learned from India and Africa to his own "native bourgeoisie." In the mid-1950s, Frazier was enthusiastic about the civil rights movement, glad to see that "Negro college students are for the first time showing a militant spirit in regard to segregation and discrimination."[47] At the same time, he was worried that "although it is a good revolt, they don't even understand their class position." He recognized that this new generation of militant students did not share the same outlook as the "black bourgeoisie . . . because those people wouldn't sit-in anything." But he felt that they "ought to have a realistic picture of the modern world,"[48] otherwise they would be easily misled or coopted or divided by an expanded middle class, living in its "world of delusions" and conspicuous consumption. "The attempt of the middle class Negro to escape from the realities of his position in American life," wrote Frazier in 1955, "is really an attempt to escape from himself. . . . The middle class Negro pretends that he is proud of being Negro while rejecting everything that identifies him with Negroes. He pretends that he is a leader of Negroes when he has no sense of responsibility to the Negro masses and exploits them whenever an opportunity offers itself."[49]

Frazier also addressed this issue in a controversial article written for John Davis's *Africa: Seen by American Negroes*. Increasingly, Frazier was impressed by nationalism in Africa and was much more hopeful about its revolutionary potential than about the potential of its counterpart in the United States. He warned the new African nations to look out for "American Negroes [who] may go to Africa as advisers and specialists" because "they will go as Americans representing American interests, not African interests." Frazier recapitulated the arguments of *Black Bourgeoisie,* noting that colleges had produced "a type of respectability and snobbishness that has alienated Negro intellectuals from the masses." Most Afro-American artists and intellectuals, continued Frazier, "sought only acceptance by the white world" and "developed a crude philosophy of opportunism, which seems to satisy their segregated existence in the white man's world." He questioned whether black Americans, who "have never been free, physically or psychologically," had anything spiritual or cultural to offer Africa. "The new Negro middle classes in the United States appear only to seek an opportunity to share in the exploitation from which they have been excluded and continue to be excluded except on an insignificant scale."[50]

A few weeks before he died in 1962 Frazier's last essay was published in *Negro Digest*. Like one of his first articles, "The Negro and Non-resistance," which appeared in *Crisis* in 1924, it too was a polemic, "The Failure of the Negro Intellectual." He was concerned that in fighting for integration, the leaders of the civil rights movement were focusing only on "the superficial aspects of the material standard of living among Negroes and the extent to which they enjoy civil rights." If the fate of black people were left to the middle class, "it would slough off everything that is reminiscent of its Negro origin." Unlike his African counterpart, argued Frazier, the typical American Negro intellectual is "seduced by dreams of final assimilation" and "can only see assimilation beyond integration." For Frazier, it was also necessary to examine "the economic and social organization of American life" into which the civil rights movement sought entry. Frazier called on his colleagues to "dig down into the experiences of the Negro." Do not "run from Du Bois and Paul Robeson," he told them.[51]

15

The Racial Question

In the realm of theory, Frazier based his work on the assumptions of Robert Park's race relations cycle and the sociological constructs of the Chicago School, yet he continually subverted their boundaries, challenged their political implications, and exposed their analytical weaknesses. The *enfant terrible* of the civil rights movement functioned as a loyal opposition within academia, a conscientious critic but one who had difficulty finding a unique theoretical voice.

Although Frazier's framework was quite eclectic and derivative, he also tried to generate systematic propositions about the nature and root causes of racism in his case studies of Afro-American families, culture, and class structure. Until he wrote *Race and Culture Contacts in the Modern World* near the end of his life, he did not undertake in any one place a comprehensive analysis of "the racial question." It is possible, however, to find the building blocks of this 1957 book in certain themes and concerns that permeate his writings from the 1920s onward.

A Question of Fear

Frazier was an astute observer of the machinery of racism and its impact on black communities. From his earliest writings, he understood that one of his responsibilities was exposing racism by demystifying its benevolent rationalizations and concretely describing the damage that it caused to Afro-Americans' physical and mental health, self-respect, resources, work life, education, culture, and family organization. After his death, Frazier would be accused of overestimating the damage caused by racism and underestimating the resilience and defiance of Afro-Americans. However, in the 1920s and at least through World War

156

II, Frazier was writing in a political and intellectual climate in which the dominant views about Afro-Americans ranged from the unabashed defense of Anglo-Saxon superiority to charitable paternalism. Not until the publication of Gunnar Myrdal's *An American Dilemma* in 1944 and the Kerner Report in 1968 did the human damage caused by institutionalized racism begin to receive serious recognition by the public at large.

Frazier was always interested in the organization and structure of racism, from its political and economic foundations to its seemingly trivial codes of interpersonal etiquette. His interest was not merely academic. "Living in the South as I do," he wrote in an editorial published in *Crisis* in 1924, "I must breathe in daily the stench of race prejudice."[1] Although he was victimized by racism and understood that the practice of racism involved individual attitudes and choices, he constantly argued that racism was not just a matter of personal prejudice. When, for example, he received an inquiry from a northern liberal in 1926 requesting examples of "cases in which Negroes have been discriminated against in criminal procedure," he responded that such an approach missed the point. "I am afraid," replied Frazier, "that you have no conception of the status of Negroes before the courts in the South. To begin with I might say that it may be taken as generally true in the South that a white man may do anything to a Negro, including murder, and not even be arrested."[2] In another article, written two years earlier, he was already convinced that racism was an institutionalized phenomenon. He noted that black defendants were presumed guilty and, if too impudent to admit their guilt, were routinely "clubbed and tortured" into confession. "A civilized man cast among cannibals would have a better chance of justice than a Negro in an Atlanta court where a white man is involved."[3]

Frazier had no sentimental affection for the South where the white man "lynches in the name of Chivalry and steals in the name of the Law." Between 1889 and 1921 Georgians lynched 414 Afro-Americans, the most in any state in the country. "As long as white Georgia commemorates the insensate dead upon Stone Mountain and turns stonier hearts to the cry of children in her mills," concluded Frazier in an incisive essay written for the *Messenger,* "and shuts her ears alike to the groans of her black peons and to the golden voice of Roland Hayes, one of her sons, because he is black, Georgia might as well be at the bottom of the sea from which she rose."[4]

Frazier's article on Georgia for the *Messenger* was one of a series of reports on "These 'Colored' United States." When he read with shock in another report on West Virginia that black miners supposedly were well paid and lived in "comfortable houses," he angrily fired off a letter protesting "this piece of fiction." If he had read this apology in the *New York Times,* he would have "passed it over as the usual propaganda of the capitalist press." Appalled to find this kind of misrepresentation in the "pages of the spokesman of labor," he documented the brutal conditions and economic insecurities of miners in West Virginia. "Any sketch, however brief," he concluded, "that undertakes to portray a community, does not tell the truth when it sets before us a few successful men and ignores not only the situation of the few independent farmers, but the thousands of servants and industrial serfs. We might as well take the recent progress of a few Atlanta Negroes as representative of the conditions of thousands of Negroes in the State of Georgia who live in peonage without educational opportunities and suffer all the other consequences of being black in the South."[5]

Frazier's exposés of racism ranged from argumentative polemics, such as his writings for the *Messenger,* to policy analyses. For example, he conducted one of the first comprehensive surveys of the state of black education in the South, documenting the impact of racism on the school system. He demonstrated how white children in Georgia, who constituted fifty-seven percent of the state's school-age children, were allotted ninety-one percent of educational funds. In 1924 Georgia spent $4.59 a year on every black child compared with $24.66 for every white child.[6] In another case study, Frazier explored the "deliberate and continued discrimination against Negro schools" in South Carolina, a state that "has lynched 134 Negroes in the last 38 years and is, next to Louisiana, the most illiterate state in the Union."[7] These studies, written in a measured style and documented with statistical evidence, helped policymakers and reformers to articulate the social damage caused by racism.

But Frazier did not limit himself to empirical studies. He was also one of the first researchers to explore the more subtle, but no less damaging, consequences of racism. In an article published in 1925 in the *Journal of Social Forces,* he took up the "question of fear." Noting that racism required a "social atmosphere of repression" and the "ever present effort to terrorize Negroes," he argued that "self-realization" was impossible under such conditions. In his travels through the South, he met many people who were "constantly afraid that they will overstep the bounds set for them by white people"—a man who "felt as if he was sitting on a keg of powder" every time he rode the streetcar, a woman who was warned by a policeman that "we string up niggers down here for that" when she crossed the street on the wrong signal, and a man who told him, "Makes me sick every time I get on a Jim Crow car." Frazier concluded that, "to the extent that the Negro lives under the domination of fear, he is unhealthy."[8]

Accommodation to racism meant that a psychological price had to be paid. "In adjusting themselves to the social system of the South," he wrote in 1924, "Negroes have developed a psychology difficult to describe. It may be called the psychology of negation, or the psychology of people in subjection. In not appearing to assert themselves in the face of the dominant white overlord, they have developed the psychology of the sick."[9] This attitude, concluded Frazier, "appears to be purely a defense mechanism. Subjectively, it affords the Negro that defense against self-depreciation that is intolerable."[10]

Negro Complex

In the early 1920s, influenced by his training and experience in social work, he used the prevailing psychological discourse to explain or at least frame his observations on the systemic nature of racism. In a discussion of the health problems of rural blacks, for example, Frazier alluded to the "psychosis of the white South in which fear of the Negro has dominated." This pathological fear meant a lack of money for health programs, the exclusion of black doctors from hospitals, and a medical definition of black patients—if they were fortunate enough to be treated—as "experimental material." Southern whites became genuinely concerned about the health of Afro-Americans, observed Frazier, only when they felt threatened by the "menace of unhealthy Negroes."[11]

Frazier pursued the metaphorical use of health and illness to its logical conclusion in his 1927 article "The Pathology of Race Prejudice," in which he deliberately satirized social psychology as well as searched for a structural explanation of racism.[12] In this notorious article, Frazier drew upon familiar psychological constructs to make the case that racism was a form of "abnormal behavior" and that whites were driven mad by the Negro complex in much the same way that paranoid schizophrenics were driven mad by their delusions and projections. "Just as the lunatic seizes upon every fact to support his delusional system, the white man seizes myths and unfounded rumors to support his delusion about the Negro."[13] Racists, argued Frazier, justify their "abnormal behavior" through rationalization—for example, "lynching becomes a holy defense of womanhood"—and through "fear, hatred, and sadism."

Then, touching the exposed nerve of southern racism that led to his flight from Atlanta in 1927, Frazier applied popular psychology to that most dangerous of topics, white women and black men:

> Perhaps more justly to be classed as symptoms of insanity are those frequent hallucinations of white women who complain of attacks by Negroes when clearly no Negroes are involved. Hallucinations often represent unacceptable sexual desires which are projected when they can no longer be repressed. In the South a desire on the part of a white woman for a Negro that could no longer be repressed would most likely be projected,—especially when such a desire is supposed to be as horrible as incest. It is not unlikely, therefore, that imaginary attacks by Negroes are often projected wishes.[14]

Finally, Frazier turned liberalism on its head by identifying racist behavior as not only irrational but also "distinctively antisocial," a sign of "social incapacity." Using the prevailing vocabulary of welfare policy, he concluded that "Southern white people afflicted with the Negro-complex show themselves incapable of performing certain social functions."[15]

Instead of portraying the victims of racism as mentally disturbed, Frazier accused racists of suffering from deficiencies and inadequacies. Instead of cataloguing the "social incapacities" of blacks, he used the disinterested language of professional psychology to assess the "abnormal behavior" of whites. Instead of developing social policies to uplift Afro-Americans into "civilization," he argued for restrictions on whites. Thus, in this one short, memorable essay, Frazier lampooned racists, liberal reformers, social workers, and psychologists.

Etiquette

From the early 1920s Frazier kept notes on his personal experiences with the etiquette of race relations. He did so partly to document his own efforts to break the rules and partly to document his sociological observations and insights. It was not unusual for Afro-American intellectuals to keep such records in the 1920s. These notes were even a genre of journalism, and the Afro-American press was full of personal accounts that documented humiliations, absurdities, ironies, and small victories.[16] During his years in the South, Frazier wrote several essays and stories that illuminated his analysis in "The Pathology of Race Prejudice." In particular, he explored the mundane social rules of race relations, focusing on how the system of racism was constructed and reproduced in everyday life.[17]

In his one published story he recounted his experience visiting a white optometrist on the thirteenth floor of a building in Atlanta. He walked up the stairs rather than ride in a Jim Crow elevator. "I am still young," wrote Frazier, "and can use my legs and save my self-respect." But he chose "insult and discomfiture" over "blindness" when he met the doctor, who called him by his last name "as if I were his bootblack or office boy or life-long friend," and the doctor's assistant. He put up with the doctor's "Southern incivilities" and restrained himself from smiling at the assistant because "in a room with a white woman in the South, a Negro's smile would be equal to an attack."[18]

In his other, unpublished observations, Frazier often focused on the rules that governed black-white relations in public places—especially buses, trains, and hotels.[19] He was intrigued by the flexibility of these rules and their selective enforcement. On one occasion in 1925 he came close to fighting with a bus conductor when he sat in a seat in front of a white man. It made no difference to the conductor that the back of the bus was filled with black passengers and there were ten empty seats up front for the only white passenger to sit in. Eventually the white passenger voluntarily moved forward so that Frazier avoided jail. Another time he noted that the head of the hospital at Morehouse College was arrested and fined for sitting one seat beyond the middle of the bus when there were no white passengers. These incidents taught Frazier that the specific rules were incidental to the enforcement of relations of superiority and inferiority.[20]

Frazier argued that Jim Crow policies in the South were not based on physical repugnance or personal hatred but rather on the enforcement of social inequality. "The presence of a dirty Negro in a menial position" was taken for granted, whereas "a cultivated Negro of pleasing manners and features becomes offensive, especially to southerners, if he occupies any place where the superiority of the white is not asserted. A white girl who sits in the lap of the Negro servant who drives her home daily, stands up from Washington to Philadelphia rather than sit beside a colored passenger."[21]

The rules concerning travel in the South often varied within states as well as from state to state. Frazier noted that on a trip to the South in 1943 "I was able to eat my meals in various ways. . . . At first I ate in the Pullman car. The next morning I ate in a dining-car, with a curtain behind me. The next day I ate in the dining-room with white people. It seems that the dining-car waiters and the dining-car stewards have a sixth sense for determining exactly where it is possible, or rather I should say, safe, for a Negro to eat with white people in the South."[22] Close to the end of his life, Frazier reported that these "customary regulations" still operated in the South, where "the most distinguished Negro, for example, cannot enter the front door of a hotel or a railway station, but a Negro butler or nurse may do so as long as it is known that he is a servant."[23]

Racialism

Frazier was interested in the ideological underpinnings, as well as the etiquette, of racism. Having studied with Frank Hankins at Clark, he was quite familiar with the language, theories, and logic of "racialism." When an article defending eugenics appeared in *Crisis* in 1924 written by a young Afro-American writer, Frazier gently but firmly rebuked its views and assumptions. "Moral traits are not inherited," he wrote. Even in the case of such physical problems as tuberculosis and rickets, Frazier argued that more could be done through "environmental control" than through any breeding program. "Pre-natal clinics can do more than eugenic control."[24]

Frazier had a knack for taking official logic and conventional wisdom and turning them against their proponents. In his research on the family, he agreed with those who said that Afro-Americans did not meet the standards of "Western civilization," then demonstrated that it was the civilizers who caused the problem. In his famous article on race prejudice, he used the clinical notion of pathology to expose the sickness of racists. Similarly, he used the logic of eugenics to expose its contradictions. "The whole social system in the South," he wrote in 1925, "favors the propagation of the least socially desirable (in a civilized environment) among Negroes. The less energetic and resourceful fit easily into the role the white man has assigned the Negro, while the more energetic and resourceful leave or often fail to reproduce."[25] If the "racialists" really wanted to preserve the "best endowed stocks," he observed, then why was "ostracism, caste, and every form of gross and refined brutality . . . used to eliminate the exceptional Negro?" Eugenics in the hands of racists was simply "rationalizations to shield the fear and cowardliness of inferior white men who are afraid to compete with black men. . . . A mulatto Dumas or Pushkin or a black Carver or Toussaint is worth a million mediocre pure blooded, god-fearing, 100% white Americans."[26]

Over the years, Frazier maintained his interest in racial ideologies, especially their role in legitimating and perpetuating relations of oppression. Well aware of the racist assumptions of sociology's founding fathers, he regularly reminded his professional colleagues about their legacy.[27] Later in his life, Frazier traced the continuities in racist ideology from Joseph-Arthur Gobineau through the myth of Anglo-Saxon superiority—"the main justification for imperialism"—to the defenders of slavery and legal segregation.[28]

This interest in ideology was two-fold. Frazier understood that racism was sustained and reproduced in everyday life as much by the ideas of "objective" scholars as by the lynch mob. And he understood that the seemingly trivial aspects of racism—etiquette, eugenics textbooks, Jim Crow rules in public transportation—also played an important role in making racism systemic and structural as opposed to a problem of individual prejudice or personal choice.

Caste and Class

In the late 1920s Frazier began to develop a theoretical framework for explaining the origins, persistence, and future of racism. In his award-winning essay for *Opportunity* in 1925, he expressed the prevailing optimism of the Negro Renaissance in his view that American society was slowly realizing the democratic ideal of social equality. In particular, he was hopeful that "as the Negro may become an integral part of the proletariat, . . . the feeling against his color may break down in the face of a common foe."[29]

With the onset of the Depression, which "laid bare the general economic insecurity of the Negro masses," his optimism was renewed about the "spread of radical ideas among working class Negroes through cooperation with white workers."[30] Influenced by the class-based theories of left intellectuals and organizations, by the 1930s his approach was predominantly economistic,[31] and his writings tended to reinterpret the history of race relations through a prism of exploitation, as demonstrated in a typical piece written in 1935:

> The introduction of the Negro into America was due to the economic expansion of Europe. . . . The fate of Negro slavery was determined by economic forces. . . . The economic dependence of the Negro in the South furnishes the key to the understanding of his status. . . . The Negro's status in the United States . . . has been bound up, in the final analysis, with the role which the Negro has played in the economic system. . . . In the urban environment [the Negro] is showing signs of understanding the struggle for power between the proletariat and the owning classes, and is beginning to cooperate with white workers in this struggle which offers the only hope of his complete emancipation.[32]

Because of his sensitivity to cultural issues and his personal experience with racism, Frazier was careful not to reduce every aspect of race relations to a crude economic determinism. Nevertheless, for several years he became more and more convinced that solutions to racism had to be found in far-ranging structural changes in the political economy. This view was expressed most fully and thoughtfully in *The Negro in Harlem,* his study of the 1935 Harlem riot that was unfortunately never published during his lifetime. Here he combined an economic analysis of unemployment with a critique of institutionalized racism in welfare, health care, housing, education, and criminal justice to demonstrate that the riot was the result of "the smouldering resentments of the people of Harlem against racial discrimination and poverty in the midst of plenty."[33]

According to Frazier, "the generally low economic status of Negro workers is, of course, due fundamentally to the operation of our competitive capitalist system." He was particularly critical of racial discrimination in the privately controlled public utilities and thought that "only through collective or public ownership" could "the Negro . . . enforce his right to employment on the same basis as other races." Though Frazier advocated modest reforms in New York's social services, he also felt that "the economic and social ills of Harlem, which are deeply rooted in the very nature of our economic and social system, cannot be cured by any administration under our present political and civic institutions."[34]

In his other writings he found himself at odds with social scientists who negated the significance of class relations in their analysis of stratification. He thought, for example, that the Lynds' second book on Middletown was hopelessly muddled because "in lumping the white collar workers and professional men in a so-called 'Business Class,' the authors have confused class as a mere category based upon similiarities in superficial aspects of behavior, with the more fundamental conception of class based upon divergent economic interests." Frazier also thought it was unnecessarily mystical to "ascribe the behavior of the ruling class to the culture in which they have been bred" when it was clear that their behavior was rooted in their class interests.[35]

Frazier's focus on the economic and class-based aspects of race relations put him at odds with the caste hypothesis that dominated race relations research from the mid-1930s through the 1940s. He was critical, for example, of Charles Johnson's study of the tobacco industry because of its emphasis on caste divisions between workers as an explanation for the lack of labor solidarity. To Frazier it was clear that Johnson had "left out of his analysis the most important factor—the economic conditions controlling the working relations in the industry."[36]

In 1942 he tried unsuccessfully to persuade Gunnar Myrdal to abandon the "concept of caste and class which is the present vogue in studying the Negro in the United States." He argued that "caste is a static concept" and "has not added anything to our understanding of the cause of present race relations or how they actually operate."[37] A few years later he was still convinced that the caste theorists had not offered any "new insights" and that the need was urgent for a "dynamic sociological theory of race relations."[38]

Frazier also broke with Robert Park, his mentor from Chicago, on this issue. In his classic 1928 article, "The Bases of Race Prejudice," Park argued that race relations had changed from horizontal to vertical relations. Previously all whites had dominated all Afro-Americans. Now, wrote Park, "on one side of this [vertical] line the Negro is represented in most of the occupational and professional classes; on the other side of the line the white man is similarly represented. . . . The races no longer look up and down; they look across."[39] Park's "different but equal" philosophy was derived from Germanic notions of "romantic racialism" that were fashionable in the United States during the 1920s.[40] Frazier was always opposed to Park's biracial conception of race relations because it did not change "the status of the Negro in any fundamental sense."[41]

Over the years Frazier refined his critique of Park's biracialism and the caste hypothesis. For Frazier the cultural and religious emphasis of caste did not make sense as a systematic framework. It was too fatalistic, too divorced from materialism, too social-psychological.[42] As for biracialism, Frazier argued that the concept precluded equality because "the biracial organization is imposed by whites" and "wherever a biracial organization exists, there are discriminations in favor of whites." He compared the United States and South Africa, noting that biracialism had meant poor land, inadequate housing, and low wages for blacks in both countries. "Despite the theory that that there is no implication of difference in social status in a biracial organization, the colored section of the organization is always stigmatized as unfit or ineligible for normal human association."[43]

Disinterested Social Science

Frazier's theoretical analysis of race relations owed a great deal to the Chicago School, especially Park. He appreciated Park's personal experiences in the South, his empirical rigor, and his efforts to generate a systematic theory of a race-relations cycle.[44] Frazier believed that Park's work was an authentic effort to depart from the tradition of scientific racism. Moreover, he remembered what Park had done for his career at a time when few Afro-Americans were allowed into academia. Nevertheless, there were some significant differences between Park and Frazier regarding sociological theory.

Frazier, for example, did not accept the moral neutrality that was supposedly the bedrock of the Chicago School. It is true that many of his academic writings became increasingly technical and divorced from social policy, while he expressed his political persona in journalistic and popular articles. But this duality was not so much a personal preference as an enforced requirement of survival in academia. Throughout his life Frazier felt much the same as he did in his 1925 letter to the *The Nation* in which he argued that it was the responsibility of progressives to expose racism through "pitiless publicity."[45] He always admired intellectuals whose work demonstrated that the "race problem was *made*" and therefore people "can *unmake* it."[46]

Occasionally. Frazier's views on this issue penetrated his more academic essays. He wrote in a 1937 review of John Dollard's *Caste and Class in a Southern Town:*

> However much one may agree with the general proposition that social science should show the same objectivity as the natural science it is difficult to accept the author's injunction that, "No one should judge even the most incredible acts of violence. We should attempt to identify and understand rather than deplore them." Nor does it appear pertinent to the issue of passing judgments on the behavior of southern whites to warn northern whites: "Can we be so sure that we would do differently if the problem of dealing with masses of Negroes were to come home to us locally?" To be sure the scientist *qua* scientist should strive to understand behavior, but moral beings who are members of society should not be satisfied merely to contemplate cruelty and violence simply because it is an expression of human nature. Men are not satisfied merely to understand the nature of cancer. Certainly, when it is a question of a system that makes a race subject to the sadistic impulses and cruelty of their overlords and destroys their personal dignity, civilized men will judge such a system.[47]

It was Myrdal's willingness to inject social policy into sociology that made Frazier so receptive to *An American Dilemma.* "Your study of the Negro problem in the United States comes at a fortunate time," Frazier told Myrdal in 1942. "I think that American social scientists will be forced to rethink their attitude to a 'disinterested social science.'" He appreciated Myrdal's efforts to make sociology "more than an aesthetic contemplation of a purely mechanical process" and hoped that it signaled the end of "fatalism" in the social sciences.[48]

Race-Relations Cycle

Critics of Frazier's work argue that, like Park, he advocated the "complete assimilation" of Afro-Americans into American society.[49] Park's race-relations cycle—contact, competition, accommodation, and assimilation—was based, in St. Clair Drake's words, on "long-run sociologistic optimism" and was quite consistent with the "melting pot" concept.[50] Though Park recognized the possibility of racial conflict in the short run, his cycle envisioned the withering away of prejudice in an evolutionary process.[51]

Frazier's views on assimilation are not so evident. At times, he too expressed an idealistic hope that racism would recede under the combined pressure of enlightened reason and a united proletariat.[52] But even in these moments of utopian optimism, there was a persistent undercurrent of mordant cynicism, fueled by his own experiences. As early as 1927, for example, he argued that social equality would not be possible in the United States until the "darker world" was sufficiently developed to "force the white world . . . to treat the darker races as equals."[53]

To Frazier the road to racial equality was filled with impediments, detours, and wrong turns. Unlike Park, he stressed that it would take a "struggle for power" and determined human agency to solve the worldwide problem of the racial question. He ruled out "any notion of a unilinear evolutionary process."[54] For a while after World War II, encouraged by Myrdal's *An American Dilemma* and the resurgence of a legal assault on segregation, he predicted the possibility of a "common humanity."[55] But when he left the country to work with UNESCO in Paris, he once again corrected his optimism and could not "foresee what crisis in American life may bring about a radical change" in U.S. race relations.[56]

Frazier made an important distinction between integration and assimilation, or, as it was once known, amalgamation. He consistently advocated the importance of economic and political integration as the only means to achieve power. He rejected nationalist and separatist strategies as both unrealistic and defeatist.[57] However, particularly by the end of his life, he thought that assimilation—that is to say "complete identification"—was both unlikely and undesirable. In 1957 he was encouraged that the "colored peoples of the world are developing a solidarity of interest which is based in part upon race consciousness."[58] He was critical of the leadership of the civil rights movement at home for envisioning only "assimilation beyond integration" and for seeking "self-effacement" and a future without a sense of "identification."[59]

Some thirty-five years earlier, no doubt influenced by Park's race-relations cycle, Frazier had predicted that "absolute equality will naturally lead (in how many centuries I dare not say) to amalgamation."[60] By the end of his life, with integration still not in sight, Frazier knew that there was nothing natural or inevitable about the achievement of social equality. He now felt that the defeat of imperialism and coloni- alism would be necessary before we might consider the possibility of "racial and cultural differentiation without implications of superiority and inferiority."[61]

By the time that Frazier wrote *Race and Culture Contacts in the Modern World*, his only effort to develop a comprehensive analysis of race relations, he had moved far beyond Park's race-relations cycle and stretched it almost beyond recognition. The monograph was not so much an original theoretical formulation as it was a profound critique of prevailing social scientific theories and a call for new perspectives and new directions in race relations theory and research. More than any of his previous academic writings, *Race and Culture Contacts in the Modern World* is unambiguously interdisciplinary, bridging the tradi- tional chasms between sociology and economics, history and political science, culture and class, and theory and practice.

Ideology

Enfant Terrible

The major dilemma facing an Afro-American intellectual of Frazier's generation, noted John Hope Franklin, was "whether he should turn his back on the world, concede that he is the Invisible Man, and lick the wounds that come from cruel isolation, or whether he should use his training, talents, and resources to beat down the barriers that keep him out of the mainstream of American life and scholarship."[1]

Beating Down the Barriers

In the 1920s Frazier took on the barriers. He did this intellectually (when he was not writing conventional academic essays) in his diatribes against the black bourgeoisie and the pathology of racism. But his non-conformity was not restricted to the realm of ideology, nor was the pen his only weapon. Although he generally preferred not to participate in collective or organized struggles, he was very much an activist who put his beliefs into action as a statement of his commitment. His political practice, like his writing, was highly individualistic and personalized. "Frazier could not have been in any kind of organization for more than one week," recalled a former student.[2]

He valued his independence and, though socially outgoing and personable, was essentially a "loner."[3] This independence gave his activism, in the words of Everett Hughes, an "edge of danger," especially in the South during the 1920s, where to be merely outspoken was enough to risk death.[4] His attempts at self-protection were minimal, inconsistent, and mostly cosmetic. He was prudent in some of his articles (writing now and then as a neutral academic); he published as "E. Franklin" rather than "Edward F."; and occasionally he thought it wise to publish anonymously or with a French title. But often he was more rash than prudent; in many situations he threw caution to the wind and often found himself in situations that could quickly turn into violent confrontations.

During the 1920s especially, Frazier made a point of personally challenging Jim Crow practices that interfered with his freedom of movement and speech. It was a matter of principle with him to oppose any concessions to the slightest insult, to practice what he preached. When asked by a friend for advice about how to challenge segregation in a small college in Arkansas, he replied, "I feel that one must decide quite frankly what price he is willing to pay for the carrying out of certain ideals."[5]

Frazier was willing to risk paying a high price. He expected and demanded too that "northern white people in general . . . give their moral support at least to every attempt of the Negro to occupy the place that belongs to every member of a democratic civilized society."[6] Frazier felt that any kind of accommodation to racism only gave it new life. He thought that intellectuals had a responsibility to expose and publicize racism;[7] like his father before him, he was a tireless writer of letters to the editor.[8] He regularly lodged protests against his professional peers who held conferences in locations known for segregated practices. He applied the same logic of his beliefs to his daily round of activities. He sent a letter of protest and stopped buying at a grocery store in Atlanta where a clerk insisted on calling him "Doc." When the store owner had trouble understanding why Frazier objected to the term, he explained that the "man in your store nicknames patrons simply bacause they are colored."[9] Similarly, he complained to the vice-president of his bank in Atlanta when a clerk addressed him as "Frazier" rather than "Mr. Frazier."[10]

Throughout the 1920s Frazier's life was filled with these kinds of incidents, which invariably involved his defiance of some seemingly trivial ritual of racist etiquette. The fact that each incident had within it the seeds of explosive violence demonstrated that such everyday routines were by no means trivial. To Frazier they were the threads that held together and shaped the fabric of racism. Also, not incidentally, he was personally and deeply offended by any racist restrictions on his personal freedoms. Frazier, clearly proud of his stubborn resistance, kept a record of many confrontations, most of which took place in public arenas—buses, trains, hotels, and conferences. The locale of these personal skirmishes in the 1920s would become the battleground of the civil rights movement thirty years later. For example, he refused to move out of segregrated seating when ordered to do so by a Pullman conductor in Georgia; in Florida, he risked confrontation with the local police by trying to make a reservation on a whites-only Pullman car; he walked out of a meeting of social workers at Atlanta's Chamber of Commerce to protest Jim Crow seating arrangements; he physically challenged a white employee of the local gas company who was disrespectful to his wife and refused to take his hat off "in any nigger's house"; and he stood his ground in the lobby of a fancy Atlanta hotel when told that he had to wait "behind the bootblack stand." [11]

Visions of Justice

It is not at all easy to get a clear picture of Frazier's politics and worldview only through his interpreters. To sociologist G. Franklin Edwards, a colleague at Howard University, Frazier at one time "espoused a belief in democratic socialism." [12] St. Clair Drake recalled that Frazier always lined up with "the communists" and was identified as a fellow traveler of the Communist Party during the 1930s at Howard University. [13] However, Michael Winston, a former student of Frazier's, had no doubt that Frazier was "never a communist and was always openly critical of the position of the [Communist] Party concerning the problem of racism in the United States." [14] Harold Cruse went even further and located Frazier within a tradition of cultural nationalism that "cut the ground from under much of what later became Communist Party dogma about the Negro working class." [15] Others did not even consider Frazier a leftist. Oliver Cox found in Frazier only a "red thread" of cynicism and doubt; [16] to Pierre van den Berghe, he was one of the "establishment blacks," a darling of the white liberals; [17] and Manning Marable, in a survey of the radical tradition among Afro-American intellectuals, damned Frazier with faint praise. [18] It is not difficult, then, to appreciate David Southern's conclusion that Frazier was an ideological chameleon who "held a multitude of competing ideas, and which ones came forth depended on the situation." [19]

These various readings of Frazier's politics, though seemingly inconsistent, are not inaccurate. His positions on issues often changed and were sometimes contradictory. Moreover, his ideology was often concealed or disguised, and he never expressed and probably did not even hold a comprehensive world-view. However, continuities can be found in his political ideas and vision, his sense of personal commitment, and his relations with organizations. He was a highly politicized intellectual who was consistently committed to the struggle against racism, who regularly took anticapitalist stands and had an affinity for socialism, who imbued his research with global and political-economic perspectives, and who refused to bow to the considerable pressures exerted by anticommunist forces.

In order to understand the shifts in Frazier's political viewpoint, it is necessary to take into account the changes in political climate from era to era, as well as his own ideological development. After World War I and during the 1920s Frazier confronted a conservative and racist academic system that expected its young Afro-American intellectuals to be compliant, apolitical, pious, and grateful for the opportunity to enter its doors. If Frazier's politics were not always self-evident, that is partly because it was risky for academics to express any viewpoint to the left of conventional liberalism.[20] In the 1920s, when Frazier was working in the South, such a viewpoint was literally life-threatening, as Frazier found out in Atlanta.

In the 1930s, when the left and a militant labor movement created a genuine political discourse in the United States, for a few years radical intellectuals made a space for themselves in academia. This opening gave Frazier the confidence, for example, to appear in public as the main speaker at a May Day event in Washington, D.C., in 1937.[21] Following World War II and the decline of the left, progressives on campus again found themselves isolated, a process further compounded by McCarthyism. Frazier, for example, was identified by the House Un-American Activities Committee as working with various "Communist front" organizations as early as 1944, and he continued to be redbaited until his death in 1962.[22]

From the time of his undergraduate days at Howard through the 1920s politics played a central role in Frazier's life, inspiring his intellectual development and guiding his interests. Though his primary concern was the struggle against racism, his political interests were quite broad and eclectic. His first article, published in the campus newspaper, was a defense of women's suffrage.[23] His first pamphlet, which he had published privately, was a polemic against U.S. involvement in World War I, not written from a pacifist perspective, for he defended "just wars" such as the French Revolution and Civil War but was against "unjust wars" such as those based on "international commercial competition and 'Spheres of influence'" and European exploitation of Africa.[24]

After World War I Frazier consistently tried to combine his interest in socialism with being an uncompromising race man. For a short while he was able to resolve these separate spheres of his political ideology by relating to the *Messenger* wing of the Socialist Party. By 1920 Frazier was convinced that "the new radicalism, represented by the *Messenger,* . . . is the most fundamental and thorough movement initiated among Negroes."[25] Throughout the 1920s Frazier subscribed to and wrote for the *Messenger,* to whose views he was much closer than he was to the views of the NAACP's *Crisis,* edited by Du Bois. Between 1924 and 1927 Frazier had one article, one survey response, and one letter published in the *Messenger.*[26] By 1928, however, he had parted ways with the *Messenger* because it was no longer the "organ of the struggling working masses" and had deteriorated into a "mouthpiece of Negro capitalists."[27]

Frazier related to the *Messenger* group in much the same way that he related to all organizations throughout his life. He supported it from outside, participated in it at a distance, and maintained his independence. A maverick to some, an opportunist to others, Frazier recognized the political necessity for organization but chose not to submit to any kind of political discipline. One positive result of this independence was his ability to bridge differences between factions and organizations. Though he was closest to the *Messenger* group in the early 1920s, he also maintained close ties with the left wing of the NAACP and left liberals in NUL. This flexibility enabled him to bring the *Messenger*'s politics into the mainstream of the Afro-American movement. For example, *Crisis* published his controversial article "The Negro and Non-resistance," which expressed relatively extreme views about self-defense, and *Opportunity* gave him a forum to present his first cautious critique of the black bourgeoisie.[28]

At the same time, Frazier did not feel obligated to follow the *Messenger* on every issue. For example, whereas Randolph and Owen attacked Marcus Garvey and called for his deportation,[29] Frazier thought that it was dangerous to write Garvey off as a "common swindler" or simply to reduce his movement to an expression of religious fanaticism. Like Du Bois, the *Messenger,* and other Afro-American leaders, Frazier was critical of Garvey's cultural nationalism, but he thought that it was a mistake to ignore somebody who "aroused the Negroes of Georgia as much as those of New York. . . . He has the distinction of initiating the first real mass movement among American Negroes."[30]

Until the late 1920s Frazier's politics were vaguely socialist, an expression of the evolutionary and utopian beliefs in vogue among progressive intellectuals. On international issues, he shared the Socialist Party's anti-imperialism and was a minority voice in the black movement against U.S. entry into World War I, which he regarded as "essentially a conflict between imperialistic powers."[31] Domestically, his economic views were influenced by the *Messenger* and by the small-scale, rural cooperatives that he studied in Denmark in 1921–1922. For several years he held out the hope that southern black communities might be able to become economically self-sufficient, small oases of "industrial democracy" within capitalism.[32]

He especially favored cooperatives as a form of business enterprise that would counter the "tendency at present to over-emphasize the importance of a few extremely wealthy men among Negroes" and create a "wide distribution of the economic surplus of the group."[33] By the 1930s, when Du Bois advocated a similar program, Frazier had abandoned the possibility and was contemptuous of Du Bois's romanticism and economic stupidity. "When Garvey proposed a grandiose scheme for building a black commercial empire Du Bois ridiculed his naivete. But what could be more fantastic than his own program for a separate non-profit economy within American capitalism?"[34]

Even while he was promoting self-reliant cooperatives in the South, Frazier recognized that Afro-American workers were becoming increasingly urbanized and proletarianized. In the early 1920s he began to explore the possibility of an organized, interracial, working-class movement. His study of New York longshoremen focused on how the unions reproduced a racist division of labor and created barriers to class solidarity.[35] By 1925 Frazier was hopeful that unions would be inclined to accept black workers on an equal footing.[36] Writing for *The Nation* in 1927, Frazier was critical of white labor leaders in the South for treating black workers as "an alien subordinate group," thus reinforcing the efforts of employers to maintain a divided and divisive working class. Frazier was still hopeful, however, that economic necessities would force unions to combat racism within their ranks. "As the industrialization of the South grows, the white working class will become class-conscious and resist through organization the present unchallenged supremacy of capital," Frazier predicted. "Faced with this situation, white capital will not hesitate to turn to the black worker, as it has always turned in such situations to an unorganized group of workers. The unions will, therefore, be forced to recognize the Negro as they have done—in self-defense—in the North."[37]

Frazier did not venture further into economic and labor issues in the 1920s. He continued to advocate cooperatives for rural workers and integrated unions for urban workers, even while recognizing the ineffectiveness of both strategies. It was not so much that he abandoned his interest in socialism, however vaguely it was expressed, but rather that the left was incapable of attracting and holding militant black intellectuals like Frazier because of its own racism, paternalism, or disinterest.[38]

Moreover, during Frazier's years in the South, the politics of socialism receded into the background for him—an abstract topic to be read about or discussed with friends on visits north—as he found himself in battle with racism's daily humiliations and occasional atrocities. Later, when Frazier returned to Chicago in 1927 to complete his doctorate in sociology, he would be once again in a political milieu where socialism was on the agenda and where the interconnections of racism and capitalism—the National Question—informed theory and strategy. Meanwhile, he liked to think of himself as an *enfant terrible* whose job it was to "destroy the illusions which keep colored people in bondage."[39]

17

Black and Red

Until the late 1920s Frazier had little contact with the Communist Party (CP); it equally had little contact with progressive Afro-American intellectuals such as Frazier and exercised an insignificant influence on black political life through most of the 1920s.[1]

There is no record of any black participation in the foundation of the party in 1919, and the first serious political discussion of the Negro Question took place not in Harlem or Chicago but in the Soviet Union at the Comintern's Second World Congress in 1920.[2] In 1928, of a total estimated CP membership of about fourteen thousand, fewer than two hundred were Afro-Americans. Even in Harlem, the center of activism and debate, as late as 1929 black membership in the CP was minuscule.[3] At the end of the 1920s, however, the CP began to exert a significant influence on leftist politics and the struggle for racial equality. Recognizing its failure to recruit Afro-American cadre and under prodding and criticism from the Comintern, in 1925 the CP initiated the American Negro Labor Congress (ANLC), supposedly a broad-based mass organization that would reach and politically educate the black working class and serve as a conduit into the party.[4] In 1928 the Comintern's Sixth World Congress issued its new position that Afro-Americans constituted an oppressed nation and had a right to self-determination in the Black Belt of the South.[5]

During and after the Depression, the CP quickly grew into a leading left-wing organization and was recognized widely for its prominent role in the struggle for civil rights and racial equality. In 1930 the party recruited some one thousand new Afro-American members, and the number of black party members increased to about twenty-seven hundred in 1935 and to a high of over five thousand in 1939.[6] It organized sharecroppers in the South and unemployment councils in the North, made the Scottsboro case a subject of worldwide concern, led demonstrations against evictions and police brutality in Harlem, and challenged racial discrimination in Alabama's welfare system.

Those who supported or participated in the CP's struggles against racism during the 1930s felt that this period was a high point of leftist organizing and that it led to a deepening of popular understanding about racism. "I don't recall the communists pulling their punches on any aspect of black rights," noted Len De Caux. "They fought for black social, civil, political, as well as job rights."[7] Similarly, Al Richmond, a former member of the CP, thought that "the perception of the national character of the black liberation struggle was a great leap from prior radical approaches, which were crudely racist at worst, and at best humanist or marked by the simplistic class analysis that the condition of blacks was just part of the overall working class condition."[8]

Frazier and the Communist Party

Frazier related to the CP in much the same way that he related to other organizations. On issues in which he was in agreement, he did not hesitate to work with communists or CP-led organizations. On matters of difference, he did not hesitate to express his disagreements. He was certainly never a cadre or loyal follower (however much the FBI and other intelligence agencies wanted him to be), not exactly a fellow traveler, but much more than a sympathetic spectator. Ideology aside, Frazier moved in CP circles because they provided an interracial forum in which to mix and discuss important political issues and international events. Frazier liked to be around smart, stimulating people, and it was a rare opportunity for him to be able to engage class-conscious, worldy intellectuals.

Frazier's first serious contact with the CP was in Chicago in 1927, when he moved there to complete his doctorate. Chicago was a center of CP organizing and the location of its headquarters from 1923 to 1927.[9] By 1927 Frazier was already familiar with the CP and its ideas. While in Atlanta, he was a subscriber to the *New Masses* and regularly ordered books from International Publishers. Paul Robeson was a close friend, and he was on first-name terms with William Patterson and

Benjamin Davis, leading Afro-American communists. Patterson regarded Frazier and Abram Harris as "two of the foremost thinkers of our group, which in my opinion, contains few real thinkers, or if I am mistaken in that, at least few thinkers who are sufficiently fearless to speak out."[10]

While in Chicago Frazier attended a celebration of the tenth anniversary of the Russian Revolution and wrote up his impressions in an article published in *Southern Workman.*[11] He also participated in interracial social events organized by the ANLC and used the opportunity to formulate his first critical observations about the party's class analysis. He watched with some amusement as "the white and colored leaders maneuvered as skilfully as possible to break down the reserve" between immigrant whites and southern blacks. He listened to a "white man and colored woman . . . sitting together trying to converse. The man knew his Marx and Tolstoy, whereas the woman had never heard of Marx except in the advertisement of Hart, Schaffner, and Marx." Another dance attracted a large number of "pool room bums and pimps" who professed contempt for "any such thing as a class struggle or radical doctrines" and "would have quite naturally opposed any arrangement that meant their going to work."

The interracial dances failed as an organizing effort, Frazier observed, because the CP's white cadre revealed a "profound incomprehension . . . of the deeper social realities of Negro life." Class unity may have made sense as an idealistic principle, but it could not be achieved "by the magical application of an abstract formula." Too many white communists regarded Afro-Americans as a homogenous "mass of poor working people who had been deluded into a bourgeois state of mind" and were "shocked to learn that Negroes have social distinctions among themselves which they still observe when whites cross the color line." Frazier concluded that "those who presume to deal realistically with the Negro's situation by ignoring the structure and traditions within the social life of the Negro are as superficial in their approach as those against whom they bring the charge."[12]

Frazier's six pages of observations about the CP's failure to recruit Afro-Americans through its interracial dances were never published, probably not even submitted for publication. Perhaps he did not want to go public with such an explicit critique of the CP. But about the same time he expressed the same point, albeit in a more restrained and oblique manner, in his article "La Bourgeoisie Noire," published in *Modern Quarterly*.[13]

Frazier also disagreed with the CP's formulation of Afro-Americans as an oppressed nation with a right to self-determination in the Black Belt. It was not the nationalism but the separatism to which he objected. Again, he was restrained in public, though he privately endorsed the assessment of his friend "Dock" Steward, whose views on important issues he generally shared. "For the first time in my life I met the other day an honest-to-goodness communist who admitted it," Steward wrote to Frazier in 1934. "I told him I thought the party wasted too much time in denunciation and gave very little to constructive programs. . . . Then he took up something I did not know the communists advocated—a separate state for Negroes somewhere in the South. Aside from the fantastic aspects of such an objective, I would not subscribe to it did I think it were even remotely probable of accomplishment. So I am not so sure that I will ever be a communist, although I do admire many of their aims and am generally in accord with what they hope to achieve. But I am not, never have been, and never will be a separatist."[14]

Frazier's first public criticism of the CP's line on the National Question was expressed indirectly when he cosigned a letter to the *The Nation* in defense of Benjamin Stolberg, a white leftist who had criticized the CP for catering to "black chauvinism" in its search for a "'mass base' in the black world." The party, noted Stolberg, "promises to take the Negro into the Green Pastures of an independent black republic in the Deep South. . . . There is no future for the American Negro in chauvinism, right or left. There can be no black economy or black autonomy."[15]

Frazier tried to steer an independent course, along with many other leftist intellectuals who in some way did not fully support or did not want to place themselves under the discipline of the CP. He was part of a group that was respectful of the CP but had its differences.[16] Given his attitude toward working in organizations, it is doubtful his relationship to the CP would have been any different if he had been in total agreement with all its lines and policies. "People who knew him well," observed Marie Brown Frazier, "knew that he would not stand for that kind of discipline."[17]

Frazier wrote for publications that included communists or were in agreement with the CP on selected issues. He published "La Bourgeoisie Noire" in *Modern Quarterly* at a time when its editor, V. F. Calverton, was an enthusiastic supporter of the CP.[18] He allowed Nancy Cunard, a British fellow traveler, to reprint his essay on "The Pathology of Race Prejudice" in her 1934 anthology, *Negro.* In 1935 he joined the editorial board of *Race,* a short-lived journal that believed "the special system of discrimination against the Negro in America is so deeply rooted in the very foundations of the present social order and the vested interests of dominant capitalism that there is no complete 'solution' of this basic problem of American life short of a fundamental reconstruction of society, a social upheaval that will plow up our institutions to their very roots and substitute a socialist order for the present capitalist-imperialist order."[19] In 1936 he also agreed to serve as a contributing editor to *Science and Society,* a "Marxian Quarterly" that included independent leftists, socialists, and communists on its board and among its contributors.[20]

Despite his differences with the CP, he had no reservations about speaking at forums with communists or participating in events organized by the party. As we have seen, in 1932 he was the only faculty member at Fisk who was willing to introduce James Ford, an Afro-American communist running for U.S. vice-president on the CP ticket, at a campus forum.[21] Soon after he arrived at Howard to take over the direction of the department of sociology, he helped organize a major conference on the impact of the economic crisis on Afro-American communities and politics. The conference, which was held under the auspices of the Joint Committee on National Recovery, included the high-level participation of socialists and communists.[22] Their inclusion alone was enough to bring the university under suspicion by the Department of the Interior (which in part funded Howard) for promoting "communistic tendencies."[23] Still, it made little difference to Frazier. He worked closely with the leftist American Federation of Teachers and was president of the Howard local in 1937.[24] Another indication of Frazier's receptivity to the CP was his willingness to be the main speaker at a May Day rally in Washington, D.C., in 1937. Speaking to a crowd of some five hundred people at the CP-organized event, he talked about the need to build a labor movement that organized black and white workers in a common struggle.[25]

Frazier's closest contact with the CP during the 1930s occurred when he was hired as research director by a commission appointed by Mayor

LaGuardia to investigate conditions in Harlem following the riot of March 19, 1935. Frazier's final report was never released by the mayor, in part because it not only acquitted the CP of any responsibility for the riot but also complimented the party for its role both in preventing a full-scale race riot and in educating the public during the Commission's hearings:

> While one, in view of the available facts, would hesitate to give the Communists full credit for preventing the outbreak from becoming a race riot, they deserve more credit than any other element in Harlem for preventing a physical conflict between whites and blacks. . . . The charge has been brought against the Communists especially that they attempted to "steal the show" or used the hearings as a platform to promulgate their doctrines. It was perfectly natural that the Communists should have utilized to the full [the] opportunity which the public hearings offered to act as the defenders of an expressed minority. Not only did they play this role with consummate skill, and this assertion does not imply any lack of sincerity, but the experienced and shrewd lawyers of the International Labor Defense translated the groping, and often incoherent, queries of the common man into clear, searching questions which prevented equivocation and subterfuge on the part of the witnesses. . . . In the final analysis, the main role which the Communists played at the public hearings was by no means that of professional agitators and propagandists; they only defined and gave direction to the often vague dissatisfaction of the people, and attempted to interpret injustices which were regarded merely as racial persecution as a phase of the general expression of the submerged classes.[26]

Several commissioners tried to get Frazier and the rest of the Commission to eliminate all references to the CP and communists, as well as all anticapitalist phrases. Frazier told the Commission that he had written the truth; but the content of the final report was theirs to decide. Most of the objectionable sections were retained, although the Commission ended up badly split and therefore politically ineffective.[27]

During the 1930s Frazier was more politically active than at any other time in his life. The Chicago School and his elevation into the ranks of professional sociology had done nothing to quench his rambunctious spirit. On the contrary, the more secure he was in academia, the more he was active on a variety of political fronts. In 1935 alone, he gave a talk on the "Negro Middle Class" to a summer school in New York organized by the League for Industrial Democracy; he went to

Philadelphia to speak at the opening ceremony for the Labor Institute of the Brotherhood of Sleeping Car Porters; and he traveled to Doylestown in Pennsylvania and advised a farm conference how to start a "workers' school . . . on the farm where the students would be taught to develop a new social order from the present chaotic capitalistic society."[28] In the same year he was running the sociology department at Howard and directing a huge research project for Mayor LaGuardia's riot commission.

Frazier versus Du Bois

Frazier was also prominently involved in the controversy that shook the Afro-American movement in 1934. By the early 1930s Frazier was concerned that little remained of the progressive black movement. When the NAACP awarded its annual Spingarn Medal to Robert Moton, his former employer from Tuskegee, Frazier was convinced that the longtime battle between the followers of Washington and Du Bois was finally over, and the "Negro radicals" had lost. "All shades of articulate Negro thought today," he wrote with some bitterness in 1932, "are conservative."[29] He was convinced that there could be "no fundamental changes in race relations in the South unless these changes are brought about in connection with some revolutionary movement. The accumulation of goodwill will not do it. The present racial situation is bound up with the present economic and social system."[30]

Frazier became increasingly disenchanted with the most prominent Afro-American leaders. He found the "common sense" opportunism of spokespeople such as James Weldon Johnson equivalent to the "Uncle Tomism" of house slaves who used to say, "Since slavery is here, don't be abolitionist. Only ask that the slaves be treated kindly."[31]

Through the early 1930s a political crisis had been developing within the NAACP. The New Deal was having minimal economic impact on black communities, and activists increasingly were at odds with the NAACP's old guard, who "remained true to the faith that ignorance was the root cause of exploitation and that meaningful progress would be achieved once men of goodwill became aware of desperate conditions."[32] The second Amenia Conference, held in the summer of 1933, was an effort by Spingarn, Du Bois, and other civil rights leaders to forge a new NAACP-led coalition and to find a new direction in the wake of the economic devastation caused by the Depression and the slow pace of integration.[33]

Among the thirty-three men and women who gathered at Spingarn's estate was a group of younger radicals—including Abram Harris, Ralph Bunche, Ira DeA. Reid, Louis Redding, Sterling Brown, and Frazier—who wanted the NAACP to take militant action. They discussed the need for black power, with Frazier leading the way in his call for "the conscious development of nationalistic sentiment" and black control of the "betterment organizations."[34] Following the Amenia Conference, the NAACP appointed a special committee—chaired by Harris, Frazier's colleague from Howard—to reconsider the NAACP's direction and strategy. Harris recruited his friends, including Frazier, to work with him in the hope that the committee could move the NAACP to the left. But the old guard held firm, and the radicals left to form new organizations.[35]

The failure of the Amenia Conference to develop a new progressive agenda and strategy was compounded by Du Bois's increasing alienation from both the NAACP and the left. By the time he resigned from the NAACP in June 1934, Du Bois was convinced that race prejudice was so enduring and intractable that it was futile to fight for social justice through the courts, as the NAACP suggested, or through the labor and leftist movements, as the CP and socialist organizations advocated.[36]

Du Bois's new program turned out to be a retreat to the politics of economic and spiritual self-reliance. "If segregated homesteads and segregated land will give us more secure employment and higher wages, we cannot for a moment hesitate," argued Du Bois. "If segregated schools will give us better education, then we must have segregated schools. If segregated housing will give us decent homes, we have no right to choose for our children and families slums for the sake of herding with the white unfit. Our first business in the midst of the great economic revolution, which is going on, is to secure a place for ourselves." Arguing that "there is no automatic power in socialism to override and suppress race prejudice," Du Bois warned that "one of the worst things that Negroes could do today would be to join the American Communist Party and any of its many branches. The Communists of America have become dogmatic exponents of the inspired word of Karl Marx as they read it. They believe, apparently, in immediate, violent and bloody revolution, and they are willing to try any and all means of raising hell anywhere and under any circumstances. This is a silly program even for white men. For American colored men, it is suicide."[37]

Frazier hurled himself into the center of the storm caused by Du Bois's dramatic political shift to the right. In May 1934, just before Du Bois's resignation, Frazier wrote a long letter to the NAACP's Walter White in which he expressed his differences with Du Bois and the NAACP, and clarified how his own nationalism differed from that of Du Bois. First, he expressed his philosophical disagreement with Du Bois's view of human agency, which stressed the futility of the fight against segregation. "This may be so. It is conceivable that institutions and social arrangements can not be affected by human effort. But, even the Communist, with his materialistic conception of history, does not believe it. Marx and Lenin both controverted the idea that since human arrangements were dependent upon impersonal economic forces, nothing could be done through human effort."

Second, Frazier went to the heart of his critique when he accused Du Bois of taking "refuge in a tame and harmless racialism" because he was "too old or is afraid to risk his livelihood in coming out in favor of Communism or the destruction of competitive capitalist society as the only solution to the Negro's problem." He told White that it was a mistake to confuse Du Bois's "racial separateness" with Frazier's advocacy of the development of group morale and solidarity, a position that he had taken at the Amenia Conference. "I did not envisage a Negro ghetto, stratified according to bourgeois society. I was advocating a revolutionary nationalism," continued Frazier, "that is, the development of racial solidarity as a cohesive force among a people who were exploited by the white master class in this country."

Finally, as an afterthought, Frazier made clear that whatever criticisms he had of Du Bois, he was also dissatisfied with the NAACP. "My present criticism of it is that what was radical and militant twenty years ago is not radical and militant today. . . . The NAACP ought to become more militant and enlist every form of strategy to break down the walls of segregation."[38]

A year later Frazier began to express his critique in public. In July 1935 he cosigned the letter sent to *Crisis* and *The Nation* in defense of Stolberg, whose article in the *The Nation* had attacked Du Bois for "black chauvinism" and the NAACP for its "sheer impotence."[39] About the same time, Frazier began to align himself with the Conference on Social Economic Aspects of the Race Problem, a group of leftist Afro-

Americans and whites who earlier in the year had met at Shaw University in Raleigh, North Carolina, to discuss new strategies for combatting racism. This group, which was far to the left of the NAACP but disagreed with the CP's separatist position on the National Question, invited Frazier to join the board of its new journal, *Race*. Frazier accepted the invitation and also agreed to "write the article criticizing Du Bois's position" for the first issue.[40]

Frazier's three-page essay made his letter to Walter White appear mild in comparison. He made no concessions to Du Bois's historical role in the Afro-American movement or his personal role in inspiring Frazier's development as an undergraduate at Howard or his defense when Frazier was under attack in Atlanta. Instead Frazier used all his considerable abilities as a satirist and polemicist to debunk his former mentor in what was "perhaps the bitterest attack of the decade upon the older race men in general and Du Bois in particular."[41]

> Du Bois remains an intellectual who toys with the idea of the Negro as a separate cultural group. He has only an occasional romantic interest in the Negro as a distinct race. Nothing could be more unendurable for him than to live within a Black Ghetto or within a black nation—unless perhaps he were king, and then probably he would attempt to unite the whites and blacks through marriage of the royal families. . . . If a fascist movement should develop in America, Du Bois would play into the hands of its leaders through his program for the development of Negro racialism. . . .
>
> Since Du Bois is an intellectual who loves to play with ideas but shuns reality, whether it be in the form of black masses or revolution, he likes to display a familiarity with Marxian ideology. In an article in the *Crisis* he demonstrated, in a few hundred words, the error of applying Marxian conceptions to the economic condition of the Negro in America. Later, in his *Black Reconstruction,* he played with Marxian terminology as a literary device. This is all at it should be, for Du Bois has said that there shall be no revolution and that economic justice and the abolition of poverty shall come through reason (the intellectual speaks), sacrifice (the romanticist speaks), and the intelligent use of the ballot (in the end he remains a liberal).

Frazier concluded by noting that, like Douglass and Washington before him, Du Bois had failed to provide "the kind of social criticism which is needed today in order that the Negro may orient himself in the present state of American capitalism."[42]

As it turned out, no individual or organization was capable of generating the "kind of social criticism" and new strategic thinking that Frazier envisioned. The group that formed around *Race* lasted less than a year; the CP's new united-front policy, initiated in 1935, brought it into alliances with the increasingly conservative NAACP and NUL; Roosevelt's New Deal coopted much of the independent left; and the promising National Negro Congress, formed in part by radicals who broke with the NAACP, quickly deteriorated into sectarianism.[43]

With the outbreak of World War II in 1939, the struggle for racial equality once again receded into the background. For Frazier, the war meant the end of his hopes for a purely domestic solution to the problem of racism. Now he would increasingly look outside the United States for the development of a "common humanity." "Today," he noted in 1943, "once more Negroes are called upon to participate in a struggle in which the issue between democracy and the equality of races, on the one hand, and autocracy and the doctrine of racial inequality, on the other, is more clearly drawn. As a result of this struggle, their own battle for freedom and equality can no longer be an isolated domestic problem."[44]

Keeping the Faith

It is not surprising that Frazier had a political affinity with the CP on many issues during the 1930s. Most progressive intellectuals placed themselves somewhere within its orbit. But given the decline of the party and the rise of a virulent anticommunism in the 1940s, it is unusual that he remained evenhanded, even sympathetic at times to the CP. He never reneged on his support, never apologized for past positions, never reinterpreted the party through Cold War assumptions, as did so many liberal intellectuals.[1] In fact, the more the CP, communism, and the Soviet Union came under attack, the more Frazier made a point of acknowledging their positive contributions. As Martin Duberman has noted about Paul Robeson, "Opposition, typically, emboldened him; pressure brought out his intransigence."[2] So it was also with Frazier.

Heresies

In his academic publications, Frazier refused to bow to anticommunist hysteria. Whatever his differences with leftist organizations, he always gave credit where credit was due. As Cold War pressures swept through academia, Frazier refused to be intimidated or coopted. Statements that would have seemed trivial or inconsequential in the 1930s drew hostile attention like a red flag in the 1940s.

His 1940 book, *Negro Youth at the Crossways,* included a summary of the activities and projects of various "militant organizations." Frazier was sympathetic but factual in his description of the Washington Council of the National Negro Congress. Noting that it "has been accused of communist affiliations," Frazier observed that the Council "has attempted to arouse the masses to protest against wrongs which could be dramatized. While its mass meetings have seldom brought the masses out, members of the Council through skilful publicity and working in cooperation with labor unions and other organizations have been able to influence to some extent the thinking of a large number of Negroes."[3] Frazier repeated this assessment in *Black Bourgeoisie,* in which, albeit briefly and dispassionately, he also credited the CP for its short-lived success during the 1930s in its "reeducation" of the "Negro masses . . . to demand more than the appointment of middle-class Negroes to honorific posts."[4]

Frazier took a similar attitude toward the Soviet Union. Even in his most academic publications, he made a point of introducing ideas that in the prevailing anticommunist atmosphere were quite heretical. In his 1949 textbook, for example, he noted that "the influence of Russia in the struggle of the colored colonial peoples for freedom and independence is more important than it is represented to be in the propaganda contained in the newspapers of the United States. Russia has provided for the world a solution of the problem of racial and cultural minorities dwelling within a single political community. . . . Moreover, in the arena of international politics, as for example in the United Nations Organization, Russia has become the champion of the rights of the colored colonial peoples."[5]

He elaborated this interpretation in *Race and Culture Contacts in the Modern World,* noting the influence of the Soviet Union on the "revolt of Asia against Western dominance" and on the global redefinition of concepts of nationalism and self-determination. He thought that the Soviet Union was engaged in the revolutionary experiment of respecting cultural autonomy within a centralized political and economic system. "If one were to seek an answer to the question of whether the Russian policy has solved the problem of nationalism, one can only say that in World War II the various nations and peoples were loyal to the Soviet Union and fought enthusiastically in its defense."[6]

After World War II Frazier's political activism subsided. From his undergraduate days at Howard through the 1930s his commitment had been sustained and shaped by social movements and innovative radical politics that attempted to unite struggles for economic and social justice. Though he had always operated on the fringe of organizations and protected his ideological independence, he was deeply involved in the political culture of the civil rights, socialist, and communist movements. As these movements collapsed after World War II and he searched for a new identification in the context of global movements, Frazier's political commitments within the United States became increasingly sporadic and more vicarious, and Frazier became increasingly disillusioned with the possibility that such commitments by themselves could be effective.

Nevertheless, he retained a degree of activism and involvement, invariably on the left edge of political issues. In the Cold War atmosphere, it did not take much to qualify as an activist. During an investigation of radicalism at Howard, Sterling Brown was asked by the FBI whether he was a communist; he supposedly replied: "Listen son, any Negro who has been to the seventh grade and is against lynching is a Communist. I have been to the eighth grade and am against a hell of a lot more than lynching."[7]

Frazier and Robeson

In the 1940s and 1950s Frazier did more than enough to bring himself to the attention of intelligence agencies and right-wing Congressional committees. In 1941 he joined the leftist Council on African Affairs (CAA), which was founded in 1937 and chaired by Paul Robeson. Frazier had known Paul and Essie Robeson since the 1920s, and over the years they stayed in touch, personally and politically.[8] The CAA was a small educational organization, a progressive conduit to bring information about Africa into the United States. When Frazier joined the CAA, it had become too left and too identified with the CP for Howard's Ralphe Bunche and Mordecai Johnson, who resigned. In 1941 the CAA had only nineteen members, including its officers. In 1946 membership grew to seventy-two, most of whom were radical Jewish intellectuals. After the Attorney General included the CAA on his list of subversive Communist-front organizations in 1947, a split developed within the organization, led on one side by Max Yergan, the CAA's executive director, and by Robeson on the other. Frazier gave his proxy to Robeson, who eventually, after a long and bitter struggle, prevailed over Yergan, who denounced the CAA as a communist organization.[9] Benjamin Davis, the black communist councilman from New York, sent Frazier a letter thanking him for his support of the Robeson faction. "I commend your courage," wrote Davis, "for standing up for what you believe to be right at a time when sinister pressures are coming from all sides. The best I can say is that I am not at all surprised."[10]

Frazier continued to side with Robeson on other issues. After the "battle of Peekskill" in 1949, when Robeson and his supporters had to fight white mobs in order to hold a concert, there was a national debate about who was to blame for the violence. Eleanor Roosevelt, A. Philip Randolph, and most liberals condemned both sides equally. However, at a meeting in Washington, D.C., Frazier defended Robeson as a "fearless and independent thinker" who refused to act out the white-assigned role of "humility and forgiveness."[11]

Frazier was also among a group of seventeen Afro-American leaders who issued a statement defending Robeson's "inalienable right to speak and sing to all who wish to hear him" in Washington, D.C.[12] After Robeson's successful concert there, he wrote Frazier a note to thank him for his support. "Whatever the hostile press and our so-called leaders may say or fail to say," Robeson wrote, he felt that his reception "from east to west served to confirm the correctness of the stand I have taken and the people's support of my stand."[13]

Frazier's relationship with Robeson and the stands he took regarding the CAA and Peekskill were typical of his politics during and after World War II. Late in 1943 Frazier accepted an invitation from Corliss Lamont and Elizabeth Moos of the National Council of American-Soviet Friendship to present a paper in New York at a conference commemorating the tenth anniversary of diplomatic relations between the United Sates and Soviet Union.[14] Frazier participated in a panel, "The Soviet Union: A Family of Nations in the War," along with Anatoly Yakovlev from the Soviet Union and Louis Adamic.[15] Though the wartime alliance between the two countries was in effect, Frazier's speech went beyond the usual niceties about antifascist cooperation. He argued that "the two most important obstacles that stand in the way of world unity [were] the competition of capitalist countries for world markets and the exploitation of the colored races." Praising the Soviet Union as a "country free of race prejudice," he pointed out that, "despite propaganda about the dire economic and moral consequences of a communistic society, the Negroes knew that a society that treated all races as equals possessed some virtue." Frazier concluded by noting the similarities between Nazi and white supremacist ideology and by explicitly urging Afro-Americans to learn from the Soviet Union's battle against racism. "If a family of nations is achieved in the post-war world, we feel certain that Soviet Russia's stand in regard to the equality of races and colonial peoples will be an important factor in the Negro's struggle for freedom and equality in American life."[16]

Frazier continued to regard himself as a leftist, and in 1945 he was furious when at least two newspapers, the *People's Voice* from Harlem and the *Black Dispatch* from Oklahoma, carried a picture of him, his wife, and two friends under the caption "We Are Hungry" sitting in Frank's Restaurant in Harlem while a picket line marched outside protesting the restaurant's racist labor policies.[17] Frazier claimed that he mistook the picket line for a fight and "milling mob," and "once we heard that the restaurant was being picketed because no Negroes were employed there, Mrs. Frazier and I got up and went out." Frazier was so angry with the story that he twice went to the office of the *People's Voice* and unsuccessfully tried to meet with Doxey Wilkerson, the general manager. He then wrote a long letter to Wilkerson refuting the newspaper's "lies" and "irresponsible attitude," and defending his own progressive credentials. "You know as well as I," he wrote Wilkerson, "that this is a vicious attack with no basis in fact. I need not repeat here my position in regard to the labor movement and the revolution which is going on in the world today." [18]

The significance of this seemingly trivial incident is that it mattered a great deal to Frazier that the left-wing press had identified him as "reactionary Negro leadership." For the most part, though, the left-wing press reported on his activities and positions favorably, a fact that did not escape the attention of the FBI and witch hunters in Congress.[19]

Frazier continued to move in the ever-diminishing circles of the public left. For example, in October 1944 he went to New York to participate in a forum organized by the *Daily Worker* to discuss Howard Fast's recently released *Freedom Road*;[20] in 1945 he agreed to write a pamphlet on "The Integration of the Negro into American Life" for the Women's International League for Peace and Freedom; in the same year he wrote to the *Afro-American* expressing his disgust at the "upper class colored citizens" who attended a segregated ball in celebration of the president's birthday, not unlike "slavery days [when] benevolent whites would often visit the 'quarters' to see how the 'darkies' were enjoying themselves";[21] and in 1948 the Fraziers accepted an invitation from the Soviet ambassador to the United States to attend a reception commemorating the thirty-first anniversary of the "Great October Revolution."[22]

Frazier and Du Bois

In his political activities throughout his life Frazier constantly searched
for ways to integrate his commitment to racial equality with his interest
in socialism and economic justice. The *Messenger* group had provided
the context for these overlapping commitments during World War I and
in the early 1920s; the CP and left wing of the civil rights movement
had provided it during the 1930s. And in the last decade of Frazier's
life Du Bois gave him another unexpected opportunity.

Frazier's personal relationship with Du Bois went back to 1924,
when Du Bois, then editor of *Crisis,* published Frazier's highly controversial article advocating retaliatory violence by Afro-American communities under attack by the Ku Klux Klan. The following year Du
Bois sought out the promising young scholar in Atlanta and asked him
whether he would be willing to do some confidential research on black
education in Georgia, Alabama, and South Carolina. Frazier immediately accepted this offer, thus initiating a collaboration that would
weather some stormy moments and last until his death. Despite Frazier's political differences with Du Bois on some significant issues—
notably Afro-American participation in World War I and the debate
about nationalism in the mid-1930s—he retained a high degree of affection and respect for the man who raised the "big moral questions
having to do with racism, exploitation, and imperialism."[23]

Du Bois, like Robeson, was a heroic figure to Frazier, not only because of his political views but also because he stood up to all kinds of
establishments—whether they were racist bigots or anticommunists or
the black bourgeoisie or university bureaucrats—and held his ground,
no matter how unpopular. Ideology aside, Frazier admired this kind of
intransigence of principle and personal stubbornness. So late in 1950
he was pleased to accept an invitation to serve as chair of a committee
sponsoring a dinner to honor Du Bois on his eighty-third birthday.

Though Du Bois again was a controversial figure—he had been
speaking out in Europe and at home against U.S. imperialism and had
participated in a Soviet peace conference[24]—Frazier naively assumed
that the celebration would be uncontroversial and that his role would be
largely symbolic and ceremonial. A major hotel had been reserved for
the event, and 250 distinguished leaders had indicated their willingness
to sponsor the dinner. All quickly changed on February 9, 1951, when
Du Bois and others associated with the Peace Information Center were
indicted as unregistered foreign agents of the Soviet Union.[25]

Though the charges had no substance and were dismissed when the case eventually came to court in November 1951, Du Bois was tried and found guilty in the press. Anticipating problems with attendance at the dinner, a letter was sent out in Frazier's name quoting Du Bois's response that the Center was an "entirely American organization whose sole objective was to secure peace and prevent a third world war." Frazier called on the sponsors to make the dinner into a "historic event," not to surrender to political pressures.[26]

But the damage had been done; many sponsors and supporters abandoned the dinner out of fear of being associated with Du Bois. "Many Negroes, at first sight, listened to no facts and convicted me out of hand without a hearing," recalled Du Bois, "until to their amazement not even the Department of Justice could prove this frame-up."[27] The three main speakers withdrew from the event, as did the hotel where the dinner was scheduled. Some simply canceled their reservations; others sent apologies. "For a private and confidential reason," wrote a Harvard professor, "I cannot participate in the Du Bois celebration. . . . The reason is that a member of my family is just now being worked over by one of our 'security' boards. . . . The inquisition of course is probably more of me (because I know you and some other good people) than it is anything else."[28]

Not many Afro-American leaders were willing to give their support to Du Bois. Most were silent, and a few, like the NAACP leader Walter White, sided with the Department of Justice and "joined in the jackals' chorus."[29] It was an act of courage for somebody like Hubert Delany, a prominent Afro-American lawyer, to send in a letter of solidarity even though a prior commitment made it impossible for him to attend the dinner. "I have decided that failure to attend, or to leave in the midst of the dinner to keep my appointment, . . ." Delany wrote Frazier, "might be interpreted as an indication that I believe in the theory of guilt by association. I therefore enclose my check to you for a reservation for the dinner so that all who can read and see may not misinterpret my absence from the dinner or my inability to remain until its conclusion. . . . I salute Dr. Du Bois, a distinguished American who has fought with courage for sixty years in the battle for Civil Rights for all the American people."[30]

Like Delany, Frazier was one of a handful of leaders to keep his public commitment to Du Bois. He stayed with the diminishing committee, signed press releases in defense of Du Bois, and on February 23rd chaired the event, which was moved to a restaurant and attended by some six hundred people. He found two new speakers, Bishop J. W. Walls and attorney Belford Lawson. When the bishop did not show, he asked Alain Locke to say a few words, but Locke refused. At the last minute, after the dinner had already begun, he saw Robeson in the audience and recruited him to give an impromptu speech.[31]

Frazier played a prominent role at the dinner. He not only chaired the event but also gave a moving and thoughtfully prepared tribute to Du Bois:

> When I accepted the chairmanship of the committee which sponsored this dinner to honor Dr. DuBois, I felt that I was attempting in a small way to repay a great personal debt which I owed to our greatest leader. This personal debt is, in fact, a debt which is shared by all educated Negroes of my generation. The educated men and women of my generation are indebted to Dr. Du Bois for two major contributions which he made to our personal development under the trying circumstances of American life. We are indebted to him, first, because he demonstrated to us by his scholarly productions and intellectual orientation toward life that the Negro was capable of the highest intellectual achievements as measured by European standards. We are indebted to him, secondly, for providing an example of courage and personal dignity in the struggle of the Negro to achieve freedom and equality in American life. . . . Since Du Bois first devoted his life to human welfare and an honest search for truth, he has always been opposed to war, violence, and hatred. Throughout his life he has attempted to show that war, stripped of all its false glory, and race prejudice, divested of its rationalizations, both grow out of and contribute to human exploitation.[32]

A few weeks after the dinner, Du Bois sent a letter to Frazier, personally thanking him "for your courageous stand in my defense. . . . Ordinarily the stand such as you took was what could be expected of any American and particularly of any educated Negro. It happened however that the number of people with guts and ordinary clarity of thought was astonishingly small among both black and white. That made your stand all the more fine and creditable. I thank you for it very deeply. You may suffer some, but I do not think in the long run you will find anything but praise and approbation among people who think and know. I shall want to see you as soon as possible and have a long talk."[33]

Apparently, Frazier and Du Bois never had that long talk. For the next several years Du Bois was treated as a political pariah in his own country and, denied a passport by the State Department until 1958, was unable to travel outside the United States.[34] In 1958–1959 he went on a tour of Western and Eastern Europe and China. "It was a most extraordinary journey," he wrote Frazier, "and has changed my outlook on current affairs." By this time Frazier was quite sick with cancer; Du Bois and his wife Shirley Graham sent their good wishes for his recovery. "I hear that you have not been well, and I am very, very sorry. You must get rest and care for yourself, which I imagine is easier said than done," said Du Bois in his last letter to his colleague of some thirty-four years.[35]

In 1961, as a last act of defiance, Du Bois formally joined the CP and left his country for good. He died two years later, August 27, 1963, at the age of ninety-five in Nkrumah's Ghana.[36] Frazier did not join the party nor did he physically leave the country before he died in May 1962, but he expressed his solidarity with Du Bois's "example of courage" and with Nkrumah's revolutionary nationalism by bequeathing his vast library to Ghana. Fittingly, it was Shirley Graham Du Bois who on behalf of Marie Brown Frazier presented Frazier's books to the University of Ghana on July 9, 1963.[37]

19

Hounded

Frazier was constantly disappointed that more of his colleagues did not live up to the standards set by Langston Hughes, Du Bois, Robeson, and others who provided "the soul of a people."[1] At the same time, however, he was aware of the objective constraints that limited individual choices and action. He recognized that Afro-American intellectuals were likely to pay a price for critical thought. "If they show any independence in their thinking they may be hounded by the FBI," wrote Frazier just before he died, "and find it difficult to make a living. At the present time many of them find themselves in the humiliating position of running around the world telling Africans and others how well-off Negroes are in the United States and how well they are treated."[2]

Racism and Academic Freedom

It is instructive to use Frazier's career as a case study in the repressive constraints that limit the creativity and productivity of progressive Afro-American intellectuals. Typically, studies and accounts of violations of academic and intellectual freedom in the United States are based on notorious cases of individual persecution or on institutional complicity in redbaiting and McCarthyism or on exclusion and discrimination based on race, ethnicity, and gender.[3]

Frazier's life allows us to draw on all these approaches to explore both the dramatic and mundane ways in which academic freedom is defined, invaded, and curtailed. In many ways, Frazier's experience is more typical than that of most victims of repression because he does not readily come to mind as a sensational victim of racism or McCarthyism. True, he was involved in leftist politics; he was an uncompromising race man; and he was a self-proclaimed atheist and critic of organized religion. But he was also a committed academic; a loner more than a joiner, who remained aloof from political parties and organizations; a thinker more than a doer, an intellectual who was committed primarily to the exploration and articulation of ideas. Moreover, he was sufficiently conventional to become the first Afro-American president of the American Sociological Association in 1948 and to be recruited as an American representative to UNESCO in 1951.

When we examine Frazier's career, however, we find a lifetime of repressive constraints, some monumental and some almost trivial or incidental, which looked at separately may not be striking but when examined in their cumulative totality reveal a massive rupture between the ideal and the reality of academic freedom. Before examining how Frazier was "hounded by the FBI" after World War II, we need to summarize what he encountered as an Afro-American intellectual in the repressive atmosphere of university life prior to the 1940s.

Politics aside, institutionalized racism severely limited Frazier's capacity to participate fully in academia. After graduating from Howard in 1916, he could teach only in a black college, which meant that he was restricted to the South until he got a job teaching at his alma mater in 1934. Despite a lifetime of productive scholarship and international recognition, he was never offered a full-time, tenure-track job in a leading university. As a result of racism, inequality of resources interfered with Frazier's ability to develop fully his intellectual craft. Between 1916 and 1934 especially, when he was mostly in the South, he had no choice but to accept inadequate libraries, minimal funding of research, scarce travel funds, and limited access to university and research facilities.

For at least the first half of his life, and after that it was too late to change, a black social scientist like Frazier had no choice but to specialize in "Negro studies" and to aspire to becoming a competent "Negro sociologist." Frazier apparently never had any regrets about his area of specialization and probably would have chosen to focus on race relations if he had been given any options. But Afro-American intellectuals of Frazier's generation were not given such a choice.

These kinds of constraints routinely circumscribed the work of all Afro-American intellectuals prior to World War II. Frazier faced additional problems because he was interested in radical ideas, because he was a militant race man in both his political orientation and his personal life, and because he was outspoken and bold to the point of being rash in expressing his views. The consequences ranged from death threats and loss of his job in Atlanta in 1927 to restrictions on what and where he could publish.

It took him three years to find a journal that would publish "The Pathology of Race Prejudice," an article that subsequently became a classic in the race-relations literature. He changed his pen name from Edward F. to E. Franklin Frazier—admittedly not a very compelling subterfuge—in order to avoid being harassed for his ideas. He thought it necessary to publish some articles anonymously (such as his reports on southern education in *Crisis* in the 1920s and his articles for the *Afro-American* in the 1930s), and he used an incongruous French title for his controversial 1928 article on the Afro-American middle class. Moreover, it took nearly thirty years before Frazier's *Black Bourgeoisie* was published in the United States. As with James Baldwin's *Giovanni's Room,* it was too controversial for U.S. publishers and was first published in Europe.[4]

Even in the 1930s and beyond, when his academic reputation was established, he still found that his ideas were subjected to censorship. His 1935 study of the Harlem riot, considered by Herbert Blumer to be a major contribution to the literature on collective behavior,[5] was, as we have seen, never released by Mayor LaGuardia because of its controversial analysis and findings. Several years later when he was revising *The Negro Family in the United States* for an abridged edition for Dryden Press—"in which they were taking out footnotes, and tables and graphs, so the illiterates could read it"—his editor tried to get him to remove a reference to the increase in intermarriage on the grounds that such an observation was undiplomatic.[6] After World War II, however, Frazier faced much more serious obstacles to his career than censorship.

Crazy Racialist

On the basis of important new studies[7] and recently released files from the FBI, it is possible to reconstruct how intelligence agencies targeted and harassed Frazier over twenty years during the last third of his life.[8] Frazier was first identified as a possible security risk in 1936 in a public document issued by the intelligence division of the Department of the

Interior, which had been authorized by a Senate resolution to investigate "communistic activities" at Howard following the use of the university for a conference on "The Position of the Negro in Our National Economic Crisis."[9] Frazier recalled that investigators came to the university to question him.[10] He was not the major target of investigation and was mentioned in only two insignificant references in the Congressional report.[11]

The FBI's interest in Frazier was part of a broad program of surveillance of Afro-Americans that was initiated in 1919. Under J. Edgar Hoover's direction, this program was expanded in the 1920s and 1930s to involve regular infiltration of every civil rights and nationalist organization. By the early 1940s Hoover was sending weekly reports on "Negro trends" to government agencies and the White House.[12] In 1942, according to Kenneth O'Reilly, the FBI launched its "most systematic Negro Question investigation, a nationwide survey of 'foreign inspired agitation' in 'colored areas and colored neighborhoods.'"[13]

Between 1941 and 1962 Frazier was subjected to three major security investigations—one in the early 1940s in association with the Hatch Act and two, initiated in the 1950s, regarding his employment by UNESCO.[14] In 1941, under authority of Public Law 135 (77th Congress), the FBI was authorized "to investigate the employees of every department, agency, and independent establishment of the Federal Government who are members of subversive organizations or who advocate the overthrow of the Federal Government." Because Howard received part of its funding from the Department of the Interior, Frazier and other faculty members were classified by the Federal Security Agency's Committee on Subversive Activities as government employees.[15] The investigation was guided by section 9A of the 1939 Hatch Act, which made it unlawful for any federal employee to "have membership in any political party or organization which advocates the overthrow of our constitutional form of government."

The first serious investigation of Frazier was conducted by the FBI's Washington, D.C., field office in 1941–1942. Although some informants reported that Frazier had spoken in 1937 at a May Day demonstration organized by the CP and that he was a "crazy racialist," there was no evidence that he was a member of the CP or its front organizations. In February 1942 Frazier was called into FBI headquarters, where he responded to questions under oath, though he later refused to sign the transcribed interview. Frazier said that he was not a member of any "subversive" organization—"I'm a social scientist and don't belong to any isms"—but begrudgingly conceded that he might have participated in activities organized by the Washington Committee for Democratic Action and American Youth Congress.

Though the FBI filled its report with every scrap of evidence and innuendo that it could extract from informants and intelligence data bases—including reports that Frazier subscribed to *New Masses,* was on the "contact list" of the League of Industrial Democracy, and had once sent a contribution of two dollars to the United American Spanish Relief Committee—the Federal Security Agency informed Frazier that "we have found nothing in the report showing that you have engaged in any activities which might properly be characterized subversive or disloyal to our Government. You have, therefore, been exonerated and the Federal Bureau of Investigation has been so notified."[16]

Despite Frazier's "exoneration" in 1942, from then on he was regularly targeted by intelligence agencies and Congressional committees for his alleged subversive and communist activities. When he testified to the Senate Internal Security Subcommittee (SISS) in 1955, he was interrogated about his participation in "communist front" organizations back to 1937.[17]

Once Hoover's FBI opened a file on a suspect, especially somebody considered a "very strong racialist" who "would follow any movement or organization with a strong racial interest," agents were under pressure to provide data that would confirm the original suspicions. Thus, Frazier's purchase of city maps in January 1943 was reported to FBI headquarters by the Washington, D.C. field office as a possible indication of espionage; the text of Frazier's 1944 speech to the National Council of American-Soviet Friendship found its way into his FBI file from the Baltimore field office; and by 1950 the Washington, D.C., police department had Frazier's name in its files on "suspected Communist Party participants."

Between 1944 and 1956 the FBI made sure that Frazier's name appeared often on the lists of communists, alleged communists, and communist sympathizers that were such a regular feature of the endless reports issued by the House Un-American Activities Committee (HUAC). Of course, it did not take much to make it onto these lists. Though Frazier was not as politically active in the 1940s as he had been in previous years, he willingly gave his name as a sponsor or endorser to all kinds of progressive petitions, organizations, coalitions, ad hoc committees, and conferences. As an established academic and head of Howard University's sociology department, his name had symbolic value, and his endorsement of an event or demand made its way into leftist newspapers. Investigators for the FBI, HUAC, and SISS seemed to do most of their research in the back issues of the CP's *Daily Worker.*

In HUAC's 1944 investigation of "un-American propaganda activities in the United States," Frazier was cited twelve times for his involvement in eight "Communist fronts," including the National Citizens' Political Action Committee, the American Youth Congress, the magazine *New Masses,* and the Washington Committee for Democratic Action.[18] Three years later he was identified by HUAC as a supporter of CP leader Earl Browder and a "sponsor" of the Southern Conference for Human Welfare, a broad-based coalition of liberal and left-wing organizations, characterized by HUAC as "perhaps the most deviously camouflaged Communist-front organization" which "shows unswerving loyalty to the basic principles of Soviet foreign policy" and "has displayed consistent anti-American bias."[19]

In 1951 he made another HUAC list, this time as a member of the American Sponsoring Committee for the World Peace Congress, as a signer of the Stockholm Appeal, and as a sponsor of the Mid-Century Conference for Peace, all part of the "most dangerous hoax ever devised by the international Communist conspiracy."[20] Finally, in 1956 he appeared in HUAC's report on "political subversion" for cosigning in 1948 a letter circulated by the Civil Rights Congress to protest pending anticommunist legislation and for serving in 1949 on the National Non-Partisan Committee to Defend the Rights of the 12 Communist Leaders.[21]

Somehow Frazier managed to avoid being subpoenaed by any of the Congressional committees until 1955. When HUAC held its hearings in 1949 on "Communist infiltration of minority groups," Frazier was not among the friendly witnesses who were called to repudiate Paul Robeson's "disloyal" attitude toward the U.S. government.[22] Jackie Robinson testified that the "Negro's loyalty" could be counted on "against Russia or any other enemy that threatened us"; NUL's Lester Granger reaffirmed the League's opposition to "the Communist who seeks to destroy the democratic ideal and practice which constitute the Negro's sole hope of eventual victory in his fight for equal citizenship"; and Charles Johnson, Frazier's long-time nemesis, testified that "Negroes, like Americans generally, are profoundly loyal to the higher purposes and future of our democratic form of government, our democratic way of life."[23] Such testimony was neither Frazier's politics nor his style. He hated public posturing and self-abasement.

Not long after HUAC held its hearings on the "Negro's loyalty," Frazier was battling to get his passport approved by the State Department so that he could go to France as chief of the Division of Applied Social Sciences in UNESCO.[24] The appointment was an extraordinary honor for Frazier, as well as an opportunity to get out of the United States and live in Paris for a couple of years. He applied for the position (which required State Department approval) in January 1951, just before Du Bois's birthday celebration.[25]

Frazier had a great deal to lose by refusing to back down from his responsibilities as chair of the Du Bois dinner. When it came time to get his passport approved, a State Department functionary asked him about his relationship with Du Bois, who at that time was under federal indictment. Frazier, as the story goes, refused to be apologetic with the examiner, who asked him, "Didn't you know that Du Bois was a communist?" "Well, I heard people say that," replied Frazier. "But we had a fine dinner. He may be a communist to you but to me he is the dean of black American scholars and I was honoring him in that role." At that point, Frazier started to leave and said, "Look, you people pushed my name forward to go over there because you simply want to show that white people in the United States have one Negro academic that you can win some points with by showing that the country isn't prejudiced. I don't need to go to Paris. I've got plenty of work to do here." Before Frazier could leave, the examiner quickly pulled out the passport and told Frazier to "represent your country worthily abroad."[26]

In 1953, at the request of the Department of Health, Education and Welfare (formerly the Federal Security Agency), the FBI began a "full security investigation" of Frazier under the Hatch Act but quickly put it on hold when it was reported that Frazier was on leave from Howard and was serving as chief of UNESCO's Division of Applied Social Sciences in Paris. Again, the FBI managed to continue its surveillance by referring the case to its unit responsible for investigating the loyalty of U.S. citizens employed by the United Nations (under Executive Order 10422).

Frazier, who had been in Paris since November 1951, managed to avoid an investigation until early 1953, a few months before he was due to return home. In February 1953 he belatedly filled out a background questionnaire; in June FBI headquarters assigned the case to "mature and experienced agents," launched a "full field investigation," and sent out inquiries to the State Department and CIA. The final report was based on memoranda from field agents in Puerto Rico, Los Angeles, San Francisco, Memphis, Charlotte, Richmond, Cleveland, Atlanta, Mobile, New York, Baltimore, Boston, Chicago, St. Louis, and New Orleans, as well as from State Department intelligence agents in Paris and Brazil.

With no evidence of his direct participation in CP organizations, agents all over the country scoured their *Daily Worker* clippings, sent out a call to informants for incriminating evidence, and tried their best to construct a plausible case against Frazier. A file was opened on Herbert Blumer, now a professor of sociology at Berkeley and one of Frazier's references, because an informant reported that thirteen years earlier Blumer had supported the NAACP's efforts to stop *The Birth of a Nation* from being shown in Chicago. Frazier's contacts from Atlanta in the 1920s reported that he had a reputation for "making argumentative and antagonistic statements with respect to political theories," that he had a tendency to make ''ill-advised remarks.'' The Atlanta field office dug up the allegation that he had been fired from the Atlanta School of Social Work in 1927 because he had "shown a lack of sufficient administrative ability and was apparently distracted from his duties by outside interests such as speeches and writings." Encouraged by this evidence of Frazier's subversive past, agents were dispatched to interview a high school teacher in Baltimore who told them that forty-one years earlier young Edward had been an "independent thinker."

The best source of information, however, remained the Howard professor who back in 1942 had called Frazier a "crazy racialist." The informant, who was traced to New York and reinterviewed, confirmed that Frazier was "personally ambitious and self-assertive." Other contacts reported on Frazier's involvement in the Council on African Affairs, his ties to Robeson and Du Bois, and his willingness to lend his name as a sponsor to leftist petitions and letters. The New York field office interviewed informants who, though unwilling to testify under oath, told them that Frazier was a "leading Negro Communist," "a joiner and supporter of Communist front organizations," and "a fellow traveler and supporter of Communist causes." Another informant in Washington, D.C., reported that Frazier was "not one of the most charming representatives of his race or of humanity in general." Most contacts, however, reported Frazier to be loyal and reliable.

After some three months of intensive research, the investigation was called off when it was discovered that Frazier had returned to Howard from UNESCO. Meanwhile, the FBI flagged his name "for unresolved question of loyalty." His file was kept open and made available to Congressional intelligence committees.

Frazier's Testimony

Frazier spent two years in Paris with UNESCO and returned to Howard in 1953. Just when it appeared that he had managed to avoid the Congressional committees, he found himself "commanded" to appear before SISS, chaired by Mississippi's James Eastland.[27] He was served with a subpoena the day before his appearance and was forced to cancel his lectures on campus.[28] Frazier testified in executive session for two hours on March 30, 1955.[29] He was not a friendly witness, and SISS was not a friendly committee. Eastland, one of the leading, die-hard advocates of segregation in the South, had a particular animosity to Frazier, whom he regarded as the "chief brainwasher" of the U.S. Supreme Court in its decision in *Brown* v. *Board of Education*.[30]

The hearing was a dull sparring match. Eastland's investigators relied on FBI reports and clippings from the *Daily Worker* and other leftist newspapers to build a case against Frazier. The committee's attorneys went through a series of rote questions and a desultory cross-examination, while Frazier restrained himself to mostly brief, ambiguous, and uninformative answers. Given the privacy of the hearing, there was no stirring oratory on either side, and Frazier even kept a rein on his usual sarcasm.

Frazier refused to answer any questions about his own political beliefs—"If you want to hear me discuss Communism," he told the committee, "then you come to my class in Sociology and hear what I have to say about Communists, all aspects of Communism." He also managed to avoid naming names without perjuring himself by identifying as communists only people who were well known members of the CP, such as James Ford, Browder, Benjamin Davis, and Doxey Wilkerson. Regarding other alleged communists who had asked him to sign this petition or that statement, Frazier's razor-sharp memory suddenly failed him. To many questions about specific people or events, he replied, "I don't remember" or "I don't recall" or "I forget how many years" or "I didn't know that" or "I didn't know of his Communist record."

Occasionally, Frazier gave longer answers and defended his politics and associations. "If a person happens to be a Communist and I have known him personally," he said in response to a series of questions about his relationship with Du Bois, "he does not become a taboo person as far as I am concerned. . . . I knew he had been smeared as a Red, yes, I knew that. . . . I revered Dr. Du Bois as a Negro leader, without any relationship to any of his political beliefs, Communism, nothing. I don't even know that Du Bois is a Communist. . . . I have deep affection and respect for Dr. Du Bois."

By the end of the hearing, the committee had not been able to get any specific information from Frazier. They extracted Frazier's concession, false of course, that his friends "aren't Communists [and] they have nothing to do with Communists." He was even provoked into one brief ideological response: "Now, you know as well as I do that the Communists say they are working for the welfare of mankind, and I say I am working for the welfare of mankind, so the objective is common. . . . But when it comes to the specific objectives of the Communists and their methods and so forth, I have nothing to do with that at all."

For the most part, however, the committee's attorney and Frazier parried the following kind of exchange: "You have had Communist friends. You have quite a number of Communist friends, don't you?" asked the chief counsel. "Well," replied Frazier, "and this is a reflection upon me, I don't have many friends." Eastland's committee soon gave up, recognizing that Frazier was "not at all awed by this committee."[31]

Paying the Price

Frazier weathered SISS with his integrity intact, but Eastland, the State Department, and the FBI would have the last word and Frazier would end his life on a note of bitter defeat. In the spring of 1960 Alfred Métraux, chief of UNESCO's Department of Social Sciences in Paris, approached Frazier about his interest in working on a project on "industrialization and race relations." Frazier was enthusiastic about the proposal and agreed to do a detailed research plan and outline of the book that might result from the research.[32] On his way home from

Edinburgh, where he received an honorary degree in July, Frazier stopped in Paris and met with his contacts at UNESCO to discuss the project. A few months later, Métraux let him know that the research was likely to be funded for a two year period. Frazier would be in charge of the project and work with a team of researchers and writers under his direction. "I think that I could put enough money at your disposal to make the venture possible," wrote Métraux on January 27, 1961, "and we should like you to cover two regions: the U.S.A. and South Africa. . . . I think you are the only person who could assume the responsibility of such an undertaking."[33]

Frazier immediately replied, confirming that "the subject is one in which I have been extremely interested and if I undertook the direction of it I would look forward to having the cooperation of people who would make a real contribution in this field."[34] Frazier completed the research proposal, a "splendid and most useful memorandum" according to Métraux, who forwarded Frazier's name from UNESCO to the State Department some time in March.[35]

On March 22 Frazier received personnel forms and a fingerprint chart from the State Department. Frazier delayed in returning the forms, which required him once again to list all his previous jobs and his arrest record, and to answer the "Are you now, or have you ever been . . ." questions. He was angry at having to spend so much "valuable time" and to submit to the "humiliating red-tape" required by the State Department. "It is difficult to understand," he wrote Métraux, "why it is necessary to fingerprint an American scholar each time that he undertakes some scholarly task for an international organization."[36] Nevertheless, he filled out the forms in May and sent them off. In September, Métraux was worried because the normally routine appointment had not yet been processed. Frazier did not know why his clearance had been held up.[37]

Meanwhile, on May 18, 1961, the FBI had reopened a full field investigation when the U.S. Civil Service Commission reported that Frazier was being considered for a new appointment with UNESCO. The main allegation against him this time was that he had been "affiliated as member, sponsor, supporter, speaker, or signer of communications in behalf of" twenty-two organizations designated by the Attorney General or Congress as "communist fronts."

In November Frazier realized why his appointment had been delayed. He received a letter from the Civil Service Commission's Loyalty Board saying that it had received "certain unevaluated information of a derogatory nature which, if true, might create a doubt concerning your loyalty to the Government of the United States." He could not get approval for the UNESCO job, he was told, until the "unevaluated information" was properly evaluated. With the letter came an eleven-page interrogatory that he was expected to complete under oath and return in ten days.

The interrogatory asked him to give detailed answers about his involvement in twenty-four "communist or communist-front groups" and his affiliation with eighteen specific "projects and undertakings which have been deemed of interest to the communist cause." One allegation was that "in or around September 1958 your name, position, and address were given by one Soviet diplomatic official to another, as the author of books on Negro questions." He was also asked to state "where your sympathies lie in the current ideological conflict between the United States and the Soviet Union." Finally, he was asked to "discuss in detail the nature and extent of [his] association" with sixteen individuals, especially if they had attempted to "induce" Frazier to "become a communist or be sympathetic to communism."[38]

By this time Frazier was seriously ill with cancer; he had to undergo surgery in December. He refused to answer the interrogatory. In March 1962 Métraux sent him a letter apologizing for his "protracted silence" and explaining that UNESCO could not wait any longer and had awarded the project to the Institute of Race Relations in London.[39] On March 23rd Frazier sent Métraux a bitter letter giving his perspective on what had happened:

> I underwent the investigation by the FBI. This investigation included, as you probably know, being fingerprinted many times and a whole history of my activities ever since I was a child. Some time after the investigation, the FBI sent me a letter. . . . Along with this letter they sent a long interrogatory which I would have ten days to fill out. This interrogatory contained a request for all kinds of information, as, for example, to give a complete history of all my contacts with sixteen persons, four of whom I had never heard of in my life. Three of them had what looked like Russian names. Explain why I had been invited to the Czechoslovakian Embassy and other embassies in Washington. Explain why a Communist paper in California had once written an unfavorable review of my book, *Black Bourgeoisie,* and then had changed and written a favorable review. An analysis of my sympathies with reference to the ideologies of Russia and the United States. . . .
>
> I had planned to write a letter to Secretary of State, Dean Rusk, telling

him that I did not intend to be subjected to any further harassment on the part of the FBI and that this was not just a routine procedure but it was a deliberate effort to see that an American Negro would not have an opportunity to perform an important task in the intellectual field. But, as it turned out, I had to go to the hospital and undergo major surgery for a very serious condition from which I am just recovering. . . .

As soon as I am well enough, I intend to write the letter to the Secretary of State and I shall even go further and inform the learned societies in the United States about this action on the part of the FBI. How can American scholars and intellectuals participate in an international organization if they have got to be subjected to a lot of foolishness initiated by policemen?[40]

Frazier never got well enough to launch his campaign against the State Department. He was already suffering from terminal cancer.[41] On May 17, less than two months after writing to Métraux, he died of a massive heart attack. Whether or not his death was accelerated by the stress of being "hounded by the FBI" is pure speculation, but it cannot be ruled out.

Epilogue

To Hell with 'Em All

In December 1950, in the midst of the Korean War and the pervasive climate of Cold War politics, Frazier began his first serious diary, which, as he put it, "is especially necessary at this time when the Fascist minded men who are going to preserve American 'democracy' are preparing padlocks first for the mouths of teachers."[1] Less than three weeks later he ended his diary on a note of despair after reading in the newspaper that there had been a sharp increase in the stocks of "the airplane industry and other industries profiting by war and human misery." Observing that "capitalism feeds on war and mass murder," he was reminded of the last three lines of an antiwar poem written by Carl Sandburg in 1919:

> To hell with 'em all,
> The liars who lie to nations,
> The liars who lie to The People.[2]

Estrangement

"To hell with 'em all" accurately expresses the defiance and alienation that Frazier felt in his last decade. Although he became increasingly hopeful about prospects for equality in the world, he became more and more despondent about his own country. Through the 1950s Frazier was increasingly disenchanted with the possibility of fundamental reforms in race relations in the United States. He also began to question strategies of integration that denied the unique cultural legacy of Afro-

Americans. These preoccupations, doubts, and reservations were shaped by his own experiences and his deepening political critique of U.S. foreign policy.

His last essays, although as biting and insightful as ever, carry an embittered message. "What can the American Negro contribute to the social development of Africa?" he asked in a 1959 article published by Présence Africaine. "Very little" was his answer.[3] His previous polemics and social criticism had generally included proposals or counterproposals. By the 1950s, however, they had become one-sided, mostly critique with little program. There was now a predominant edge of cynicism to the *enfant terrible*.

Although the Moynihan Report cited Frazier to legitimize the technocratic liberalism of the Johnson administration, Frazier himself had grave doubts about the possibility or even desirability of the assimilation of Afro-American people into a Western, capitalist model of society. In 1955, while supporting all efforts toward integration following the Supreme Court's decision in *Brown* vs. *Board of Education,* he nevertheless warned black leaders that "personal dignity and peace within themselves" could not be achieved unless they accepted "their racial identification and their real position in American economic life."[4]

In the nascent days of the civil rights movement, he was encouraged by the "militant spirit" of college students,[5] but he was increasingly critical of the "opportunism" and "servile conformity" of the black middle class, who "by insisting upon being only Americans . . . become nobody." Integration into what, for what? asked Frazier. "Africa is demanding an intellectual and spiritual leadership that has caught a vision of a new world—a world freed from racism, colonialism and human exploitation. But the new Negro middle classes in the United States appear only to seek an opportunity to share in the exploitation from which they have been excluded."[6]

Whereas he had been an actor within the civil rights and social movements of the 1920s and 1930s, in the 1950s he did not have an organic relationship to the new civil rights movement and its new generation of activists, who were once again assaulting the walls of segregation. In 1961 his heroes were from his own generation and that of his parents—Denmark Vesey, Harriet Tubman, Langston Hughes, W.E.B. Du Bois, and Paul Robeson. There is no mention of the new heroes—Martin Luther King, Jr., or James Baldwin or Rosa Parks.[7]

It was not that he turned his back on the movement. He was still firing off letters to the press—including one to the *Washington Post Times Herald* denouncing William Faulkner, "that distinguished apostle of moderation"[8]—and he was still in regular contact with activists and progressive intellectuals.[9] He also welcomed the rise of the New Negro in the South who "don't scare any more."[10] He appreciated the militancy of black college students and the "new spirit among southern Negroes" as exemplified in the Montgomery bus boycott.[11]

But his support came from afar and with a sense of estrangement that was not simply a generational problem. His critiques sounded increasingly dogmatic because in these last years he tended to apply an analysis that was well grounded prior to World War II but did not take into account changing conditions in the 1950s. For example, his last book, *The Negro Church in America,* published posthumously, stressed the "stifling domination" that religious leaders exercised over Afro-American communities.[12] It was an old and plausible argument that he had made for several years, quite consistent with his overall assessment of the middle class. But in the mid-1950s, when he was writing this book, sectors of the Negro church had begun to play a prominent and militant role in the civil rights movement. His failure to address these contradictions and the possibilities they generated made Frazier's analysis rigid and revealed how much he was out of touch with the new activism.[13]

In the last years of his life, Frazier's sourness about politics, race relations, and academic life in the United States was no doubt in part the result of being investigated and harassed by the FBI, the State Department, and the SISS. But there were also other pressures, as well as important changes in how he viewed and related to the world. After World War II he found himself ostracized for his political views. His defense of Robeson and support of Du Bois placed him in the ranks of a small and beleaguered Afro-American left. He maintained tangential relationships with a defensive and weakened CP, and an increasingly anticommunist and legalistic NAACP. His tendency to go it alone and stand apart from organizations, even those with which he agreed, had always made him vulnerable to this kind of isolation. But through the 1920s and 1930s he had found a niche within vital social movements that encouraged a cross-fertilization of ideas and activities among civil rights, nationalist, and socialist organizations. The postwar decline of activism, combined with the rise of McCarthyism, thrust Frazier into a political wilderness.

Does It Provide Answers to Important Questions?

During the 1950s Frazier became increasingly dissatisfied with academic life. Howard became more and more a disappointment to him. In his undergraduate days it had been the "capstone of Negro education," alive with stimulating intellectual and political debates. Here he had first heard Du Bois, learned about socialism, and gained confidence in his own abilities. When he returned again in 1934, this time as a professor, the campus was a center of activism, and he was surrounded by some of most progressive Afro-American intellectuals in the country, including Alain Locke, Ralph Bunche, Abram Harris, Charles Thompson, Sterling Brown, Rayford Logan, Charles Wesley, and, a few years later, Eric Williams and John Hope Franklin.

After World War II, however, political ferment and intellectual vitality declined at Howard. Without significant funding or a doctoral program, the sociology department was not an encouraging environment for research. Frazier retreated more and more into his own writing.[14] Over the years his solitary style began to take its toll. He became more abrasive, more quickly disappointed in the administration, his colleagues, even his students at times. "Howard graduates only nitwits," he wrote in his diary after attending a Charter Day dinner in 1956, "not the slightest gleam of intellectual culture. . . . Howard is becoming worse each year."[15] His decision to leave his library to the University of Ghana was not only a statement of his support for Nkrumah's politics but also an expression of his alienation from Howard.[16]

Meanwhile, during the 1950s he also became quite discontented about sociology. Although he had always taken his discipline seriously and worked within its professional norms—being rewarded with the presidency of the American Sociological Association in 1948—it had never been enough for him to be a dutiful sociologist. He always tried to broaden the definition and responsibilities of an intellectual. Certainly, he never confused scientific rigor with political detachment.

Frazier hated the fact that academia and sociology had put him in a box, a distinguished and decorated box, but a box all the same. He was the "leading Negro sociologist," the "expert on the Negro family," a "scholar of race relations." Of course these assessments were correct, and he defended his accomplishments.[17] But he brought a great deal more to sociology that went unrecognized and unrewarded. He was grappling with the political role of intellectuals and the relationship between ideas and activism throughout his life, long before they became fashionable topics in the 1960s.

Several years before C. Wright Mills's critique of sociology was published, Frazier was putting forward his own views about "abstracted empiricism" and the crisis in sociological theory.[18] He was concerned that sociology was becoming too microscopic—"it has become fashionable to turn sociological problems into psychological problems," he noted in 1953—and that sociologists were elevating techniques of research over substantive issues of theory and policy.[19] He had already thought a great deal about these issues by 1951. "Very often when empirical studies are based upon sociological concepts, they are concerned with minutiae and almost microscopic phases of the social process. This criticism applies to both the statistical and the case study method. Technical perfection in either method is important but the crucial point is that if either method is used in a study, does it provide answers to important questions?"[20] Throughout the 1950s he increasingly felt that sociology had lost its mission and the vision that had characterized its early days in Chicago. "Virtuosity in the use of methods and techniques becomes an end in itself" with the result that "important generalizations have been ignored or forgotten."[21]

He was a persistent advocate of an interdisciplinary social science that broke down the artificial barriers between professionally defined bodies of knowledge. It made absolutely no sense to him that race relations, for example, could be studied only within the theoretical confines of sociology. "The sociological analysis of race and cultural contacts," wrote Frazier in 1957, "must include the study of the influence of the geographic environment and the technological development of peoples as well as the effect of economic and political institutions upon the relations of men of different races and cultures. Therefore, it is necessary to draw upon the findings of all the social sciences: human geography, anthropology, economics, and political science."[22]

The increasing narrowness of sociology was reinforced by McCarthyism, which discouraged social scientists from integrating economic and political issues into their studies. "These days," he confided in his diary in 1950, "it is safe to talk about interpersonal relations." He noted with contemptuous amusement that "anthropologists are really becoming courageous when they admit that there are classes in the U.S."[23]

Frazier recognized that his students were bearing the brunt of this trivialization of knowledge as sociology turned inward and away from political and economic issues. "Found as usual," he noted in 1950, "that my graduate students after four years of college had no more conceptions of economics or the economic system of the western world than a cat. Spent some time giving an elementary notion of such ideas as profits, capital, etc."[24] Ten years later, little had changed. "I do not see how anyone can finish college and not know the difference between wages and interest, wages and dividends, and wages and profit. But it is true that most of the students who finish social science in Negro schools don't know the difference. . . . We pretend we believe in democracy and that people should help to make decisions. Imagine someone who has finished college and who has had social science and doesn't know the difference between wages and profit. . . . People like that," he concluded, "are dangerous."[25]

A Common Humanity

By 1962 Frazier was looking to the revolutionary nationalism of Nkrumah rather than John F. Kennedy's liberalism as a model for the black movement. As he matured intellectually and politically, he became increasingly aware of the global context of racism and of the limits of both cultural nationalism and paternalistic reforms. In his last years Frazier moved further and further away from New Deal liberalism, which, culminating in the Moynihan Report, advocated a technocratic strategy of social engineering to provide a stratum of Afro-Americans with the opportunities of white society. His views about racism had become much more global and grounded in political economy than was the reformist, social-psychological perspective that guided the war on poverty.[26]

Frazier was not sure what it would take to achieve racial equality in the United States, but he was by now quite pessimistic and suspicious about statist efforts to legislate social justice. He had expressed these views for quite some time, but they become sharply focused during the

1950s. In his textbook, *The Negro in the United States*, and in his book *Race and Culture Contacts in the Modern World*, for example, Frazier located the fundamental roots of racism in the dynamics of class relations on a global scale. "The integration of the Negro into American society," he wrote in 1949, "will be determined largely by the reorganization of American life in relation to a new world organization. The so-called 'Negro Problem' is no longer a southern problem or even an exclusively domestic problem." [27] For Frazier the race problem had to be approached as "a part of the regional power systems which have supplanted Europe as a center of world power."[28]

The Korean War confirmed his increasingly global understanding of domestic issues. He confided in his diary his private fears that Harry Truman ("the haberdasher") and General Douglas MacArthur ("that glorified Boy Scout") were seriously "considering throwing atomic bombs on another colored nation in order to maintain western civilization." It outraged him that "Negro regiments were thrown against Chinese and North Koreans to prove that there was no racial discrimination." In his worst moments he envisioned a "Pax Americana with Chinese, Hindus and everyone chewing gum, reading comics and listening to Margaret [Truman]'s wonderful voice!"[29]

Frazier's cynicism about the United States was matched by his optimism about Third World revolutionary movements. He had always had a tendency to view experiences outside the United States through an idealist lense. In the 1920s, after a few months in Denmark, he was convinced that folk schools and rural cooperatives could be transplanted to the South. When he traveled to Latin America and the Caribbean in the early 1940s, he quickly and naively concluded that there was "no race problem in Brazil."[30]

In the early 1950s he spent two years in Paris with UNESCO and traveled through Europe, Africa, and the Middle East. It must have been an extraordinary experience for him to get away from Howard and the United States. At UNESCO, where he was chief of the Division of Applied Social Sciences, he received a level of professional recognition that he never received at home. With the respect came the privileges of first-class travel and accommodations,[31] and contact with progressive, sophisticated intellectuals from all over the world.

From his vantage point in Paris, Frazier witnessed a world that was bursting with revolutionary and nationalist movements, a striking contrast to the defeatism that reigned in the United States. Communist

China was emerging as a world power; the Soviet Union was leading anticolonial struggles within the United Nations; in Indochina, Ho Chi Minh's revolt against French rule presaged a united, socialist Vietnam; and, in Africa, Nkrumah's revolutionary nationalism offered a model for the rest of the continent and all nonaligned nations emerging from colonial rule.[32]

After his experience at UNESCO Frazier was convinced that the fate of the Third World and of Afro-Americans were inseparably intertwined, a view that Du Bois had expressed around the turn of the century and that Malcolm X would popularize again a few years later. "When the political relations of white and colored people are viewed in world perspective," wrote Frazier, "they are seen to be a phase of the developing social organization of the world."[33]

Just as his pessimism at home overestimated the power of the state and underestimated the possibilities of revolt, so his optimism about the world overestimated the strength of anticapitalist movements and underestimated the resiliency of capitalism and imperialism. The Soviet Union, as it would turn out, had not solved the problem of reconciling ethnic and national interests; in Vietnam it would take nearly two decades and a full-scale war to achieve independence; Nkrumah would be deposed in Ghana a few years after Frazier's death; and the United States would soon complete its economic and political domination of Latin America.

Frazier was hopeful that a new "international community" was in the process of birth, that "a world based upon federated cultures" was in the making. "As imperialism and colonialism based upon color disappear, racial and cultural differentiation without implications of superiority and inferiority will become the basic pattern of a world order."[34] Whatever despair he felt about the struggle against racism in the United States and however much he felt personally discouraged, he left life as he lived it, with a sense of outrage at the world's injustices and an unshakable vision of "a common humanity and a feeling of human solidarity that transcends racial and national differences."[35]

As a final expression of Frazier's internationalism and the optimism that was buried beneath his cynicism, he bequeathed his library to the University of Ghana, home of Nkrumah's revolutionary nationalism, home away from home to an exiled Du Bois, and the site of what Frazier hoped might be the birthplace of a new humanity. It was even more fitting that Frazier's last epitaph was written by Du Bois, who, a few weeks before he died, sent a message to commemorate Frazier's gift to Ghana. "In the best sense of the words, E. Franklin Frazier was more fundamentally American than most Americans. He believed the ideals of democracy were genuine and that men equally sharing responsibility could and would improve themselves. He pursued Truth and revealed the reasons for society's confusions and fears."[36]

Notes

Prologue

1. Frazier's unpublished essay "Southern Scenes" was written around 1923 and is in the E. Franklin Frazier Papers, Moorland-Spingarn Research Center, Howard University (hereafter cited as Frazier Papers), box 131-77, folder 31.

2. E. Franklin Frazier, "The Negro and Non-resistance," *Crisis* 27 (March 1924):213.

3. See, for example, James O. Young, *Black Writers of the Thirties* (Baton Rouge: Louisiana State University Press, 1973), 50–51, 239.

4. For this tendency to damn Frazier with faint praise and consign him to the outer periphery of the progressive Afro-American intelligentsia, see Manning Marable, "Black Studies: Marxism and the Black Intellectual Tradition," in *The Left Academy: Marxist Scholarship on American Campuses*, vol. 3, ed. Bertell Ollman and Edward Varnoff (New York: Praeger, 1986), 35–66.

5. See, for example, G. Franklin Edwards, "E. Franklin Frazier," in *Black Sociologists: Historical and Contemporary Perspectives*, ed. James Blackwell and Morris Janowitz (Chicago: University of Chicago Press, 1974), 85–117.

6. G. Franklin Edwards, ed., *E. Franklin Frazier on Race Relations* (Chicago: University of Chicago Press, 1968), xvi.

7. Frazier's statement was first quoted by Howard Odum, *American Sociology: The Story of Sociology in the United States Through 1950* (New York: Longmans, Green & Co., 1951), 238.

8. One critic even accused Frazier of rejecting "the philosophy and life-style behind the blues." See Young, *Black Writers of the Thirties*, 53.

9. E. Franklin Frazier, "La Bourgeoisie Noire," *Modern Quarterly* 5 (November 1928):84.

10. For a discussion of these critiques, see Chapter 11.

11. E. Franklin Frazier, "The Failure of the Negro Intellectual," *Negro Digest* 11 (February 1962):36.

12. Oliver Cox, "Introduction," in Nathan Hare, *The Black Anglo-Saxons* (New York: Collier Books, 1970), 30.

13. James Baldwin, *The Fire Next Time* (New York: Dell, 1988), 127.

14. Quoted in Odum, *American Sociology,* 238.

15. See generally Ellen Schrecker, *No Ivory Tower: McCarthyism and the Universities* (New York: Oxford University Press, 1986).

Chapter 1. Son of the Crossways

1. Howard Zinn, *The Twentieth Century: A People's History* (New York: Harper & Row, 1984), ch. 1; Congressional Research Service, Foreign Affairs Division, *Background Information on the Use of U.S. Armed Forces in Foreign Countries* (Washington, D.C.: U.S. Government Printing Office, 1975).

2. W.E.B. Du Bois, *The Souls of Black Folk* (1903; reprint, Greenwich, Conn.: Fawcett, 1961), 49.

3. For general information on the milieu of the New Negro movement, see two important case studies: Arnold Rampersad, *The Life of Langston Hughes,* (New York: Oxford University Press, 1986), vol. 1, *1902–1941: I, Too, Sing America;* and Martin Duberman, *Paul Robeson* (New York: Knopf, 1988).

4. Frazier's work built on an earlier prospectus by W.E.B. Du Bois, *The Negro American Family* (Atlanta, Ga.: Atlanta University Press, 1908).

5. Letter from E. Franklin Frazier to C. S. Brown, January 28, 1928, Frazier Papers. (All letters can be found in alphabetical order in the correspondence files of the Frazier Papers.)

6. Interview with Marie Brown Frazier by the author, November 2, 1975 (hereafter cited as MBF Interview).

7. MBF Interview. See also Grace Harris, "The Life and Work of E. Franklin Frazier" (Ph.D. diss., University of Virginia, 1975), 20.

8. Richard Bardolph, *The Negro Vanguard* (Westport, Conn.: Negro Universities Press, 1959), 236; Harris, "The Life and Work of E. Franklin Frazier," 18.

9. MBF Interview. Information about Frazier's height, physique, and appearance can be found in medical records and photographs, available in the Frazier Papers, especially box 131-2, folder 11, and box 131-141, folder 1–7.

10. E. Franklin Frazier, "The Role of the Social Scientist in the Negro College," in *The Civil War in Perspective: Papers Contributed to the Twenty-Fourth Annual Conference of the Division of Social Sciences,* ed. Robert Martin (Washington, D.C.: Howard University Press, 1961), 12.

11. MBF Interview; Harris, "The Life and Work of E. Franklin Frazier," 19–20.

12. Quoted in Harris, "The Life and Work of E. Franklin Frazier," 28.

13. Arthur P. Davis, "E. Franklin Frazier (1894–1962): A Profile," *Journal of Negro Education* 31 (Fall 1962):430.

14. Davis, "E. Franklin Frazier," 430; MBF Interview.

15. Letter from Alain LeRoy Locke to Whom It May Concern, June 16, 1916, Frazier Papers.

16. Letter from G. Stanley Hall to Carl Seashore, March 30, 1920, Clark University Archives.

17. Davis, "E. Franklin Frazier," 429.

18. Adelaide Cromwell Hill, testimonial for Frazier, c. 1962, Frazier Papers, box 131-1, folder 5.

19. Samuel Hoskins, "He Defied Mob Violence, Was Unmoved by Storm over His 'Black Bourgeoisie,'" *Afro-American*, May 26, 1962, p. 21.

20. Interview with St. Clair Drake by the author, January 22, 1975.

21. A draft of this article, written around 1928, is on file in the Frazier Papers, box 131-75, folder 18.

22. Shirley Graham Du Bois, "Presentation of E. Franklin Frazier's Library to the University of Ghana," Legon, Ghana (July 9, 1963), Frazier Papers, box 131-5, folder 24.

23. Frazier wrote that it is the "family history of a young woman who teaches in a Negro college." The original quotation, somewhat edited by Shirley Graham Du Bois, can be found in E. Franklin Frazier, *The Negro Family in the United States* (Chicago: University of Chicago Press, 1939), 18.

24. MBF Interview.

25. Frazier had a longstanding debate with various scholars about this issue. See in particular Melville J. Herskovits, *The Myth of the Negro Past* (1941; reprint, Boston: Beacon Press, 1958).

26. MBF Interview.

27. This term was widely used in Frazier's day to describe activists who "didn't believe in sitting by waiting for economic forces to abolish segregation." Frazier "felt that Negroes, themselves, had to organize as a battering ram." St. Clair Drake, "Introduction to the 1967 Edition," in E. Franklin Frazier, *Negro Youth at the Crossways: Their Personality Development in the Middle States* (New York: Schocken Books, 1967; originally published, 1940), ix.

28. MBF Interview.

29. Davis, "E. Franklin Frazier," 430; see also G. Franklin Edwards, "E. Franklin Frazier: Race, Education, and Community," in *Sociological Traditions from Generation to Generation: Glimpses of the American Experience,* ed. Robert Merton and Matilda White Riley (Norwood, N.J.: Ablex, 1980), 109–129.

30. These scrapbooks, inscribed "from James E. Frazier to his children," are available in the Frazier Papers, box 131-143, folders 1–3.

31. Bardolph, *The Negro Vanguard,* 236.

32. Drake, "Introduction," viii–ix.

33. MBF Interview. "My father died when I was ten years old, and since then to the present time I have always supported myself," said Frazier in his testimony to the Subcommittee to Investigate the Administration of the Internal Security Act and Other Internal Security Laws, Senate Judiciary Committee, vol. 349 (March 30, 1955), 2; hereafter cited as SISS (Senate Internal Security Subcommittee).

34. Quoted in "Quotes and Unquotes," *Common Sense* 11 (November 1942):editorial page.

35. MBF Interview.

36. MBF Interview.

37. The Frazier–Du Bois correspondence is available in the Frazier Papers. Du Bois died in self-imposed exile in Ghana fifteen months after Frazier's death.

38. Edward Franklin Frazier, *God and War* (privately printed, c. 1918), Frazier Papers, box 131-75, folder 24.

39. MBF Interview.

40. See, for example, E. Franklin Frazier, *The Negro Church in America* (New York: Schocken, 1964).

41. See diary entry for December 10, 1950, Frazier Papers, box 131-2, folder 6.

42. MBF Interview. Frazier died of a heart attack, but he had pancreatic cancer and was not expected to live long following surgery at the end of 1961.

43. Du Bois, *The Souls of Black Folk*, 16–17.

44. Horace Cayton, "E. Franklin Frazier: A Tribute and Review," *Review of Religious Research* 5 (Spring 1964):137.

45. "The Negro race, like all races, is going to be saved by its exceptional men," wrote Du Bois in his famous 1903 essay, "The Talented Tenth." It is reprinted in Andrew G. Paschal, ed., *A W.E.B. Du Bois Reader* (New York: Collier Books, 1971), 31–51.

46. "In Defense of John Henry" is available in the Frazier Papers, box 131-75, folder 13. It was written sometime after December 1925, when Langston Hughes's controversial poem "Cross" appeared in *Opportunity*. The original poem, reprinted in *Selected Poems of Langston Hughes* (New York: Random House, Vintage Books, 1974), 158, read as follows:

My old man's a white old man
And my old mother's black.
If I ever cursed my white old man
I take my curses back.
If I ever cursed my black old mother
And wished she were in hell,
I'm sorry for that evil wish
And now I wish her well.
My old man died in a fine big house.
My ma died in a shack.
I wonder where I'm gonna die,
Being neither white nor black?

Chapter 2. Keep Well Thy Tongue

1. Most black colleges remained under the control of white trustees, faculties, and administrators until World War II. Howard had its first Afro-American president in 1926; Hampton was still governed by whites in the 1940s; and Fisk had to wait until 1946 for its first black president. See generally on this topic Raymond Wolters, *The New Negro on Campus: Black College Rebellions of the 1920s* (Princeton, N.J.: Princeton University Press, 1975); and Bardolph, *The Negro Vanguard*, pt. 2.

2. Wolters, *The New Negro on Campus*, ch. 3; Rayford W. Logan, *Howard University: The First Hundred Years, 1867–1967* (New York: New York University Press, 1969), ch. 5; A. Walter Dyson, *Howard University, The Capstone of Negro Education: A History, 1867–1940* (Washington, D.C.: Howard University, 1941).

3. Wolters, *The New Negro on Campus*, 86; Logan, *Howard University*, 171–172.

4. MBF Interview.

5. Frazier, "The Role of the Social Scientist in the Negro College," 12.

6. Dyson, *Howard University*.

7. W.E.B. Du Bois, *The Autobiography of W.E.B. Du Bois* (New York: International Publishers, 1971), 240.

8. See Wolters, *The New Negro on Campus*, passim; Du Bois, *The Autobiography*, 132–235.

9. Wolters, *The New Negro on Campus*, 3, 81–82.

10. James Weinstein, *The Decline of Socialism in America 1912–1925* (New York: Random House, Vintage Books, 1969).

11. W.E.B. Du Bois, "Socialist of the Path" and "Negro and Socialism" (1907), reprinted in Francis L. Broderick and August Meier, eds., *Negro Protest Thought in the Twentieth Century* (Indianapolis: Bobbs-Merrill, 1965), 52–54.

12. Weinstein, *The Decline of Socialism*, 63–74.

13. Du Bois, *The Autobiography*, 256.

14. A greal deal has been written on this topic. For an overview of the various positions and debates, see Broderick and Meier, *Negro Protest Thought*, passim; Wolters, *The New Negro on Campus*, ch. 1; Henry Lee Moon, ed., *The Emerging Thought of W.E.B. Du Bois* (New York: Simon & Schuster, 1972); Paschal, *A W.E.B. Du Bois Reader;* Francis L. Broderick, *W.E.B. Du Bois: Negro Leader in a Time of Crisis* (Stanford, Calif.: Stanford University Press, 1959); Rayford W. Logan, ed., *W.E.B. Du Bois: A Profile* (New York: Hill and Wang, 1971). For a succinct statement of Du Bois's critique of Washington, see *The Souls of Black Folk*, ch. 3. For Washington's perspective, see Louis Harlan, *Booker T. Washington: The Wizard of Tuskegee, 1901–1915* (New York: Oxford University Press, 1983).

15. Jervis Anderson, *A. Philip Randolph: A Biographical Portrait* (New York: Harcourt Brace Jovanovich, 1972), chs. 5 and 6. See also Weinstein, *The Decline of Socialism*, 63–74, and Theodore Draper, *American Communism and Soviet Russia* (New York: Random House, Vintage Books, 1986), ch. 15.

16. Frazier's analysis of the *Messenger* was a central focus of this thesis, "New Currents of Thought among the Colored People of America" (master's thesis, Clark University, 1920). For his views on self-defense, which owe a great deal to the *Messenger*, see Frazier, "The Negro and Non-resistance," 213–214.

17. See, especially, Harlan, *Booker T. Washington*, ch. 14.

18. *Howard University Journal* 9 (May 3, 1912).

19. *Howard University Journal* 10 (November 8, 1912):1.

20. *Howard University Journal* 10 (March 14, 1913):1.

21. David A. Shannon, *The Socialist Party of America: A History* (Chicago: Quadrangle Books, 1967), 54–55; Weinstein, *The Decline of Socialism*, 74–75.

22. *Howard University Journal* 13 (March 10, 1916):8.

23. *Howard University Journal* 13 (November 5, 1915):1.

24. *Howard Year Book* 1 (1916):107; *Howard University Journal* 13 (December 10, 1915):5; *Howard University Journal* 13 (February 18, 1916):1.

25. "The Onslaught of Injustice," *Howard University Journal* 11 (May 23, 1913):1–3.

26. *Howard Year Book* 1 (1916):197.

27. *Howard University Journal* 11 (October 31, 1913):1, 5.

28. *Howard University Journal* 13 (October 8, 1915):1; *Howard Year Book,* 1 (1916): 107. *The Birth of a Nation* was released and shown in New York in 1915. It was met with major protests, led by the NAACP. For a discussion of the movement against the film, see Thomas R. Cripps, "The Reaction of the Negro to the Motion Picture Birth of a Nation," *The Historian* 25 (May 1963):344–362.

29. "Opinion of W.E.B. Du Bois," *Crisis* 22 (July 1921):102.

30. *Howard University Journal* 10 (November 8, 1912):3.

31. *Howard University Journal* 10 (January 31, 1913):5.

32. *Howard University Journal* 11 (April 17, 1914):3

33. A collection of these essays was published in an anthology, Kelly Miller, *Out of the House of Bondage* (New York: Neale, 1914).

34. *Howard University Journal* 10 (October 4, 1912):1.

35. *Howard University Journal* 10 (April 4, 1913):1.

36. *Howard University Journal* 11 (April 17, 1914):2–3.

37. W.E.B. Du Bois, *The Negro* (New York: Holt, 1915), 231, 241, 242.

38. *Howard Year Book* 1 (1916):29; *NIKH Year Book* (College of Arts and Sciences, Howard University) (1914): 86; Davis, "E. Franklin Frazier," 430.

39. *Howard Year Book* 1(1916):48.

40. Letter from Frazier to Bertha Lomack, September 9, 1924, Frazier Papers.

41. Frazier, "The Role of the Social Scientist in the Negro College," 11–12. Frazier's undergraduate transcript confirms that he took two years of English language and two years of English literature.

42. Quoted in Odum, *American Sociology,* 234.

43. Miller's relationship to Washington and President Taft is discussed by Harlan, *Booker T. Washington,* 95, 351–352.

44. Davis, "E. Franklin Frazier," 430.

45. I am grateful to Michael Winston for providing me with a copy of Frazier's undergraduate transcript.

46. "Quotes and Unquotes," *Common Sense* 11 (November 1942):editorial page; interview with Michael Winston by author, November 3, 1975.

47. *Howard Year Book* 1 (1916):29. The quotation came from "The Maunciples Tale." Lines preceding the ones chosen by Frazier read: "My son, keep well thy tongue and keep thy friend./ A wicked tongue is worse than a fiend."

48. Edwards, *E. Franklin Frazier on Race Relations,* x.

49. Du Bois, *The Autobiography,* 222.

50. In the class vote taken in his senior year, he received the second most votes for "nerviest." See *Howard Year Book,* 1 (1916):48.

51. Davis, "E. Franklin Frazier," 430–431. Davis mistakenly says that this took place during Frazier's last year at Howard in 1916. An article in the *Howard University Journal* (10 (March 14, 1913): 1) refers to "some hitch as to marching position in the Inaugural parade." For a general description of the parade, see also *New York Times,* March 5, 1913.

52. Davis, "E. Franklin Frazier," 430–431.

53. Interviews with St. Clair Drake (January 22, 1975), G. Franklin Edwards (No-

vember 23, 1970), A. Philip Randolph (September 18, 1969), and Marie Brown Frazier (November 2, 1975) by the author and Renetia Martin.

54. Quoted in Odum, *American Sociology,* 234.

55. Edward Frazier, "Woman Suffrage," *Howard University Journal* 13 (January 14, 1916):2–3.

Chapter 3. A Cruel and Devastating War

1. *Howard Year Book* 1 (1916):29.

2. For general background, see Harlan, *Booker T. Washington,* 143–173.

3. Harlan, *Booker T. Washington,* 155–156.

4. E. Franklin Frazier, "A Note on Negro Education," *Opportunity* 2 (March 1924):75.

5. Frazier, "A Note on Negro Education," 144.

6. Wolters, *The New Negro on Campus,* ch. 4; Earl Ofari, *The Myth of Black Capitalism* (New York: Monthly Review Press, 1970), 31–36.

7. Quoted in Wolters, *The New Negro on Campus,* 138–139.

8. MBF Interview.

9. Horace R. Cayton, *Long Old Road* (Seattle: University of Washington Press, 1970), 199.

10. Wolters, *The New Negro on Campus,* 142–143, 147–148.

11. Cayton, *Long Old Road,* 198–199.

12. E. Franklin Frazier, *Black Bourgeoisie* (Glencoe, Ill.: Free Press, 1957), 245.

13. Frazier, "The Role of the Social Scientist in the Negro College," 11.

14. Frazier, "New Currents of Thought," 12–13.

15. Quoted by Wolters, *The New Negro on Campus,* 143.

16. Cayton, *Long Old Road,* 205.

17. The Selective Service Act provided for enlistment of all able-bodied men from twenty-one to thirty-one years old, and by July 5th, registration day, more than seven hundred thousand blacks had registered. See Peter M. Bergman, *The Chronological History of the Negro in America* (New York: Harper & Row, 1969), 382.

18. E. Franklin Frazier, "A Community School: Fort Valley High and Industrial School," *Southern Workman* 54 (October 1925):459–464.

19. Quoted in Odum, *American Sociology,* 234.

20. Correspondence in Clark University Archives from Edward Frazier to Dr. G. Stanley Hall, June 22, 1917; G. Stanley Hall to Edward F. Frazier, June 24, 1918; G. Stanley Hall to Edward Frazier, July 5, 1917; Edward Frazier to Frank H. Hankins, September 12, 1918.

21. MBF Interview.

22. Quoted in Odum, *American Sociology,* 234.

23. A copy of Frazier's World War draft registration card, which was issued in Baltimore, is on file at the National Archives (Atlanta branch). On this card Frazier noted that his mother was "solely dependent" on him for financial support.

24. Interview with G. Franklin Edwards by author, March 30, 1989.

25. A copy of the completed (undated) form, "Identification and Personnel Data for Employment of United States Citizen" (Department of State), is on file in the Frazier Papers.

26. *Year Book of the Young Men's Christian Associations of North America* (May 1, 1918–April 1919):476.

27. This contract, dated July 19, 1918, is available in the YMCA of the USA Archives, University of Minnesota.

28. Frazier's wartime record, about which he was quite reticent, was pieced together through his registration card (available in the National Archives) and detailed records of his YMCA service (including his work card, dated June 18, 1918), made available by David Carmichael, YMCA of the USA Archives, University of Minnesota. Unfortunately, Frazier's official military service record was destroyed in a fire at the National Personnel Records Center, St. Louis.

29. MBF Interview.

30. Office of Training Camp Activities, *Handbook of Camp A. A. Humphreys* (Washington, D.C.: U.S. War Department, c. 1918), passim.

31. Weinstein, *The Decline of Socialism,* ch. 3.

32. Frazier, "A Note on Negro Education," 76.

33. W.E.B. Du Bois, "Close Ranks," *Crisis* 16 (June 1918):111.

34. Moon, *The Emerging Thought of W.E.B. Du Bois,* 244–245. According to Moon, Du Bois later had doubts about the position he had taken.

35. B. Joyce Ross, *J. E. Spingarn and the Rise of the NAACP, 1911–1939* (New York: Atheneum, 1972), 98–101.

36. The NAACP led an "extensive and sustained campaign of publicity and political lobbying" to stop southern states from eliminating blacks from the draft. Afro-Americans were allowed into the Navy only as mess boys and were barred entirely from the Marines. The Army accepted enlisted men but not officers. See August Meier and Elliott Rudwick, *From Plantation to Ghetto* (New York: Hill and Wang, 1970), 218–219; and Ross, *J. E. Spingarn,* 95.

37. Ross, *J. E. Spingarn,* 86–87.

38. The first segregated camp for training black officers was established at Fort Des Moines, Iowa, in June 1917. See Ross, *J. E. Spingarn,* 88, 97.

39. Ross, *J. E. Spingarn,* 92–94.

40. Anderson, *A. Philip Randolph,* 98.

41. From an editorial in the *Messenger,* quoted in Anderson, *A. Philip Randolph,* 98.

42. In a copy available in the Frazier Papers (box 131-75, folder 24), a handwritten date, possibly added by Frazier, indicates that this pamphlet was written in 1918.

43. Du Bois, *The Autobiography,* 197.

44. Frazier, *God and War,* passim.

45. This unpublished, untitled memoir is available in the Frazier Papers, box 131-73, folder 13. From type style and pagination, it likely was originally one of several anecdotes "Embodying Stories of Experiences with Whites, Particularly in the South," submitted by Frazier as a memorandum to Gunnar Myrdal for *An American Dilemma,* published in 1944. Frazier decided for some reason not to submit this story to Myrdal. The manuscript is not dated. Probably Frazier wrote the final version of this story in

the 1930s based on notes or a first draft written in the 1920s. This genre of storytelling was popular among Afro-American intellectuals in the 1920s, and Frazier typically wrote about his personal experiences in this way.

Chapter 4. Learning Sociology

1. E. Franklin Frazier, *The Negro in the United States* (New York: Macmillan, 1957), 558. (The original edition of this book was published in 1949. Unless otherwise noted, all references are to the 1957 revised edition.) See also Michael R. Winston, "Through the Back Door: Academic Racism and the Negro Scholar in Historical Perspective," *Daedalus* 100 (Summer 1971):689–694; Bardolph, *The Negro Vanguard*, 310.

2. Jay R. Mandle, "The Plantation Economy and Its Aftermath," *Review of Radical Political Economics* 6 (Spring 1974):32–48; Gilbert Osofsky, *Harlem: The Making of a Ghetto* (New York: Harper & Row, 1963); Allan H. Spear, *Black Chicago: The Making of a Negro Ghetto* (Chicago: University of Chicago Press, 1967); Bardolph, *The Negro Vanguard*, 134; Olivier Zunz, *The Changing Face of Inequality: Urbanization, Industrial Development, and Immigrants in Detroit, 1880–1920* (Chicago: University of Chicago Press, 1982), ch. 14.

3. Sterling Spero and Abram Harris, *The Black Worker: The Negro and the Labor Movement* (1931; reprint, New York: Atheneum, 1968), ch. 8.

4. Ray Marshall, *The Negro and Organized Labor* (New York: Wiley, 1965); Spero and Harris, *The Black Worker*, ch. 8.

5. Spero and Harris, *The Black Worker*, 467. See also Bernard Mandel, "Samuel Gompers and the Negro Workers, 1886–1914," *Journal of Negro History* 40 (January 1955):34–60.

6. Frazier, *Black Bourgeoisie*, 99.

7. Elliott Rudwick, *Race Riot at East St. Louis, July 2, 1917* (New York: Atheneum, 1972); Carl Sandburg, *The Chicago Race Riots, July, 1919* (New York: Harcourt, Brace and Howe, 1919); Chicago Commission on Race Relations, *The Negro in Chicago: A Study of Race Relations and a Race Riot* (Chicago: University of Chicago Press, 1922); William M. Tuttle, Jr., *Race Riot: Chicago in the Red Summer of 1919* (New York: Atheneum, 1970); Meier and Rudwick, *From Plantation to Ghetto*, 220–222.

8. W.E.B. Du Bois, "Returning Soldiers," *Crisis* 17 (May 1919):13–14.

9. See generally Frazier, *Black Bourgeoisie*.

10. Frazier, "The Role of the Social Scientist in the Negro College," 9.

11. Alfred H. Stone, "Is Race Friction between Blacks and Whites in the United States Growing and Inevitable?" (1907–1908), reprinted in Robert Park and Ernest Burgess, *Introduction to the Science of Sociology* (Chicago: University of Chicago Press, 1924), 639, 640.

12. Frazier, "A Note on Negro Education," 77.

13. Schrecker, *No Ivory Tower*, ch. 1.

14. Du Bois's pioneering studies done at Atlanta University prior to World War I

were generally ignored by academics. See John Bracey, Jr., August Meier, and Elliott Rudwick, eds., *The Black Sociologists: The First Half Century* (Belmont, Calif.: Wadsworth, 1971), 2–5; and Elliott Rudwick, "W.E.B. Du Bois as Sociologist," in Blackwell and Janowitz, *Black Sociologists*, 25–55.

15. The Chicago Commission, established after the 1919 riots, called on "both races . . . to understand that their rights and duties are mutual and equal." The Commission concluded that "race friction and antagonism are largely due to the fact that each race too readily misunderstands and misinterprets the other's conduct and aspirations." See Chicago Commission on Race Relations, *The Negro in Chicago*, xxiv, 644.

16. See, for example, I. A. Newby, *Jim Crow's Defense: Anti-Negro Thought in America, 1900–1930* (Baton Rouge: Louisiana State University Press, 1965). For a critique of the racist underpinnings of early theories of race relations, see John Stanfield, "The 'Negro Problem' within and beyond the Institutional Nexus of Pre-World War I Sociology," *Phylon* 43 (Fall 1982):187–201.

17. E. Franklin Frazier, "Sociological Theory and Race Relations," *American Sociological Review* 12 (June 1947):265–271. This paper was originally read at a conference in 1946.

18. Frazier did not take sociology courses at Howard, but he did read widely and "came across" Giddings's textbook, originally published in 1905. Frazier was "fascinated by the subject, especially his manner of presentation." See Odum, *American Sociology*, 234.

19. Franklin H. Giddings, *The Elements of Sociology: A Text-Book for Colleges and Schools* (New York: Macmillan, 1905), 319–320.

20. John Spargo, "The Psychology of Bolshevism" (1919), reprinted in Park and Burgess, *Introduction to the Science of Sociology*, 909–915. The ideas of Giddings and Spargo coincided with a wave of government repression that was instituted immediately after World War I against the Socialist Party and a variety of progressive organizations. For a general discussion of repressive policies during this period, see Robert J. Goldstein, *Political Repression in Modern America from 1870 to the Present* (Cambridge, Mass.: Schenkman, 1978), ch. 5; William Preston, Jr., *Aliens and Dissenters: Federal Suppression of Radicals, 1903–1933* (New York: Harper Torchbooks, 1966).

21. Quoted in Odum, *American Sociology*, 234.

22. From Lydia Colby to Whom It May Concern, June 11, 1948, Clark University Archives. Frazier's graduate transcript, master's thesis, and related correspondence were provided by Suzanne Hamel, Clark University Archives.

23. Odum, *American Sociology*, 186–189.

24. See generally John Higham, *Strangers in the Land: Patterns of American Nativism, 1860–1925* (New York: Atheneum, 1967); Thomas F. Gossett, *Race: The History of an Idea in America* (New York: Schocken, 1965).

25. Gossett, *Race*, 373.

26. Gossett, *Race*, ch. 16.

27. Gossett, *Race*, ch. 15.

28. Gossett, *Race*, 369.

29. G. Stanley Hall, "A Few Results of Recent Scientific Study of the Negro in America," *Proceedings of the Massachusetts Historical Society* (1905), quoted in Winston, "Through the Back Door," 685–686.

30. For a profile of Hankins's career, see Odum, *American Sociology*, 186–189.

31. Odum, *American Sociology*, 189.

32. Frank H. Hankins, *The Racial Basis of Civilization: A Critique of Nordic Doctrine* (New York: Knopf, 1926), ix.

33. Hankins, *The Racial Basis of Civilization*, 297–298.

34. Hankins, *The Racial Basis of Civilization*, 306–307.

35. Hankins, *The Racial Basis of Civilization*, 322, 370.

36. Hankins, *The Racial Basis of Civilization*, 375.

37. From G. Stanley Hall to Dean Carl E. Seashore, March 30, 1920, Clark University Archives.

38. The review of Thomas Woofter's *The Basis of Racial Adjustment* was solicited by Hankins in May 1925 and appeared in *Social Forces* in December 1925. In a letter accompanying the review, Frazier wrote, "We know that race problems are not caused by ignorance, poverty, and lack of ability on the part of the repressed group." (From E. Franklin Frazier to Frank Hankins, July 20, 1925, Frazier Papers.)

39. From Frank Hankins to the Laura Spelman Rockefeller Memorial, April 20, 1927. This and other correspondence between Frazier and Hankins can be found in the Frazier Papers.

40. MBF Interview.

41. This observation is based on comments made during an interview with St. Clair Drake by the author, January 22, 1975.

42. Frazier, "New Currents of Thought," i.

43. Frazier, "New Currents of Thought," 2.

44. Frazier, "New Currents of Thought," 13.

45. Frazier, "New Currents of Thought," 15–16.

46. Frazier, "New Currents of Thought," 17, 19.

47. Frazier, "New Currents of Thought," 19, 39.

48. Frazier, "New Currents of Thought," 6.

49. Frazier, "New Currents of Thought," 71. These comments owe a great deal to Du Bois, *The Negro*, 231.

50. Frazier discusses the *Messenger*'s views about cooperatives on pp. 60–61 of his thesis. Frazier began publishing his own articles about the benefits of cooperatives in 1922.

51. E. Franklin Frazier, "Georgia: Or the Struggle against Impudent Inferiority," *Messenger* 4 (June 1924):173–177. Frazier also had a letter (November 1924) and survey response (January 1927) published in the *Messenger*.

52. For a critical analysis of this period in U.S. sociology, see Herman Schwendinger and Julia R. Schwendinger, *The Sociologists of the Chair: A Radical Analysis of the Formative Years of North American Sociology, 1883–1922* (New York: Basic Books, 1974).

53. Oliver Cox, whose analysis of racism and capitalism was an original contribution to U.S. sociology, was, like Du Bois in a previous era, "accorded only negative recognition during most of his long academic career." See Gordon Morgan, "In Memoriam: Oliver C. Cox, 1901–1974," *Monthly Review* 28 (May 1976):34–40. A useful anthology of Cox's work can be found in Herbert Hunter and Sameer Abraham, eds., *Race, Class, and the World System: The Sociology of Oliver C. Cox* (New York: Monthly Review, 1987).

54. Contrast, for example, his earliest writings on the topic of the black bourgeoi-

sie. Frazier expresses himself as the cautious academic sociologist in "Durham: Capital of the Black Middle Class," in *The New Negro*, ed. Alain Locke (New York: A. and C. Boni, 1925), 333–340. Frazier as the cavalier polemicist expresses very different views on the same topic in "La Bourgeoisie Noire," published in 1928.

55. Edward F. Frazier, "Scandinavian vs. American Universities," *The Nation* 114 (May 17, 1922):597.

Chapter 5. A Complete Existence

1. Letter of reference for Frazier by Porter H. Lee, August 10, 1921, Frazier Papers.

2. His notes from these classes are in the Frazier Papers, box 131-1, folders 9–10.

3. Frazier used what he learned from Glueck in a class that he taught at the Atlanta School of Social Work. A few years later he also drew upon some of Glueck's ideas in his article "The Pathology of Race Prejudice," in which he argued that racists exhibit behavior reminiscent of "insane complexes." See correspondence between Frazier and Bernard Glueck, December 29, 1924, and January 5, 1925, in the Frazier Papers. It was almost three years before the controversial article was accepted for publication. See Edward Franklin Frazier, "The Pathology of Race Prejudice," *Forum* 70 (June 1927):856–862.

4. E. Franklin Frazier, "A Negro Industrial Group," *Howard Review* 1 (June 1924):196–232.

5. Spero and Harris, *The Black Worker;* Horace R. Cayton and George S. Mitchell, *Black Workers and the New Unions* (Chapel Hill: University of North Carolina Press, 1939).

6. According to Herbert Gutman, writing in 1968, "Much concerning the Negro worker in the early decades of the twentieth century (just before and after the great migration) awaits its historians." Preface to Spero and Harris, *The Black Worker*, xi.

7. Frazier, "A Negro Industrial Group," 197, 199.

8. Frazier, "A Negro Industrial Group," 209.

9. Frazier, "A Negro Industrial Group," 213, 226.

10. Frazier, "A Negro Industrial Group," 232.

11. Frazier, "A Negro Industrial Group," 199, 201.

12. Frazier, "A Negro Industrial Group," 201, 214.

13. Frazier, "A Negro Industrial Group," 230–231.

14. Frazier, "A Negro Industrial Group," 211, 230.

15. See, for example, Rampersad, *The Life of Langston Hughes;* Blanche E. Ferguson, *Countee Cullen and the Negro Renaissance* (New York: Dodd, Mead, 1966); Du Bois, *The Autobiography;* Bardolph, *The Negro Vanguard,* 291; Phyllis Rose, *Jazz Cleopatra: Josephine Baker in Her Time* (New York: Doubleday, 1989).

16. Letter from American-Scandinavian Foundation to Frazier, May 9, 1921, Frazier Papers.

17. "Foundation Fellows for 1921–1922," *American-Scandinavian Review* 9 (July

1921):494–495. See also Dale Vlasek, "The Social Thought of E. Franklin Frazier" (Ph.D. diss., University of Iowa, 1978), 55, 92–93.

18. Frazier's comments on the film were made in a form he filled out in 1961 when trying to a get a security clearance for a job with UNESCO. See "Identification and Personnel Data for Employment of United States Citizen" (Department of State), available in the Frazier Papers, box 131-54, folder 20. The date and consequences of Frazier's arrest are derived from a security check conducted by the FBI's New York field office in 1953. See Chapter 19 for a discussion of Frazier and the FBI.

19. "Opinion of W.E.B. Du Bois," *Crisis* 22 (July 1921):102; MBF Interview.

20. MBF Interview.

21. See letter from Frazier to Du Bois, March 31, 1925, Frazier Papers.

22. Edward F. Frazier, "The Folk High School at Roskilde," *Southern Workman* 51 (July 1922):325–328.

23. Booker T. Washington, *The Man Farthest Down: A Record of Observation and Study in Europe* (New York: Doubleday, Page, 1912), ch. 17.

24. Frazier, "The Folk High School at Roskilde," 326. Frazier subtitled this article, "Where Memories of Booker T. Washington Live."

25. Washington, *The Man Farthest Down,* 340.

26. Frazier, "The Folk High School at Roskilde," 328.

27. Edwin (*sic*) Franklin Frazier, "Danish People's High Schools and America," *Southern Workman* 51 (September 1922):425–430.

28. Edward Franklin Frazier, "The Co-operative Movement in Denmark," *Southern Workman* 52 (October 1923):479–484. Frazier's views about cooperatives had clearly been influenced by the ideas of the *Messenger* group. See, for example, A. Philip Randolph, "The Crisis in Negro Business," *Messenger* 4 (March 1922):371–374.

29. Madeline Allison, "The Horizon," *Crisis* 23 (March 1922):220–221.

30. E. Franklin Frazier, "Cooperation and the Negro," *Crisis* 25 (March 1923):228–229.

31. E. Franklin Frazier, "Some Aspects of Negro Business," *Opportunity* 2 (October 1924):293–297.

32. E. Franklin Frazier, "Cooperatives: The Next Step in the Negro's Business Development," *Southern Workman* 53 (November 1924), 508.

33. Letter from Frazier to "Dock" Steward, January 3, 1925, Frazier Papers. Gustavus "Dock" Steward grew up with Frazier in Baltimore. He published political essays in the black press while working for the Supreme Life and Casualty Company in Columbus, Ohio. Frazier and Steward maintained a lively correspondence from 1924 until Frazier's death in 1962.

34. E. Franklin Frazier, "La Bourgeoisie Noire," 82–83. By the mid-1930s, Frazier dismissed the cooperative movement as a utopian, impractical vision, promising nothing but "false hopes." In 1935, for example, he ridiculed Du Bois's proposal for a "separate non-profit economy within American capitalism" as a cooperative program that "could only adopt 'Share Your Poverty' as a slogan." See E. Franklin Frazier, "The Du Bois Program in the Present Crisis," *Race* 1 (Winter 1935–1936):11–13.

35. Quoted in Odum, *American Sociology,* 235. See also *New York Times,* September 6, 1921, p. 16.

36. Frazier, "Scandinavian vs. American Universities," 597.

37. Davis, "E. Franklin Frazier," 431.
38. MBF Interview.
39. Frazier, "Durham," 333.
40. MBF Interview; see also Calvin Scott Brown's obituary in *Journal and Guide* (Norfolk, Va.), September 19, 1936; and Joseph J. Boris, ed., *Who's Who in Colored America, 1928–1929* (New York: Who's Who in Colored America Corporation, 1930).
41. MBF Interview.
42. See, for example, letter from Countee Cullen to Marie Brown Frazier, May 25, 1928, Frazier Papers.
43. Marie Brown Frazier, "In a Jar," *Opportunity* 6 (June 1928):168; Marie Brown Frazier, "White Riders," *Opportunity* 7 (March 1929):30 (Edward Frazier's article, "Chicago: A Cross-Section of Negro Life," was also published in this same issue of *Opportunity*); Marie Brown Frazier, "Dixie Snow," *Survey Graphic* 31 (November 1942):494.

Chapter 6. Practically an Outcast

1. Frazier, "Southern Scenes," 1.
2. E. Franklin Frazier, "My Relation with the Atlanta School of Social Work," unpublished memo (1927), Frazier Papers, box 131-76, folder 7.
3. See letter from the president of Howard University to Frazier, May 23, 1923, Frazier Papers.
4. See letters between Frazier and James Hubert in November and December 1924; he also corresponded with Eugene Jones, executive secretary of NUL, about the possibility of a job with the national office. This correspondence is in the Frazier Papers.
5. Letter from Frazier to Charles Johnson, January 8, 1925, Frazier Papers.
6. Letters from Frazier to Du Bois, January 18 and 27, 1927; and from Du Bois to Frazier, January 21 and 22, 1927, Frazier Papers.
7. E. Franklin Frazier, "Training Colored Social Workers in the South," *Journal of Social Forces* 1 (May 1923):445–446; E. Franklin Frazier, "Social Work in Race Relations," *Crisis* 27 (April 1924):252–254; Frazier, "My Relation with the Atlanta School of Social Work," passim.
8. All the prize winners are listed in *Opportunity* 3 (May 1925):142–143. Frazier won the essay prize for "Social Equality and the Negro," *Opportunity* 3 (June 1925):165–168.
9. This award of two hundred dollars was made for Frazier's essay "The Mind of the American Negro," *Opportunity* 6 (September 1928):263–266, 284.
10. Frazier's research was published anonymously as "The Negro Common School, Georgia," *Crisis* 32 (September 1926):248–264; and "South Carolina Negro Common Schools," *Crisis* 34 (December 1927):330–332.
11. "All God's Chillun Got Eyes," a story about his experience with a racist optometrist in Atlanta, was published in *Crisis* 29 (April 1925):254–255. Frazier's play, "The

Senator," was acknowledged by Charles Johnson, *Opportunity*'s editor, but failed to win an award. See letter from Johnson to Frazier, December 16, 1924, Frazier Papers. Frazier tried without success to get a literary agency to market his short stories. See letter from Brandt and Brandt to Frazier, February 27, 1925, Frazier Papers.

12. Frazier's photographs were used in his unsigned article "The Negro Common School, Georgia." Du Bois acknowledged receipt of the photographs in a letter to Frazier, August 11, 1925, Frazier Papers. "Years ago, when I was at Morehouse College, Dr. Du Bois carried a series in the *Crisis* on Education in the South and I did a lot of field work for him. I went after statistics, I made pictures of schoolhouses and so forth, and he published it," said Frazier in his testimony to SISS, 19–20. Frazier's photographs were also used to illustrate articles that he published in *Southern Workman* in the early 1920s.

13. In a speech at a memorial service for Frazier in 1962, Adelaide Cromwell Hill noted that "few persons who read his works know of Frazier's gift as an artist. His delicately sketched portraits of persons close to him reveal the talent of the brush as well as his familiar keen insight into the depth of his subject." This speech is available in the Frazier Papers, box 131-1, folder 5.

14. Letter from Frazier to Charles Johnson, January 3, 1925, Frazier Papers. Frazier sent two cover designs to Johnson for possible use in *Opportunity*. Johnson responded enthusiastically but had problems with the lettering and apparently did not use the designs. See letter from Frazier to Johnson, January 8, 1925, Frazier Papers.

15. David Levering Lewis, *When Harlem Was in Vogue* (New York: Oxford University Press, 1989).

16. Lewis, *When Harlem Was in Vogue*, 117–118.

17. Locke, *The New Negro*, 14.

18. Letter from Frazier to Charles Johnson, January 9, 1925, Frazier Papers.

19. Letter from Frazier to "Dock" Steward, July 17, 1925, Frazier Papers.

20. Letter from Elsa Butler Grove to Fraser (*sic*), January 2, 1924, Frazier Papers.

21. See his letter to Bertha Lomack, July 24, 1924, Frazier Papers.

22. Letter from Frazier to "Dock" Steward, June 1, 1925, Frazier Papers.

23. Letter from Frazier to Samuel Allen, March 13, 1926, Frazier Papers.

24. E. Franklin Frazier, "Family Life of the Negro in the Small Town," *Proceedings of the National Conference of Social Work* (May 26–June 2, 1926):384–388.

25. For description of this conference, see Abram L. Harris, "Brockwood's Symposium on Negro Labor," *Crisis* 34 (September 1927):226. See also letter from A. J. Muste to Frazier, May 14, 1927, Frazier Papers.

26. Frazier, "My Relation with the Atlanta School of Social Work," 2. His paper was subsequently published; see E. Franklin Frazier, "Professional Education for Negro Social Workers," *Hospital Social Service* 17 (1928):167–176.

27. Letter from Countee Cullen to Marie Brown Frazier, August 25, 1931, Frazier Papers.

28. Winston, "Through the Back Door," 695.

29. Winston, "Through the Back Door," 678.

30. Michael Harris, "Black Professors Still a Rarity at University of California and Stanford," *San Francisco Chronicle*, June 2, 1986, p. 6; James Blackwell, Maurice

Jackson, and Joan W. Moore, "The Status of Racial and Ethnic Minorities in Sociology," *Footnotes* (American Sociological Association Special Supplement) (August 1977):1.

31. John Hope Franklin, "The Dilemma of the American Negro Scholar," in *Soon One Morning: New Writings by American Negroes, 1940–1962,* ed. Herbert Hill (New York: Knopf, 1972), 71.

32. Letter from Frazier to Charles Johnson, December 1, 1925, Frazier Papers.

33. Interview by author with Michael Winston, March 30, 1989.

34. Bardolph, *The Negro Vanguard,* 179.

35. Frazier, "The Role of the Social Scientist in the Negro College," 9.

36. Bardolph, *The Negro Vanguard,* 179, 180.

37. "Answers to Five Questions Submitted to Professor Howard Odum, University of North Carolina" in letter from Frazier to Odum, undated (c. 1948), Frazier Papers. Frazier's answers, with the notable exception of this point, were published in Odum, *American Sociology,* 233–239. Frazier made this point about the inferior status of Negro studies on several occasions. See, for example, E. Franklin Frazier, "Race Contacts and the Social Structure," *American Sociological Review* 14 (February 1949):1–11; Frazier, "The Role of the Social Scientist in the Negro College," 15.

38. See generally Bracey, Meier, and Rudwick, *The Black Sociologists;* Joyce Ladner, ed., *The Death of White Sociology* (New York: Random House, Vintage Books, 1973); and August Meier and Elliott Rudwick, *Black History and the Historical Profession, 1915–1980* (Urbana: University of Illinois Press, 1986).

39. E. Franklin Frazier, "Brazil Has No Race Problem," *Common Sense* 11 (November, 1942): 364.

40. Franklin, "The Dilemma of the American Negro Scholar," 71.

41. Franklin, "The Dilemma of the American Negro Scholar," 65.

42. Frazier, "Family Life of the Negro in the Small Town," 388; Frazier, "Georgia," 175.

43. E. Franklin Frazier, review of *The Basis of Racial Adjustment* by Thomas J. Woofter, Jr., *Social Forces* 4 (December 1925):443–444.

44. Letter from Frazier to Frank Hankins, July 20, 1925, Frazier Papers.

45. E. Franklin Frazier, "The Putting Away of 'Sister Jones,'" 3–4 (unpublished story, c. 1923), available in the Frazier Papers, box 131-77, folder 11.

Chapter 7. Publish and Perish

1. Edyth Ross, *Black Heritage in Social Work* (Metuchen, N.J.: Scarecrow Press, 1978).

2. For this historical blind spot, see, for example, Walter Trattner, *From Poor Law to Welfare State: A History of Social Welfare in America* (New York: Free Press, 1979); Robert Bremner, *American Philanthropy* (Chicago: University of Chicago Press, 1960); James Leiby, *A History of Social Welfare and Social Work in the United States* (New York: Columbia University Press, 1978).

3. Clarke Chambers, *Seedtime of Reform: American Social Service and Social Action, 1918–1933* (Minneapolis: University of Minnesota Press, 1963).

4. John Ehrenreich, *The Altruistic Imagination: A History of Social Work and Social Policy in the United States* (Ithaca, N.Y.: Cornell University Press, 1985); Michael Katz, *In the Shadow of the Poor House: A Social History of Welfare in America* (New York: Basic Books, 1986).

5. For information about this aspect of NUL's program, see Guichard Parris and Lester Brooks, *Blacks in the City: A History of the National Urban League* (Boston: Little, Brown, 1971); Nancy Weiss, *The National Urban League, 1910–1940* (New York: Oxford University Press, 1974); and Meier and Rudwick, *From Plantation to Ghetto*, 222–234.

6. Frazier, "Professional Education for Negro Social Workers," 168.

7. Mary Russell, "Possibilities of Case Work with Colored Families," *The Family* 2 (May 1921):59–62; Corinne Sherman, "Racial Factors in Desertion, Part V: The Negroes," *The Family* 3 (January 1923):221–225; Helen Pendleton, "Case Work and Racial Traits," *The Family* 3 (February 1923):252–254.

8. See, for example, Edward Devine, "The Klan in Texas," *Survey* 48 (1922):10–11; and Annie MacLean, "Where Color Lines Are Drawn," *Survey* 48 (1922):453–454.

9. Russell, "Possibilities of Case Work," 60.

10. "The Southern Negro and Social Work," *Survey* 40 (1918):643.

11. Sherman, "Racial Factors in Desertion," 222, 223.

12. Pendleton, "Case Work and Racial Traits," 252.

13. "Miss Sherman Replies," *The Family* 3 (February 1923):254–255.

14. Jesse O. Thomas, *My Story in Black and White* (New York: Exposition Press, 1967), 117.

15. Russell, "Possibilities of Case Work," 61.

16. Frazier, "Professional Education for Negro Social Workers," 169.

17. Frazier, "Professional Education for Negro Social Workers," 169, 170.

18. Frazier, "My Relation with the Atlanta School of Social Work," 1.

19. Frazier, "Professional Education for Negro Social Workers," 167.

20. Frazier, "Professional Education for Negro Social Workers," 170.

21. Davis, "E. Franklin Frazier," 432.

22. Frazier, "Professional Education for Negro Social Workers," 173–174.

23. Frazier, "Training Colored Social Workers in the South," 445.

24. Edward Franklin Frazier, "Neighborhood Union in Atlanta," *Southern Workman* 52 (September 1923):437–442.

25. Frazier, "My Relation with the Atlanta School of Social Work," 1–2.

26. Frazier, "My Relation with the Atlanta School of Social Work," 2.

27. Frazier, "My Relation with the Atlanta School of Social Work," 1. See also Frazier, "Training Colored Social Workers in the South," 445–446.

28. Frazier, "Social Work in Race Relations," 252–254.

29. Frazier, "Social Work in Race Relations," 253, 254.

30. Letter from Frazier to "Dock" Steward, January 3, 1925, Frazier Papers.

31. Frazier, "My Relation with the Atlanta School of Social Work," 2.

32. The following analysis is based on documents available in the Frazier Papers,

box 131-1, folder 2, and box 131-25, folder 17. See, for example, Frazier, "My Relation with the Atlanta School of Social Work," passim; "Extract from note of what Helen B. Pendleton *did* say about Mr. Frazier" (January 1927); Frazier, "To the Board of Trustees of the Atlanta School of Social Work In Re Statement of Miss Van de Vrede to the Board" (December 14, 1926); Frazier, "To the Members of the Board of Trustees of the Atlanta School of Social Work" (December 14, 1926); Frazier, "Summary of Reasons for Asking for the Resignation of Miss Helen B. Pendleton as Supervisor of Field Work in the Atlanta School of Social Work" (December 1926).

33. For her critique of racial stereotypes in social work, see Pendleton, "Case Work and Racial Traits," 252–254.

34. Frazier, review of *The Basis of Racial Adjustment*, 442–444

35. Frazier, "The Negro and Non-resistance," 213.

36. Frazier, "Embodying Stories of Experiences with Whites," 7, 7a, 13, 13c.

37. For example, on January 15 he wrote to Walter Pettit, an influential social worker and professor at the New York School of Social Work, giving details of how his opponents were manufacturing charges against him in order to force his resignation. He still thought he had a chance of being rehired. Pettit urged Frazier to "keep a stiff upper lip" and promised to help him find another job. See letters from Frazier to Walter Pettit, January 15, 1927, January 18, 1927, and February 3, 1927, and from Pettit to Frazier, January 24, 1927, Frazier Papers.

38. Letter from W. A. Robinson to M. W. Adams, February 14, 1927, Frazier Papers.

39. Letter from M. W. Adams to W. A. Robinson, February 22, 1927, Frazier Papers.

40. Letter from W.E.B. Du Bois to Frazier, January 21, 1927, Frazier Papers.

41. Letter from Frazier to W.E.B. Du Bois, January 18, 1927, Frazier Papers.

42. Letters from W.E.B. Du Bois to Frazier, January 21, 1927, and from Du Bois to Thomas Jones, March 9, 1927, Frazier Papers.

43. Letter from Frazier to Walter Pettit, February 3, 1927, Frazier Papers.

44. Letter from Thomas Jones to W.E.B. Du Bois, March 26, 1927, Frazier Papers.

45. Letter from W.E.B. Du Bois to Thomas Jones, March 30, 1927, Frazier Papers.

46. Letter from Thomas Jones to W.E.B. Du Bois, April 11, 1927, Frazier Papers.

47. Letters from Frank Hankins to Frazier, February 10, 1927, and February 21, 1927, Frazier Papers.

48. Frazier, "My Relation with the Atlanta School of Social Work," 5.

49. See letters from Ernest Burgess to Frazier, February 1, 1927; and from Frazier to Robert Park, February 1, 1927. See also telegram from Eugene Kinkle Jones to Frazier, April 12, 1927, offering Frazier a job with a local office of NUL, Frazier Papers.

50. As early as 1923, he and Park had discussed a topic for Frazier's dissertation. See reference in letter from Robert Park to Frazier, August 2, 1924, Frazier Papers.

51. Letter from Robert Park to Frazier, April 20, 1927, Frazier Papers.

52. See letters from Frazier to Leonard Outhwaite, June 16, 1927, and to Andrew Allison, January 28, 1928, Frazier Papers.

53. Letter from Gustavus Steward to Frazier, June 14, 1927, Frazier Papers.

54. Letter from Walter White to Frazier, April 25, 1927, Frazier Papers.

55. Letter from Gustavus Steward to Frazier, June 10, 1927, Frazier Papers.

56. Frazier, "The Pathology of Race Prejudice," 856–862.

57. Letter from Willis King to the Editor of the *Afro-American*, July 8, 1927, Frazier Papers, box 131-25, folder 17.

58. Letters from Frazier to Willis King, July 14 and July 16, 1927, Frazier Papers.

59. E. Franklin Frazier, "The Negro in the Industrial South," *The Nation* 125 (July 27, 1927):84.

60. Ehrenreich, *The Altruistic Imagination*, chs. 2 and 3.

61. Katz, *In the Shadow of the Poor House*, 177.

62. Frazier, "The Negro in the Industrial South," 84.

63. Frazier, "Social Work in Race Relations," 254.

Chapter 8. Becoming a Sociologist

1. Frazier's only published comments about the flight from Atlanta appeared in a book review, "Racial Culture and Conflict," *Christendom* 2 (Summer 1937):506.

2. Letter from Frazier to Nancy Cunard, February 18, 1932, Frazier Papers.

3. Frazier, "The Pathology of Race Prejudice," 856–862.

4. See letters between Frazier and Bernard Glueck, December 29, 1924, and January 5, 1925, Frazier Papers.

5. Letter from Editors of *Atlantic Monthly* to Frazier, February 17, 1928, Frazier Papers.

6. See correspondence between Locke and Frazier in May and June 1925, Frazier Papers. See also Frazier, "Durham."

7. Letter from Emory Bogardus to Frazier, August 5, 1926, Frazier Papers.

8. Park and Burgess, *Introduction to the Science of Sociology*, 138–139.

9. Sam Small, "An Atlanta Negro's Diagnosis of the Insanity of Race Prejudice," *Constitution*, June 10, 1927, p. 6.

10. "E. Franklin Frazier," *Atlanta Independent*, June 30, 1927, p. 4.

11. E. Franklin Frazier, "How Edward F. Frazier Became E. Franklin Frazier," undated memo, Frazier Papers, box 131-1, folder 1. Even if the *Forum* had used Frazier's pen name, he would have still been threatened after Sam Small's June 10th editorial identified him as director of the Atlanta School of Social Work.

12. "Whites Threatened Him with Lynching," *Afro-American*, June 25, 1927, pp. 1,10.

13. MBF Interview. This story has been embroidered over the years, but its basic facts have been verified.

14. Drake, "Introduction," x.

15. Letter from Charles Johnson to Frazier, June 29, 1927, Frazier Papers.

16. Letters from Gustavus Steward to Frazier, June 10 and June 14, 1927, Frazier Papers.

17. E. Franklin Frazier, "The Pathology of Race Prejudice," in *Negro: Anthology*, ed. Nancy Cunard (London: Wishart, 1934), 116–119.

18. Postcard from Nancy Cunard to Frazier, October 23, 1932, Frazier Papers.

19. Letter from Gustavus Steward to Frazier, July 31, 1927, Frazier Papers.

20. Letter from Frazier to Leonard Outhwaite, June 16, 1927, Frazier Papers.

21. The following discussion of Frazier's efforts to get a scholarship relies on John Stanfield, "The Cracked Back Door: Foundations and Black Social Scientists between the World Wars," *American Sociologist* 17 (November 1982):201–202.

22. Letter from Leonard Outhwaite to John Hope, May 12, 1927, cited in Stanfield, "The Cracked Back Door," 201.

23. Letters from Will Alexander to Outhwaite, May 11, 1927, and May 23, 1927, cited in Stanfield, "The Cracked Back Door," 201, 202.

24. Letter from Hope to Outhwaite, May 17, 1927, cited in Stanfield, "The Cracked Back Door," 202.

25. Details of Frazier's graduate school grades come from his official transcript, Office of the Registrar, University of Chicago. See also letter from Robert Park to Frazier, October 25, 1923, Frazier Papers.

26. Harris, "The Life and Work of E. Franklin Frazier," 36.

27. Robert Faris, *Chicago Sociology, 1920–1932* (San Francisco: Chandler, 1967), 26.

28. Faris, *Chicago Sociology,* 37.

29. Interview by author with Herbert Blumer, April 28, 1971.

30. Quoted in Odum, *American Sociology,* 235.

31. Faris, *Chicago Sociology,* 34.

32. When Frazier returned to complete his doctorate in 1927, Blumer was an instructor who served on the committee that supervised his preliminary exam. Interview by the author with Herbert Blumer, April 28, 1971. See also two-page undated memo, "Preliminary Doctor's Examinations, Spring 1930," on file in Frazier Papers, box 131-1, folder 6.

33. E. Franklin Frazier, "Louis Wirth: An Appreciation," *Phylon* 13 (1952):167.

34. See, for example, William I. Thomas, "The Psychology of Race Prejudice," *American Journal of Sociology* 9 (1904):593–611.

35. The findings were published in Chicago Commission on Race Relations, *The Negro in Chicago.*

36. Ellsworth Faris, "Remarks on Race Superiority," *Social Service Review* 1 (March 1927):36–45.

37. Ellsworth Faris, "The Verbal Battle of the Races," *Social Service Review* 3 (1929):28, 29.

38. Harlan, *Booker T. Washington,* 291. See also Fred Mathews, *Quest for an American Sociology: Robert E. Park and the Chicago School* (Montreal: McGill-Queens, 1977); and Stow Persons, *Ethnic Studies at Chicago, 1905–45* (Urbana: University of Illinois Press, 1987).

39. Robert Park, *Race and Culture* (Glencoe, Ill.: Free Press, 1950), vii.

40. See, for example, H. L. Harris, Jr., "Negro Mortality Rates in Chicago," *Social Service Review* 1 (March 1927):58–77; Myra Hill Colson, "Negro Home Workers in Chicago," *Social Service Review* 2 (September 1928):385–413; and Irene Graham, "Family Support and Dependency among Chicago Negroes: A Study of Unpublished Census Data," *Social Service Review* 3 (December 1929): 541–562.

41. Letter from Everett Hughes to Frazier, May 18, 1929, Frazier Papers.

42. Frazier, "Embodying Stories of Experiences with Whites," 1. In this story Frazier refers to the incident as taking place in Chicago around 1929.

43. Harris, "The Life and Work of E. Franklin Frazier," 37. See also Young, *Black Writers of the Thirties,* 50–53, 239.

44. Quoted in Edwards, *E. Franklin Frazier on Race Relations,* xvi. See also "Memoir" by Everett Hughes in preface to Frazier, *The Negro Church in America,* vii–viii.

45. Vlasek, "The Social Thought of E. Franklin Frazier," 101.

46. Dale Vlasek, "E. Franklin Frazier and the Problem of Assimilation," in *Ideas in America's Cultures: From Republic to Mass Society,* ed. Hamilton Cravens (Ames: Iowa State University Press, 1982), 148.

47. Persons, *Ethnic Studies at Chicago,* 131.

48. For a more balanced view of Frazier's relationship with Park, his theoretical agreements and disagreements, see Persons, *Ethnic Studies at Chicago,* chs. 4, 5, and 8; and Edwards, "E. Franklin Frazier," 85–117.

49. See, for example, Frazier, *Negro Youth at the Crossways,* 273–274; *The Negro in the United States,* 665–668.

50. MBF Interview. Mrs. Frazier said that her husband never agreed with Park on fundamental issues, but they still remained very good friends.

51. Arvarh Strickland, *History of the Chicago Urban League* (Urbana: University of Illinois Press, 1966), 98–99.

52. See, for example, *Chicago Defender,* February 25, 1928, p. 5; *Chicago Defender,* March 24, 1928, p. 2. A copy of his five-page, unpublished and undated (c. 1928) speech, broadcast on WMAQ radio, is available in the Frazier Papers, box 131-28, folder 4.

53. Strickland, *History of the Chicago Urban League,* 86.

54. Strickland, *History of the Chicago Urban League,* ch. 4.

55. Frazier, "The Mind of the American Negro," 263–266, 284; E. Franklin Frazier, "The Negro Family," *The Annals* 140 (November 1928):44–51.

56. E. Franklin Frazier, "Racial Self-Expression," in *Ebony and Topaz: A Collectanea,* ed. Charles Johnson (New York: National Urban League, 1927), 119–121.

57. Frazier, "La Bourgeoisie Noire," 78–84.

58. E. Franklin Frazier, "Black and Red," unpublished and undated (c. 1928) essay, available in the Frazier Papers, box 131-75, folder 7.

59. E. Franklin Frazier, "A Folk Culture in the Making," *Southern Workman* 57 (June 1928):198–199.

Chapter 9. The Plantation

1. Letter from "Dock" Steward to Frazier, October 14, 1928, Frazier Papers.
2. MBF Interview.
3. Frazier, "The Role of the Social Scientist in the Negro College," 17.
4. Letter from Frazier to Will Alexander, August 6, 1927, Frazier Papers.

5. Letter from Charles Johnson to Frazier, April 13, 1929, Frazier Papers.

6. Letter from William Ogburn to Frazier, August 31, 1929, Frazier Papers.

7. Frazier, *The Negro Family in the United States,* xix.

8. Interview by author with St. Clair Drake, January 22, 1975.

9. Frazier, "The Role of the Social Scientist in the Negro College," 17.

10. Wolters, *The New Negro on Campus,* ch. 2.

11. Wolters, *The New Negro on Campus,* 34.

12. Wolters, *The New Negro on Campus,* 65–66.

13. Letters from Thomas Jones to W.E.B. Du Bois, March 26 and April 11, 1927, Frazier Papers.

14. Wolters, *The New Negro on Campus,* 67–68.

15. Butler Jones, "The Tradition of Sociology Teaching in Black Colleges: The Unheralded Professionals," in Blackwell and Janowitz, *Black Sociologists,* 127; Stanley Smith, "Sociological Research and Fisk University: A Case Study," in Blackwell and Janowitz, *Black Sociologists,* 164–190.

16. The others were Hampton Institute, Howard University, and Atlanta University. See E. Franklin Frazier, "Graduate Education in Negro Colleges and Universities," *Journal of Negro Education* 2 (July 1933):329–341.

17. Frazier, "Graduate Education," 337–338.

18. Frazier, "Graduate Education," 339–341.

19. Frazier, "La Bourgeoisie Noire."

20. Frazier, "The Pathology of Race Prejudice."

21. Cunard, *Negro,* iv. Cunard was a British feminist and activist who had close ties with the Communist Party. On her life, see Ann Chisolm, *Nancy Cunard: A Biography* (New York: Knopf, 1979). Also see Hugh Ford's introduction to an edited and abridged version of the anthology, published in New York by Frederick Ungar in 1970. Frazier's essay was not reprinted in Ford's version.

22. Smith, "Sociological Research and Fisk University," 164–190.

23. See correspondence between Frazier and Mencken, March 27, April 3, April 6, and April 10, Frazier Papers. Nothing came of this after Mencken rejected an article that Frazier submitted.

24. Letter from W.E.B. Du Bois to Abram Harris, January 3, 1934, reprinted in Herbert Aptheker, ed., *The Correspondence of W.E.B. Du Bois,* vol. 1, *Selections 1877–1934* (Amherst: University of Massachusetts Press, 1973), 470–471. Others mutually agreed upon were Ernest Just, Allison Davies, Sterling Brown, Charles Wesley, Valvarez Spratlin, and Rayford Logan. Du Bois also recommended Robert Weaver, was "not so sure about" William Hastie and Ralph Bunche, and was "a bit leary about" Alain Locke and Charles Johnson.

25. See correspondence between Frazier and Spingarn, April 12 and April 25, 1933, Frazier Papers.

26. Ross, *J. E. Spingarn,* 178–185. For further discussion of Frazier's role in the Amenia Conference, see Chapter 17.

27. Anna Rothe, ed., *Current Biography 1946: Who's Who and Why* (New York: H. W. Wilson, 1946), 285–287. For a vivid portrait of Johnson's significance in the New Negro movement, see Lewis, *When Harlem Was in Vogue,* chs. 4 and 5.

28. Lewis, *When Harlem Was in Vogue*, 90, 97.

29. Jones, "The Tradition of Sociology Teaching in Black Colleges," 136–137.

30. Jones, "The Tradition of Sociology Teaching in Black Colleges," 137.

31. MBF Interview. For a discussion of the network of foundations that controlled Johnson and determined the direction of race-relations research, see Stanfield, "The Cracked Back Door," 193–204.

32. According to Jones ("The Tradition of Sociology Teaching in Black Colleges," 162), "Almost every black sociologist over forty and possessed of 'a Southern exposure' is aware of the long estrangement between Charles S. Johnson and E. Franklin Frazier."

33. Letter from Frazier to W.E.B. Du Bois, January 18, 1927, Frazier Papers.

34. According to Herbert Blumer, Frazier "felt himself in rivalry" with Johnson. Interview by author with Herbert Blumer, April 28, 1971.

35. Butler, "The Tradition of Sociology Teaching in Black Colleges," 162–163; MBF and Blumer interviews; Davis, "E. Franklin Frazier," 432.

36. Interview by author with St. Clair Drake, January 22, 1975.

37. Interview by author with Everett Hughes, September 22, 1972. Johnson became president of Fisk in 1946.

38. Rothe, *Current Biography 1946*, 286

39. Contrast, for example, Frazier's "The Pathology of Race Prejudice" (1927) with Charles Johnson, "The Balance Sheet: Debits and Credits in Negro-White Relations," *The World Tomorrow* 2 (January 1928):13–16.

40. E. Franklin Frazier, "Good Will, Bad Science," *The Nation* 141 (July 10, 1935):53.

41. E. Franklin Frazier, "A Critical Summary of Articles Contributed to Symposium on Negro Education," *Journal of Negro Education* 5 (July 1936):532–533. See also Charles Johnson, "On the Need of Realism in Negro Education," *Journal of Negro Education* 5 (July 1936):375–382. The reference to the "brilliant student" was based on a real incident in which Frazier and Johnson lined up on different sides of the controversy.

42. In a letter to Frazier, the editor agreed to pay him the usual rate for published copy and promised "not to use your name." Carl Murphy to Frazier, February 7, 1925, Frazier Papers. It is apparent from the files of the *Afro-American* that Frazier submitted several articles, some of which were printed.

43. Vlasek, "The Social Thought of E. Franklin Frazier," 145.

44. Vlasek, "The Social Thought of E. Franklin Frazier," 145; Davis, "E. Franklin Frazier," 432. The *New York Times* (November 8, 1931, sec. II, p. 7) reported Derricotte's death without any reference to the controversy.

45. See story, "Dead Fisk Women Suffered because Ga. Hospitals Were for Whites Only," written by Frazier, in the *Afro-American*, November 21, 1931, p. 18.

46. Frazier's account, "Seize Negro Second Door from the Dean of Women of Fisk and Lynch Him" (dated December 16, 1933), was presumably sent anonymously to various newspapers. A copy is on file in the Frazier Papers, box 131-77, folder 19. For other accounts of the lynching, see *New York Times*, December 16, 1933, p. 1; *New York Times*, December 17, 1933, p. 35; *New York Times*, December 19, 1933, p. 44.

Unlike the *New York Times*'s version, Frazier's story implies the involvement of sheriff's deputies in the lynching.

47. Harris, "The Life and Work of E. Franklin Frazier," 29; see also Frazier's testimony to SISS, 12–15.

48. See letters from William Patterson to Frazier, March 25, 1933; from John Dos Passos to Frazier, November 4, 1933; from Alfred Hirsch to Frazier, November 25, 1933; from the Writers League against Lynching to Frazier, December 9, 1933, Frazier Papers.

49. As quoted in the *Afro-American*, January 6, 1934.

50. Frazier, "Embodying Stories of Experiences with Whites," 5–5a. A version of this story can also be found in Bardolph, *The Negro Vanguard*, 323.

51. Frazier, "Embodying Stories of Experiences with Whites," 15–15c. A version of this incident, written by Frazier, was published in the *Afro-American*, June 2, 1934.

Chapter 10. Capstone of Negro Education

1. Kenneth R. Manning, *Black Apollo of Science: The Life of Ernest Everett Just* (New York: Oxford University Press, 1983), 153.

2. Young, *Black Writers of the Thirties*, 41. For a thoughtful assessment of Howard during the 1930s, see generally Joanne Gabbin, *Sterling A. Brown: Building the Black Aesthetic Tradition* (Westport, Conn.: Greenwood Press, 1985).

3. "Statement Concerning the Development of Sociology at Howard University," memorandum from Frazier to Howard Odum (c. 1948), Frazier Papers.

4. Harris, "The Life and Work of E. Franklin Frazier," 41–49.

5. Edwards, "E. Franklin Frazier," 109.

6. Harris, "The Life and Work of E. Franklin Frazier," 42.

7. Edwards, "E. Franklin Frazier," passim.

8. Edwards, "E. Franklin Frazier," passim.

9. Manning, *Black Apollo of Science*, ch. 9.

10. Mayor's Commission on Conditions in Harlem, *The Negro in Harlem: A Report on Social and Economic Conditions Responsible for the Outbreak of March 19, 1935* (New York: New York Municipal Archives, 1935). The commission's final report was never released to the public by LaGuardia. One version was published in full in the New York *Amsterdam News*, July 18, 1936. This version was reprinted, with a few errors and without proper credit to Frazier, by Robert Fogelson and Richard E. Rubinstein, eds., *The Complete Report of Mayor LaGuardia's Commission on the Harlem Riot of March 19, 1935* (New York: Arno Press and *New York Times*, 1969). For a discussion and selections of the final report, see Anthony M. Platt, ed., *The Politics of Riot Commissions, 1917–1970: A Collection of Official Reports and Critical Essays* (New York: Macmillan, 1971), 159–195.

11. This title was the one used by Frazier. His original manuscript is available in the New York Municipal Archives. This version differs in a few respects from the other published versions.

12. Interview by Renetia Martin (for author) with A. Philip Randolph, September 18, 1969.

13. Platt, *The Politics of Riot Commissions*, 161–163. Frazier's modified report was sent to LaGuardia in March 1936, a year after the riot. A few months later, Villard complained to LaGuardia that "failure to publish this report is subjecting the Commission to widespread attacks—intimations that it has been called off and that the Mayor does not wish or is afraid to print the findings." LaGuardia still refused to publish the report. See telegram from Oswald Garrison Villard to Mayor LaGuardia, September 26, 1936, Collection of the Mayor's Commission on Conditions in Harlem, New York Municipal Archives.

14. He completed the outline of a book titled "Harlem: De Wheel Widin a Wheel" (1938, available in the Frazier Papers, box 131-73, folder 14), but his only publication on the topic was "Some Effects of the Depression on the Negro in Northern Cities," *Science and Society* 2 (Fall 1938):489–499.

15. When various commissions were established to study urban riots beginning in the 1960s, Frazier's earlier work was forgotten or ignored. See Platt, *The Politics of Riot Commissions*, passim.

16. Other studies included Charles Johnson, *Growing Up in the Black Belt* (Washington, D.C.: American Council on Education, 1941), and Allison Davis and John Dollard, *Children of Bondage* (Washington, D.C.: American Council on Education, 1940).

17. Frazier, *Negro Youth at the Crossways*. This 1940 book was reprinted in 1967 by Schocken Books with a perceptive introduction by St. Clair Drake.

18. These comments are based on an unpublished paper ("E. Franklin Frazier's Brazil") and personal communication from David Hellwig, Department of Interdisciplinary Studies, St. Cloud State University, St. Cloud, Minn. 56301.

19. See, for example, Frazier, "Brazil Has No Race Problem," 363–365.

20. Gunnar Myrdal, *An American Dilemma* (New York: McGraw-Hill, 1964), lii. The study was first published by Harper & Row in 1944.

21. The summary appeared in *An American Dilemma*, 930–935.

22. Myrdal, *An American Dilemma*, lv. See also "Memorandum of Conversation between Drs. Frazier, Johnson, and Myrdal," February 2, 1940, Frazier Papers, box 131-27, folder 15.

23. Myrdal, *An American Dilemma*, lv, 982–986.

24. Letter from Gunnar Myrdal to Frazier, May 11, 1942, Frazier Papers.

25. Letter from Frazier to Myrdal, June 24, 1942, Frazier Papers.

26. Myrdal, *An American Dilemma*, lix.

27. Letter from Myrdal to Frazier, September 11, 1942, Frazier Papers.

28. For a discussion of these various responses, see David Southern, *Gunnar Myrdal and Black-White Relations: The Use and Abuse of An American Dilemma, 1944–1969* (Baton Rouge: Louisiana State University Press, 1987), ch. 4. For Afro-American critiques, see Oliver Cox, "An American Dilemma: A Mystical Approach to the Study of Race Relations," *Journal of Negro Education* 14 (1945):132–148; and Ralph Ellison, "*An American Dilemma:* A Review," in *Shadow and Act* (New York: Random House, Vintage Books, 1972), 303–317. Ellison's review was written in 1944.

29. E. Franklin Frazier, "Race: An American Dilemma,"*Crisis* 51 (April 1944):105–106, 124. See also Frazier's other review of *An American Dilemma* in *American Journal of Sociology* 50 (1945):555–557.

Chapter 11. Setting the Record Straight

1. Frazier, *The Negro in the United States*, xi.

2. Lee Rainwater and William Yancey, eds., *The Moynihan Report and the Politics of Controversy* (Cambridge, Mass.: MIT Press, 1967), 51, 75. The full report and the debates it generated can be found in this book.

3. Meier and Rudwick, *Black History and the Historical Profession*, 249.

4. Meier and Rudwick, *Black History and the Historical Profession*, 251–252.

5. For critiques of the report, see Herbert Gans, "The Negro Family: Reflections on the Moynihan Report," in Rainwater and Yancey, *The Moynihan Report*, 445–457; Eleanor Burke Leacock, ed., *The Culture of Poverty: A Critique* (New York: Simon & Schuster, 1971); Meier and Rudwick, *Black History and the Historical Profession*, ch. 4; Ulf Hannerz, *Soulside: Inquiries into Ghetto Culture and Community* (New York: Columbia University Press, 1969); and Christopher Lasch, *Haven in a Heartless World: The Family Besieged* (New York: Basic Books, 1977), ch. 7.

6. "W.E.B. Du Bois had addressed the subject in 1908 in his book *The Negro American Family*. Nearer at hand, the brilliant and defiant Frazier had taken up several of Du Bois' themes, added his own, and published in 1939 *The Negro Family in the United States*, which forecast much that seemed now to be appearing. (Frazier, though president of the American Sociological Association in 1948, met with much disapproval)." Daniel P. Moynihan, *Family and Nation* (New York: Harcourt Brace Jovanovich, 1986), 28.

7. From the author's interviews with G. Franklin Edwards (November 23, 1970), St. Clair Drake (January 22, 1975), and Marie Brown Frazier (November 2, 1975).

8. Rainwater and Yancey, *The Moynihan Report*, 7.

9. See, for example, Nathan Glazer's introduction to the 1966 edition of E. Franklin Frazier, *The Negro Family in the United States* (Chicago: University of Chicago Press); Lasch, *Haven in a Heartless World*, 158; Logan, *Howard University*, 492–493; John Stanfield, "Race Relations Research and Black Americans between the Two World Wars," *Journal of Ethnic Studies* 11 (Fall 1983):61–93; Eugene Genovese, *Roll, Jordan, Roll: The World the Slaves Made* (New York: Pantheon, 1972), 450–451; and Walter R. Allen, "The Search for Applicable Theories of Black Family Life," *Journal of Marriage and the Family* 40 (February 1978):117–129. For typical linking of Frazier and Moynihan in the media, see Lena Williams, "Blacks Debating a Greater Stress on Self-Reliance Instead of Aid," *New York Times*, June 15, 1986, pp. 1, 18; and Eric Sundquist, "A Great American Flowering," *New York Times Book Review*, July 3, 1988, p. 15. For rare exceptions to this characterization of Frazier as the father of the Moynihan thesis and for a more balanced view, see Jacquelyne Jackson, "But Where Are the Men?" *Black Scholar* (December 1971):30–41; and especially Herbert Gut-

man, "Persistent Myths about the Afro-American Family," *Journal of Interdisciplinary History* 6 (Autumn 1975):181–210.

10. Southern, *Gunnar Myrdal and Black-White Relations*, 255.

11. Charles Valentine, *Culture and Poverty: Critique and Counter-Proposals* (Chicago: University of Chicago Press, 1968), 20, 23, 29.

12. Abd-L Hakimu Ibn Alkalimat (Gerald McWorter), "The Ideology of Black Social Science," *Black Scholar* (December 1969):20.

13. Herbert Gutman, *The Black Family in Slavery and Freedom, 1750–1925* (New York: Pantheon, 1976), 9.

14. Manning Marable, review of *The Black Family in Slavery and Freedom, 1750–1925*, by Herbert Gutman, *San Francisco Review of Books* 2 (February 1977):11.

15. Hannerz, *Soulside*, 73.

16. Rainwater and Yancey, *The Moynihan Report*, 52, 75.

17. Rainwater and Yancey, *The Moynihan Report*, 64.

18. Rainwater and Yancey, *The Moynihan Report*, 94.

19. Frazier, *The Negro Family in the United States;* E. Franklin Frazier, "Problems and Needs of Negro Children and Youth Resulting from Family Disorganization," *Journal of Negro Education* 19 (Summer 1950):215–277.

20. Frazier, *The Negro Family in the United States*, 298.

21. Frazier, *The Negro Family in the United States*, 298–299.

22. Frazier, *The Negro Family in the United States*, 340–341.

23. Frazier, *The Negro Family in the United States*, 486.

24. Frazier, *The Negro Family in the United States*, 487–488.

25. Frazier, *The Negro Family in the United States*, 488.

26. Frazier, "Problems and Needs of Negro Children and Youth," 276.

27. See also E. Franklin Frazier, "The Negro Family and Negro Youth," *Journal of Negro Education* 9 (July 1940):290–299.

28. Frazier, *The Negro in the United States*, 652–653.

29. E. Franklin Frazier, "Theoretical Structure of Sociology and Sociological Research," *British Journal of Sociology* 4 (December 1953):292–311.

30. E. Franklin Frazier, "The Present State of Sociological Knowledge concerning Race Relations," *Transactions of the Fourth World Congress of Sociology* 5 (1959):73–80.

31. Herbert Gutman, "Persistent Myths about the Afro-American Family," 181–210.

32. C. Wright Mills, *The Sociological Imagination* (New York: Oxford University Press, 1959), 158.

Chapter 12. Saving the Negro's Self-Respect

1. Young, *Black Writers of the Thirties*, 53. See also Valentine, *Culture and Poverty,* passim. For a more accurate and sympathetic view of Frazier, see Harold Cruse, *The Crisis of the Negro Intellectual* (New York: Morrow, 1967), especially 155–157.

2. Frazier maintained a long friendship with Herskovits, as he did with all his serious intellectual adversaries. See Melville Herskovits, *The Myth of the Negro Past.* Also, for a full and respectful discussion of Frazier's differences with Herskovits, see Frazier, *The Negro in the United States,* pt. 1.

3. E. Franklin Frazier, "The Negro Slave Family," *Journal of Negro History* 15 (April 1930):203.

4. Frazier, "La Bourgeoisie Noire," 83.

5. Frazier, "The Negro and Non-resistance," 213.

6. Frazier uses this term in "Southern Scenes."

7. Frazier, "Georgia," 176.

8. E. Franklin Frazier, "Discussion," *Opportunity* 2 (August 1924):239.

9. Davis, "E. Franklin Frazier," 430.

10. E. Franklin Frazier, "Chicago," 70–73.

11. Unpublished, untitled, and undated (c. 1928) essay, given as a talk on WMAQ radio, available in the Frazier Papers, box 131-79, folder 8.

12. Frazier, "A Note on Negro Education," 75–77.

13. Frazier, "Neighborhood Union in Atlanta," 437–442.

14. Frazier, "A Community School," 459–464.

15. Frazier, "Cooperatives," 505.

16. Frazier, *The Negro in the United States,* chs. 5, 15, and 20.

17. Frazier, "The Negro and Non-resistance," 213, 214.

18. Letter from Ellen Winsor to W.E.B. Du Bois, reprinted in Aptheker, *The Correspondence of W.E.B. Du Bois,* 283. Winsor's views reflected prevailing liberal sensibilities. A leading sociologist, for example, argued that racist violence should be controlled through education and legislation. "Organized opposition by negroes would merely result in organized attacks by the whites." Edwin Sutherland, *Criminology* (Philadelphia: Lippincott, 1924), 248.

19. Frazier, quoted in "Opinion of W.E.B. Du Bois," *Crisis* 28 (June 1924):58–59.

20. Frazier, "Social Equality and the Negro," 168.

21. Frazier, "A Note on Negro Education," 75–77.

22. Frazier, "Chicago," 72.

23. E. Franklin Frazier, "Enfant Terrible" (unpublished and undated, c. 1928), available in the Frazier Papers, box 131-75, folder 18. It is likely that Frazier submitted this as a column to the *Chicago Defender,* but his writings were too intellectual and radical for the *Defender,* which reported mostly on crime, sports, and social events.

24. Gustavus Adolphus Steward, "The New Negro Hokum" *Social Forces* 6 (March 1928):438–445.

25. Frazier, "La Bourgeoisie Noire," 84.

26. E. Franklin Frazier, "Racial Self-Expression," 119–121. For an important statement in defense of a unique black culture, written shortly before Frazier's essay, see Langston Hughes, "The Negro Artist and the Racial Mountain," *The Nation* 122 (June 23, 1926):692–694.

27. Frazier, "A Folk Culture in the Making," 195, 197.

28. Quoted in the *Afro-American,* January 6, 1934.

29. E. Franklin Frazier, "The Negro's Struggle to Find His Soul" 3 (unpublished and undated, c. 1928), available in the Frazier Papers, box 131-76, folder 21.

30. Frazier, "The Negro's Struggle to Find His Soul," 1–9.

31. Frazier, "A Folk Culture in the Making," 198–199; Frazier, "The Negro's Struggle to Find His Soul," 8.

32. Frazier, "The Negro's Struggle to Find His Soul," 9.

33. E. Franklin Frazier, "Group Tactics and Ideals," *Messenger* 9 (January 1927):31.

34. Frazier, *Negro Youth at the Crossways*, 277.

35. Frazier, *The Negro in the United States*, xi, xii.

36. Frazier, *The Negro in the United States*, 703.

37. E. Franklin Frazier, *Race and Culture Contacts in the Modern World* (New York: Beacon Press, 1965), chap. 18. (This book was first published by Knopf in 1957.) See also Frazier, "Theoretical Structure of Sociology and Sociological Research," 293–311.

38. E. Franklin Frazier, "What Can the American Negro Contribute to the Social Development of Africa?" in *Africa: Seen by American Negroes*, ed. John Davis (Paris: Présence Africaine, 1959), 263–278.

39. Frazier, "The Failure of the Negro Intellectual," 34, 36.

Chapter 13. Scourges of the Negro Family

1. Letter from Frazier to W.E.B. Du Bois, August 2, 1939, reprinted in Herbert Aptheker, ed., *The Correspondence of W.E.B. Du Bois*, vol. 2, *Selections 1934–1944* (Amherst: University of Massachusetts Press, 1976), 193–194.

2. See, for example, R. Fred Wacker, *Ethnicity, Pluralism, and Race: Race Relations Theory in America before Myrdal* (Westport, Conn.: Greenwood Press, 1983), 3. For discussion of Du Bois's role within academia, see Bracey, Meier, and Rudwick, *The Black Sociologists*, 1–12; Rudwick, "W.E.B. Du Bois as Sociologist," 25–55.

3. Du Bois, *The Negro American Family*, 9.

4. E. Franklin Frazier, "The Changing Status of the Negro Family," *Social Forces* 9 (March 1931):386. The same point is expressed in Frazier, "The Negro Slave Family," 198.

5. Du Bois, *The Negro American Family*, 21.

6. Frazier, *The Negro Family in the United States*, 21.

7. Du Bois, *The Negro*, 187–188.

8. Frazier, "Family Life of the Negro in the Small Town," 384.

9. E. Franklin Frazier, "Is the Negro Family a Unique Sociological Unit?" *Opportunity* 5 (June 1927):165.

10. Du Bois, *The Negro American Family*, 10.

11. These various influences are summed up in Edwards, "E. Franklin Frazier," 93–103.

12. E. Franklin Frazier, rejoinder to "'Social Determination' in the Writings of Negro Scholars," by William Fontaine *American Journal of Sociology* 49 (January 1944):314. Ernest Mowrer's dissertation, *Family Disorganization: An Introduction to*

a Sociological Analysis, was written under Burgess's influence in 1924 and published in 1927 by the University of Chicago Press, just before Frazier arrived in Chicago.

13. Letter from Frazier to Robert Park, July 24, 1924, Frazier Papers.

14. Letter from Robert Park to Frazier, August 2, 1924, Frazier Papers.

15. Robert Faris, *Chicago Sociology*, 103, 137.

16. This paper is available in the Frazier Papers, box 131-1, folder 17.

17. Frazier, rejoinder to "'Social Determination' in the Writings of Negro Scholars," 314.

18. Frazier, *The Negro in the United States*, 623.

19. All these references are summarized and documented in Frazier, *The Negro in the United States*, 623–627.

20. Gutman, "Persistent Myths about the Afro-American Family," 184.

21. Frazier, *The Negro Family in Chicago* (Chicago: University of Chicago Press, 1932), 245.

22. Letter from Frazier to Rev. James B. Adams, January 22, 1930, Frazier Papers.

23. Letter from Frazier to Rev. James B. Adams, January 22, 1930, Frazier Papers.

24. Frazier, rejoinder to "'Social Determination' in the Writings of Negro Scholars," 314.

25. Ernest W. Burgess, "Editor's Preface," in Frazier, *The Negro Family in Chicago*, xii. Emphasis added.

26. See, for example, Allen, "The Search for Applicable Theories of Black Family Life," 119–120.

27. Frazier, "The Negro Slave Family," 259

28. Frazier, *The Negro in the United States*, 214.

29. Frazier, *The Negro in the United States*, 636.

30. For this point and a balanced, critical assessment of Frazier's work on the family, see Gutman, "Persistent Myths about the Afro-American Family," 181–210.

31. See, for example, Frazier, *The Negro Family in Chicago*, 245–252; *The Negro in the United States*, 21; "The Negro Family," 51.

32. Gutman, "Persistent Myths about the Afro-American Family," 181–210; Allen, "The Search for Applicable Theories of Black Family Life," 125.

33. See, for example, Frazier, *The Negro in the United States*, 311, 313.

34. E. Franklin Frazier, "Is the Negro Family a Unique Sociological Unit?" 165.

35. Frazier, rejoinder to "'Social Determination' in the Writings of Negro Scholars," 314.

36. E. Franklin Frazier, "Three Scourges of the Negro Family," *Opportunity* 4 (July 1926):210.

37. E. Franklin Frazier, "The Negro Slave Family," 259.

38. Frazier, "The Negro Slave Family," 227, 233, 253, 258, 259.

39. Frazier, *The Negro Family in the United States*, 24, 297, 487.

40. Much of the current debate has focused on William J. Wilson, *The Truly Disadvantaged: The Inner City, the Underclass, and Public Policy* (Chicago: University of Chicago Press, 1987). For various critiques of Wilson's work and Wilson's response, see "The Truly Disadvantaged: Challenges and Prospects," *Journal of Sociology and Social Welfare* 16 (December 1989).

41. Wright acknowledges his reliance on Frazier in Richard Wright and Edwin Ros-

skam, *12 Million Black Voices: A Folk History of the Negro in the United States* (New York: Viking Press, 1941), 6, 93.

42. Frazier, "Three Scourges of the Negro Family," 211, 212.

43. E. Franklin Frazier, "The Impact of Urban Civilization upon Negro Family Life," *American Sociological Review* 2 (August 1937):618.

44. Fogelson and Rubinstein, *The Complete Report of Mayor LaGuardia's Commission on the Harlem Riot*, 43, 122

45. Frazier, *The Negro Family in the United States*, 324.

46. For a summary of various criticisms, see Allen, "The Search for Applicable Theories of Black Family Life," passim.

47. Gutman, "Persistent Myths about the Afro-American Family," 181–210. For other studies that challenge the accuracy and assumptions of Frazier's research, see Genovese, *Roll, Jordan, Roll*; Gutman, *The Black Family in Slavery and Freedom*; Lawrence Levine, *Black Culture and Black Consciousness: Afro-American Folk Thought from Slavery to Freedom* (New York: Oxford University Press, 1977).

48. Rainwater and Yancey, *The Moynihan Report*, 75.

49. Paula Giddings, *When and Where I Enter: The Impact of Black Women on Race and Sex in America* (New York: Bantam Books, 1985), 252, 328.

50. In *When and Where I Enter*, Giddings stretches her citations from Frazier's books to make her point and ignores evidence that contradicts her claims. See, for example, her selective discussion of Frazier's views about the "desire of slave women to become mistresses of their masters" (p. 61) and contrast with Frazier's original, complex treatment of the topic in *The Negro Family in the United States*, ch. 4.

51. Frazier, *The Negro in the United States*, 330.

52. E. Franklin Frazier, "New Role of the Negro Woman," *Ebony* 15 (August 1960):40. Emphasis added.

Chapter 14. Black Bourgeoisie

1. Edwards, *E. Franklin Frazier on Race Relations*, xviii; Bracey, Meier, and Rudwick, *The Black Sociologists*, 10; interview with Michael Winston by the author, November 3, 1975.

2. Frazier, *God and War*, 4.

3. Frazier, "The Failure of the Negro Intellectual," 31.

4. Frazier, *The Negro Church in America*, 86. This book was published two years after Frazier's death.

5. This story, which is part of the Frazier lore, was communicated to me by Michael Winston, a former student of Frazier's, November 3, 1975.

6. Frazier, *Black Bourgeoisie*, 236.

7. Benjamin Stolberg, "Black Chauvinism," *The Nation* 140 (May 15, 1935):570. For Frazier's agreement with Stolberg, see his letter to *The Nation* 141 (July 3, 1935):17.

8. Frazier, *Black Bourgeoisie*, 147.

9. Cox, "Introduction," 15–31. Although Cox clearly has too much of an axe to

grind, another sociologist errs in the opposite direction by trying to locate Frazier within a Marxist tradition. See Bert Landry, "A Reinterpretation of the Writings of Frazier on the Black Middle Class," *Social Problems* 26 (December 1978):211–222.

10. See, for example, Frazier, *The Negro in the United States*, 292–302; *Black Bourgeoisie*, ch. 2.

11. Frazier, *The Negro in the United States*, 301.

12. Frazier, quoted in "Opinion of W.E.B. Du Bois," *Crisis* 28 (June 1924):59.

13. Frazier, *The Negro in the United States*, 91.

14. Frazier, "The Negro's Struggle to Find His Soul," 7, 8.

15. Lewis, *When Harlem Was in Vogue*, 115.

16. Frazier, "The Negro and Non-resistance," 213, 214.

17. Frazier, "A Note on Negro Education," 76.

18. See correspondence between James Bond and William Alexander, president of the Commission, February 20 and 23, 1927, Frazier Papers.

19. Frazier, review of *The Basis of Racial Adjustment*, 443.

20. E. Franklin Frazier, "The Status of the Negro in the American Social Order," *Journal of Negro Education* 4 (July 1935):303, 304.

21. E. Franklin Frazier, *Bourgeoisie Noire* (Paris: Plon, 1955).

22. Frazier, "Some Aspects of Negro Business," 293–297.

23. Letter from Charles Johnson to Frazier, October 20, 1924, Frazier Papers.

24. Letter from Alain Locke to Frazier, undated, but from Frazier's response clearly written in May 1925, Frazier Papers.

25. See letters from Frazier to Locke, May 26 and June 8, 1925, Frazier Papers.

26. Frazier, "Durham," 333, 334, 340.

27. Frazier, "Durham," 338, 339.

28. Alain Locke, "The New Negro," in Locke, *The New Negro*, 16.

29. Letter from Frazier to Gustavus Steward, January 3, 1925, Frazier Papers.

30. Frazier, "The Negro in the Industrial South," 84.

31. Letter from Steward to Frazier, December 14, 1927, Frazier Papers.

32. Letter from Steward to Frazier, January 4, 1928, Frazier Papers.

33. Letter from Steward to Frazier, December 14, 1927, Frazier Papers.

34. Steward, "The New Negro Hokum," 438–445.

35. Letter from Eileen Hood to Frazier, February 29, 1928, Frazier Papers.

36. Cruse, *The Crisis of the Negro Intellectual*, 154.

37. Frazier, "La Bourgeoisie Noire," passim.

38. Frazier, "The Du Bois Program in the Present Crisis," 11–13; E. Franklin Frazier, "Quo Vadis?" *Journal of Negro Education* 4 (January 1935):129–131.

39. E. Franklin Frazier, "Some Effects of the Depression on the Negro in Northern Cities," *Science and Society* 2 (Fall 1938): 496, 497.

40. E. Franklin Frazier, "Human, All Too Human: The Negro's Vested Interest in Segregation," *Survey Graphic* 36 (January 1947): 74–75, 99–100.

41. Frazier, *The Negro in the United States*, 409, 412.

42. For a useful summary of reviews and criticisms of the book, see Harris, "The Life and Work of E. Franklin Frazier," ch. 5. For a typical account of a speech given by Frazier to a black sorority luncheon, where "he flung critical and witty barbs at middle class colored Americans," see *Afro-American*, August 26, 1958.

43. Frazier, *Black Bourgeoisie*, 173, 237.

44. Frazier, *Race and Culture Contacts in the Modern World*. See also Frazier, "Theoretical Structure of Sociology and Sociological Research," 292–311.

45. Frazier, *Race and Culture Contacts in the Modern World*, 295, 300.

46. Frazier, *Race and Culture Contacts in the Modern World*, 293.

47. E. Franklin Frazier, "The New Negro," *The Nation* 183 (July 7, 1956): 7–8.

48. Frazier, "The Role of the Social Scientist in the Negro College," 14.

49. E. Franklin Frazier, "The New Negro Middle Class," in *The New Negro Thirty Years Afterward* (Washington, D.C.: Howard University Press, 1955), 26–32.

50. E. Franklin Frazier, "What Can the American Negro Contribute to the Social Development of Africa?" 263–278. Davis devoted almost all of his introduction to an angry refutation of Frazier's analysis.

51. Frazier, "The Failure of the Negro Intellectual," passim.

Chapter 15. The Racial Question

1. Frazier quoted in "Opinion of W.E.B. Du Bois," *Crisis* 28 (June 1924): 58.

2. Letter from Frazier to Eugene Bixby, April 28, 1926, Frazier Papers.

3. Frazier, "Georgia," 176.

4. Frazier, "Georgia," 173–177.

5. E. Franklin Frazier, "Letter to the Editor," *Messenger* 6 (November 1924):362–363.

6. No doubt out of self-protection, the article was published anonymously as "The Negro Common School, Georgia," 252–253.

7. This article was also published anonymously as "South Carolina Negro Common Schools," 330, 332.

8. E. Franklin Frazier, "Psychological Factors in Negro Health," *Journal of Social Forces* 3 (March 1925):488–490.

9. E. Franklin Frazier, "Discussion," 239.

10. Frazier, "Psychological Factors in Negro Health," 489.

11. Frazier, "Discussion," 239.

12. See letter from Frazier to Nancy Cunard, February 18, 1932, Frazier Papers, in which he admits that the article was written in a "partly satirical vein."

13. Frazier, "The Pathology of Race Prejudice," 858.

14. Frazier, "The Pathology of Race Prejudice," 859, 861.

15. Frazier, "The Pathology of Race Prejudice," 861–862.

16. For example, see Langston Hughes, *Laughing to Keep from Crying* (New York: Henry Holt, 1952).

17. See, for example, Frazier, "All God's Chillun Got Eyes," 254–255. Frazier's unpublished stories are available in the Schomburg Collection, New York Public Library, and Frazier Papers, box 131-73, folder 13.

18. Frazier, "All God's Chillun Got Eyes," passim.

19. Frazier, "Embodying Stories of Experiences with Whites," passim.

20. For Frazier's bus stories, see two undated (c. 1925) and untitled essays, on file

in the Frazier Papers, box 131-73, folder 13. These stories were not included in the memorandum submitted to Myrdal.

21. Frazier, "Social Equality and the Negro," 166. Park, in an article published three years after Frazier's, made a similar point: "A colored nurse may ride, without objection, in a Pullman coach if she has a white baby in her arms." See Robert Park, "The Bases of Race Prejudice" *The Annals* 140 (November 1928): 18.

22. University of Chicago Round Table, "Race Tensions," Radio Discussion by E. Franklin Frazier, Carey McWilliams, and Robert Redfield (July 4, 1943), 10. Transcript in Frazier Papers, box 131-77, folder 16.

23. Frazier, *Race and Culture Contacts in the Modern World,* 264, 265.

24. E. Franklin Frazier, "Eugenics and the Race Problem," *Crisis* 31 (December 1925): 92.

25. Frazier, "Eugenics and the Race Problem," 92.

26. E. Franklin Frazier, "A Note for Racialists," unpublished essay (c. 1923), Frazier Papers, box 131-77, folder 2.

27. See, for example, Frazier, "Sociological Theory and Race Relations," 265–271.

28. Frazier, *Race and Culture Contacts in the Modern World,* 271–273.

29. Frazier, "Social Equality and the Negro," 167.

30. Frazier, "Some Effects of the Depression on the Negro in Northern Cities," 498.

31. See, for example, E. Franklin Frazier, "The Economic Subordination of the Negro," unpublished essay (c. 1928), Frazier Papers, box 131-75, folder 17.

32. E. Franklin Frazier, "The Status of the Negro in the American Social Order," *Journal of Negro Education* 4 (July 1935):293–307.

33. Fogelson and Rubinstein, *The Complete Report of Mayor LaGuardia's Commission on the Harlem Riot,* 7.

34. Fogelson and Rubinstein, *The Complete Report of Mayor LaGuardia's Commission on the Harlem Riot,* 123, 124, 128. In the Commission's version of Frazier's report that was finally sent to Mayor LaGuardia, this sentence was changed to read: "The Commission fully realizes that the economic and social ills of Harlem, which are deeply rooted in the very nature of our economic and social system, can not be corrected forthwith. The process must of necessity be gradual and patiently dealt with." For discussions about Frazier's draft and the commissioners' disagreements with Frazier's analysis, see minutes of the Commission, especially for February 14, 1936, available in the New York Municipal Archives.

35. E. Franklin Frazier, review of *Middletown in Transition,* by Robert S. Lynd and Helen M. Lynd, *Science and Society* 1 (Summer 1937):573–575.

36. E. Franklin Frazier, "Caste and Class in an American Industry," *American Journal of Sociology* 42 (September 1936):252–253.

37. Letter from Frazier to Gunnar Myrdal, June 24, 1942, Frazier Papers.

38. Frazier, "Sociological Theory and Race Relations," 271.

39. Robert Park, "The Bases of Race Prejudice," 11–20.

40. George M. Frederickson, *The Black Image in the White Mind: The Debate on Afro-American Character and Destiny, 1817–1914* (Middletown, Conn.: Wesleyan University Press, 1987), 327–328.

41. Frazier, "The Status of the Negro in the American Social Order," 303.

42. See, for example, Frazier, "Sociological Theory and Race Relations," passim.

43. Frazier, *Race and Culture Contacts in the Modern World*, 284–287.

44. See, for example, Robert Park, "Our Racial Frontier on the Pacific" (1926), reprinted in Park, *Race and Culture*, 138–151.

45. Letter from Frazier to Freda Kirchwey, July 6, 1925, Frazier Papers.

46. E. Franklin Frazier, review of *The Strange Career of Jim Crow*, by C. Vann Woodward, *Saturday Review* 38 (June 11, 1955):13.

47. Frazier, "Racial Culture and Conflict," 506–507.

48. Letter from Frazier to Gunnar Myrdal, September 9, 1942, Frazier Papers.

49. See, for example, Young, *Black Writers of the Thirties*, 239.

50. St. Clair Drake, *Black Folk Here and There: An Essay in History and Anthropology* (Los Angeles and Berkeley: University of California Press, 1987), 49–53. For Park's various essays on the race relations cycle, see Park, *Race and Culture*, pt. 2.

51. Drake, *Black Folk Here and There*, 49. Some of Park's critics suggest that he minimized conflict in his prognosis of race relations, but, according to Frazier, "there was always a latent conflict" in Park's model. See letter from Frazier to Gunnar Myrdal, June 24, 1942, Frazier Papers.

52. See, for example, Frazier, "Social Equality and the Negro" (1925); "The Status of the Negro in the American Social Order" (1935); and *The Negro in the United States* (1957), 706. For a statement of his optimistic views about the labor movement after World War II, see E. Franklin Frazier, *The Integration of the Negro into American Life* (Washington, D.C.: Women's International League for Peace and Freedom, 1945). This pamphlet is available in the Peace Collection, Swarthmore College.

53. Frazier, "Group Tactics and Ideals," 31.

54. E. Franklin Frazier, "Racial Problems in World Society," in Edwards, *E. Franklin Frazier on Race Relations*, 105, 116.

55. Frazier, *The Negro in the United States*, 703–706.

56. Frazier, *Race and Culture Contacts in the Modern World*, 212.

57. See, for example, Frazier, *The Integration of the Negro into American Life* and *The Negro in The United States*, ch. 18.

58. Frazier, *Race and Culture Contacts in the Modern World*, 337.

59. Frazier, "The Failure of the Negro Intellectual," passim.

60. Frazier, "Group Tactics and Ideals," 31.

61. Frazier, *Race and Culture Contacts in the Modern World*, 338.

Chapter 16. Enfant Terrible

1. Franklin, "The Dilemma of the American Negro Scholar," 75–76.

2. Interview by author with Michael Winston, March 30, 1989. See also the personal observations of Edwards, "E. Franklin Frazier," 109–129. Another indication of Frazier's isolation was that, of his many publications, only one article and one monograph were coauthored.

3. Interview by author with St. Clair Drake, January 22, 1975.

4. Interview by author with Everett Hughes, September 22, 1972.

5. Letter from Frazier to Mildred Price, May 9, 1932, Frazier Papers.

6. Letter from Frazier to Elsa Butler Grove, January 21, 1924, discussing his racist treatment at a hotel in Washington, D.C., during a social work conference, Frazier Papers.

7. Letter from Frazier to Freda Kirchwey, July 6, 1925, Frazier Papers.

8. See, for example, E. Franklin Frazier, "Trial by Fury," *The Nation* 121 (September 16, 1925):303–304.

9. Letters from Frazier to L. W. Rogers Company, October 17 and October 21, 1925, Frazier Papers.

10. Frazier, "Embodying Stories of Experiences with Whites," 18–19.

11. Frazier, "Embodying Stories of Experiences with Whites," passim.

12. Edwards, "E. Franklin Frazier," 87.

13. Interview by author with St. Clair Drake, January 22, 1975.

14. Michael Winston, "Postface," in Frazier, *Bourgeoisie Noire* (translated from French); also interview by author with Michael Winston, November 3, 1975.

15. Cruse, *The Crisis of the Negro Intellectual,* 154, 156. According to Cruse, Frazier was "grappling with Negro class realities in a way that would have enlightened some of the more flaming revolutionaries of the time, had they not been forced to follow Moscow's dictates."

16. Cox, "Introduction," 29, 30.

17. Pierre van den Berghe, "Sociological Apartheid," letter to *American Sociologist* 6 (August 1971):257–258.

18. Manning Marable, "Black Studies," 35–66. Frazier is vaguely identified as part of the "older tradition of black sociologists," but his contributions are not discussed nor are his writings cited.

19. Southern, *Gunnar Myrdal and Black-White Relations,* 92.

20. See generally Schwendinger and Schwendinger, *The Sociologists of the Chair;* Schrecker, *No Ivory Tower.*

21. See photograph and news story, dated May 8, 1937, from untitled Washington, D.C., newspaper, in Frazier Papers, box 131-2, folder 12. This event was under surveillance by local intelligence agencies, and Frazier's participation was recorded in his FBI file; see Chapter 19.

22. In 1944 Frazier was listed in ten different contexts in U.S. Congress, House Committee on Un-American Activities, *Investigation of Un-American Propaganda Activities in the United States,* 78th Cong., 2d sess., 1944, vol. 17, 10299, 10301, 10305, 10306, 10340, 10341, 10343, 10344, 10346, 10348. See Chapter 19 for further discussion of this aspect of Frazier's life.

23. Frazier, "Woman Suffrage," 2–3.

24. Frazier, *God and War,* 4.

25. Frazier, "New Currents of Thought," 19.

26. Frazier, "Georgia," 173–177; letter to the editors, *Messenger* 6 (November 1924):362–363; and "Group Tactics and Ideals," 31.

27. Frazier, "La Bourgeoisie Noire," 83.

28. Frazier, "The Negro and Non-resistance," 213–214; "Some Aspects of Negro Business," 293–297.

29. See, for example, A. Philip Randolph, "Garveyism," *Messenger* 3 (September 1921):248–252; Editorial, *Messenger* 4 (September 1922):479–480.

30. E. Franklin Frazier, "Garvey: A Mass Leader," *The Nation* 123 (August 18, 1926):147–148. See also E. Franklin Frazier, "The Garvey Movement," *Opportunity* 4 (November 1926):346–348.

31. Frazier quoted by Odum, *American Sociology,* 234.

32. See, for example, Frazier, "The Co-operative Movement in Denmark," 127–130.

33. Frazier, "Cooperatives," 508.

34. Frazier, "The Du Bois Program in the Present Crisis," 13.

35. Frazier, "A Negro Industrial Group," 196–232.

36. Frazier, "Social Equality and the Negro," 167.

37. Frazier, "The Negro in the Industrial South," 83–84.

38. See generally Cruse, *The Crisis of the Negro Intellectual,* passim; Theodore Draper, *American Communism and Soviet Russia: The Formative Period* (New York: Random House, Vintage Books, 1986), ch. 15.

39. Frazier, "Enfant Terrible."

Chapter 17. Black and Red

1. Mark Naison, *Communists in Harlem during the Depression* (New York: Grove Press, 1984), ch. 1; Wilson Record, *The Negro and the Communist Party* (New York: Atheneum, 1971), ch. 2; Draper, *American Communism and Soviet Russia,* ch. 15.

2. Draper, *American Communism and Soviet Russia,* 320. The party remained underground until 1921, when it was known as the Workers Party; its name was changed to Workers (Communist) Party in 1925 and to Communist Party of the United States in 1930. For a discussion of the party's origins and emergence, see William Z. Foster, *History of the Communist Party of the United States* (New York: International Publishers, 1952), ch. 13.

3. Record, *The Negro and the Communist Party,* 25–26, 52; Naison, *Communists in Harlem,* 1. According to party leader William Z. Foster, the CP's sixth convention in 1929 recorded no more than two hundred black members nationwide.

4. The Congress failed in both these tasks and lasted only five years. Organizationally, it existed primarily as a paper organization outside Chicago, where it was based, and even in Chicago its functioning membership was not larger than fifty. It was superseded in 1930 by the League of Struggle for Negro Rights, which was no more successful than its predecessor. William Z. Foster even conceded that the ANLC "remained small and was largely limited to Communists in its membership." See Draper, *American Communism and Soviet Russia,* 331–332; Record, *The Negro and the Communist Party,* 31–34; Foster, *History of the Communist Party,* 268.

5. Draper, *American Communism and Soviet Russia,* 350–356; Record, *The Negro and the Communist Party,* 54–119.

6. Draper, *American Communism and Soviet Russia,* 551–552.

7. Len De Caux, *Labor Radical: From the Wobblies to the CIO* (Boston: Beacon Press, 1970), 173.

8. Al Richmond, *A Long View from the Left: Memoirs of an American Revolutionary* (Boston: Houghton Mifflin, 1972), 246.

9. In January 1927 the party moved its headquarters to New York. See Foster, *History of the Communist Party,* 261.

10. Letter from William Patterson to Frazier, May 26, 1927, Frazier Papers.

11. Frazier, "A Folk Culture in the Making," 195–199.

12. Frazier, "Black and Red."

13. "The first mistake of those who think that the Negro of all groups in America should be in revolt against the present system is that they regard the Negro group as homogenous. As a matter of fact, the Negro group is highly differentiated, with about the same range of interests as the whites. It is very well for white and black radicals to quote statistics to show that ninety-eight per cent of the Negroes are workers and should seek release from their economic slavery; but as a matter of fact ninety-eight per cent of the Negroes do not regard themselves as in economic slavery." Frazier, "La Bourgeoisie Noire," 78.

14. Letter from Gustavus Steward to Frazier, August 29, 1934, Frazier Papers.

15. Stolberg, "Black Chauvinism," 571. Frazier's letter (consigned with Sterling Brown, Ralph Bunche, and Emmett Dorsey) appeared in *The Nation* on July 3, 1935. It was many years before Frazier made this criticism in a more direct way. In the 1950s he pointed out that the CP was wrong in its expectation that the Afro-American middle class would play a leading role in the "national liberation" of the "Negro people." See Frazier, *Black Bourgeoisie,* 234–235.

16. Frazier shared many of the same views as Sterling Spero and Abram Harris, who, in public at least, were much more critical of the CP, though still within a leftist perspective. See Spero and Harris, *The Black Worker,* ch. 19.

17. MBF Interview.

18. In 1928 Calverton endorsed the CP's presidential ticket and used his journal to defend the USSR. Several years later Calverton broke with the party and became one of its staunchest critics. See Michael Nash, "Schism on the Left: The Anti-communism of V. F. Calverton and His *Modern Quarterly,*" *Science and Society* 45 (Winter 1981–1982):437–452.

19. "Editorial," *Race* 1 (Winter 1935–1936):3. Because of a lack of funds, the journal ceased publication after its second issue in summer 1936.

20. For the early history of this journal, see David Goldway, "Fifty Years of *Science and Society,*" *Science and Society* 50 (Fall 1986):260–279.

21. Harris, "The Life and Work of E. Franklin Frazier," 29.

22. "Economic Status Is Theme of Conference," *Hilltop* (Howard University newspaper), May 18, 1935. The proceedings of the conference were published in the *Journal of Negro Education* 5 (January 1936).

23. See, for example, U.S. Congress, Senate, *Letter from the Acting Secretary of the Interior: Alleged Communistic Activities at Howard University, Washington, D.C.,* 74th Cong., 2d Sess., 1936, S. Doc. 217.

24. For the involvement of the CP and other leftist organizations in the teachers' union during the 1930s, see Schrecker, *No Ivory Tower,* 52–53.

25. "Howard University Professor Criticizes White Capitalists in May Day Speech in Park," untitled Washington, D.C., newspaper (May 8, 1937), available in the Frazier Papers, box 131-2, folder 12.

26. Fogelson and Rubinstein, *The Complete Report of Mayor LaGuardia's Commis-*

sion on the Harlem Riot, 11, 23–24. For another defense of the role of "white radicals" in the riot, see Frazier, "Some Effects of the Depression on the Negro in Northern Cities," 489–499.

27. See, for example, the minutes of the Commission's meetings on file in the New York Municipal Archives.

28. Letters from Mary Hillyer to Frazier, June 17, 1935; from A. Philip Randolph to Frazier, July 24, 1935; from B. L. McLaurin to Frazier, August 30, 1935; and Jane Morgan, minutes of meeting at La Citadelle Farm, May 26, 1935. All this correspondence is in the Frazier Papers, correspondence files and box 131-28, folder 8.

29. See E. Franklin Frazier, "Where Are the Negro Radicals?" unpublished and undated (c. 1932), Frazier Papers, box 131-78, folder 10.

30. Letter from Frazier to Mildred Price, May 9, 1932, Frazier Papers.

31. Frazier, "Quo Vadis?" 129–131. For an example of his criticisms of prevailing liberal sentiment, see also Frazier, "A Critical Summary of Articles Contributed to Symposium on Negro Education," 531–533.

32. Raymond Wolters, *Negroes and the Great Depression: The Problem of Economic Recovery* (Westport, Conn.: Greenwood Press, 1970), 313.

33. Ross, *J. E. Spingarn,* 178–185.

34. Quoted by Wolters, *Negroes and the Great Depression,* 22, 320.

35. Wolters, *Negroes and the Great Depression,* ch. 12.

36. For a candid view of Du Bois's ideas during this period, see his exchange with George Streator, an Afro-American socialist who shared Frazier's political views, in Aptheker, *The Correspondence of W.E.B. Du Bois,* vol. 2, 86–96. See also George Streator, "In Search of Leadership," *Race* 1 (Winter 1935–1936):14–20.

37. W.E.B. Du Bois, "Social Planning for the Negro, Past and Present," *Journal of Negro Education* 5 (January 1936):122, 123–124. This is one of the clearest statements of Du Bois's position, but he had been expressing similar views long before 1936.

38. Letter from Frazier to Walter White, May 17, 1934, Frazier Papers.

39. Stolberg, "Black Chauvinism," 570–571.

40. Letter from Francis Henson to Frazier, October 1, 1935, Frazier Papers.

41. Young, *Black Writers of the Thirties,* 47.

42. Frazier, "The Du Bois Program in the Present Crisis," 11–13. Du Bois was used to being the object of polemical attacks and did not hold any grudges against Frazier. In 1939 Frazier sent Du Bois a copy of his recently published book *The Negro Family in the United States* with a letter expressing his debt to Du Bois's "pioneering contribution to the study of the Negro family." A few months later, Du Bois included Frazier in his list of outstanding Afro-Americans to be included in a book commemorating the seventy-fifth anniversary of the abolition of slavery. See Aptheker, *The Correspondence of W.E.B. Du Bois,* vol. 2, 193–194, 219–224.

43. On the National Negro Congress, see Wolters, *Negroes and the Great Depression,* ch. 13. Frazier supported the Congress and was at least nominally involved in its committees. See letter from Benjamin Davis to Frazier, January 21, 1936, Frazier Papers.

44. E. Franklin Frazier, "A Negro Looks at the Soviet Union," in *Proceedings of the Nationalities Panel: The Soviet Union: A Family of Nations in the War* (New York: National Council of American-Soviet Friendship, 1943), 16.

Chapter 18. Keeping the Faith

1. See, for example, Schrecker, *No Ivory Tower;* and Lillian Hellman, *Scoundrel Time* (Boston: Little, Brown, 1976).

2. Duberman, *Paul Robeson,* 363.

3. Frazier, *Negro Youth at the Crossways,* 288.

4. Frazier, *Black Bourgeoisie,* 107.

5. Frazier, *The Negro in the United States* (1949 ed.), 702–703. Significantly, despite the pressures of McCarthyism, Frazier retained a positive evaluation of the Soviet Union in his revised, 1957 edition of this book.

6. Frazier, *Race and Culture Contacts in the Modern World,* 220, 300–304.

7. Quoted in Gabbin, *Sterling A. Brown,* 51.

8. Duberman, *Paul Robeson,* 668. For example, in 1943 he received a "long chatty letter" from Essie Robeson. He replied quickly and graciously, saying that he looked forward to "spending some time with you and Paul and talking over the good old days." Essie encouraged him to see Robeson in *Othello* in New York. "You just must see it. It is a social experience, watching the play, as well as the way the audience accepts it. You will appreciate it." She told Frazier that he should go backstage to see Robeson, who would get tickets for him. See letters from Frazier to Essie Robeson, October 21, 1943; and from Essie Robeson to Frazier, December 22, 1943, Frazier Papers.

9. Though the Robeson faction won the battle, it lost the war. The internecine struggle took its toll, and the CAA declined as a functioning organization, disbanding in 1955. For a description of the CAA and the Robeson-Yergan struggle, see Duberman, *Paul Robeson,* 256–258, 330–333. Letters from Robeson and Yergan to Frazier, lobbying for his support, are available in the Frazier Papers, box 131-30, folders 5–6.

10. Letter from Benjamin Davis to Frazier, January 31, 1948, Frazier Papers.

11. Frazier made these remarks on October 13, 1949. See Duberman, *Paul Robeson,* 374, 698.

12. Duberman, *Paul Robeson,* 377.

13. Letter from Paul Robeson to Frazier, October 27, 1949, quoted in Duberman, *Paul Robeson,* 378.

14. Letters from Elizabeth Moos to Frazier, November 1 and November 3, 1943; and from Corliss Lamont to Frazier, November 16, 1943, Frazier Papers.

15. This association with Adamic would years later be resurrected as proof of his communist affiliations by the Senate Internal Security Subcommittee and the State Department. See Chapter 19 for a discussion of their investigations.

16. Frazier, "A Negro Looks at the Soviet Union," 11–16.

17. The *People's Voice* was a militant Harlem weekly. Adam Clayton Powell, Jr., was its editor until 1946 when he left because of its CP connections. Doxey Wilkerson, an Afro-American member of the CP and one-time colleague of Frazier's at Howard, was its general manager. See Duberman, *Paul Robeson,* 330.

18. Frazier even called on his friends and CP contacts to protest on his behalf. Ida Guggenheimer, a member of the International Labor Defense's Executive Committee, wrote to the *Black Dispatch*'s editor defending Frazier as an "outstanding man who has

with you been a fighter against injustice to all." As a result of his lobbying efforts, the *People's Voice* published a half-hearted retraction on September 22, though it "did not impress [Frazier] very much since it did not assume responsibility for its own misrepresentation." See letters from Frazier to Doxey Wilkerson, September 13, 1945, and Ida Guggenheimer, September 29, 1945; from Wilkerson to Frazier, October 3, 1945; from Guggenheimer to Roscoe Dunjee, September 16, 1945. All correspondence is in the Frazier Papers, box 131-33, folder 2.

19. See Chapter 19.

20. Frazier was paid thirty-five dollars by the *Daily Worker* to cover his expenses and a small fee. See letters from Samuel Barron to Frazier, September 26 and October 23, 1944; and from Frazier to Barron, October 23, 1944, Frazier Papers.

21. Letter ("Why Did Big Shots Attend Jim-Crow Birthday Ball?") from E. Franklin Frazier to *Afro-American*, February 17, 1945.

22. Letter of acceptance from Dr. and Mrs. E. Franklin Frazier to the Ambassador, undated, Frazier Papers, box 131-17, folder 31.

23. MBF Interview.

24. Manning Marable, "Peace and Black Liberation: The Contributions of W.E.B. Du Bois," *Science and Society* 47 (Winter 1983–1984):385–405.

25. The Center, formed in New York in 1950, was involved in collecting signatures for the Stockholm Appeal, a document calling for the abolition of atomic weapons. It was disbanded in October 1950, a few months before the indictment. See Marable, "Peace and Black Liberation," 397–399.

26. Letter from Frazier to the Officers, Sponsors and Invited Guests, February 10, 1951, Frazier Papers, box 131-31, folder 1.

27. Letter from W.E.B. Du Bois to Leaders of the American Negro People, February 5, 1952, Frazier Papers, box 131-31, folder 1.

28. Letter from Harlow Shapley to Frazier, January 22, 1951, Frazier Papers, box 131-31, folder 1.

29. Marable, "Peace and Black Liberation," 399.

30. Letter from Hubert Delany to Frazier, February 16, 1951, Frazier Papers, box 131-31, folder 1. Delany himself was later victimized by McCarthyism in 1955, when Mayor Robert F. Wagner, Jr., refused to reappoint him to the bench because of his left-wing tendencies.

31. Letter from Frazier to *New York World Telegram and Sun* (undated, c. February 24, 1951), Frazier Papers, box 131-31, folder 1. Frazier's letter complained about the newspaper's coverage of the event, especially its report that "Paul Robeson headed the list of speakers."

32. Unpublished, untitled, and undated (c. February 1951), Frazier Papers, box 131-31, folder 2.

33. Letter from W.E.B. Du Bois to Frazier, April 11, 1951, Frazier Papers. For a description of the event and Frazier's role, see Du Bois, *The Autobiography,* 367–369.

34. Marable, "Peace and Black Liberation," 401.

35. Letter from W.E.B. Du Bois to Frazier, July 17, 1959, Frazier Papers.

36. Marable, "Peace and Black Liberation," 403.

37. See letter from Kwame Nkrumah to Marie Brown Frazier, December 21, 1962, Frazier Papers, box 131-5, folder 24. Nkrumah invited Mrs. Frazier to come to Ghana

to participate in a "suitable ceremony for the presentation of your late husband's books." Unable to go, she asked Du Bois, who was already in Ghana, to act on her behalf. He was too sick, so Shirley Graham Du Bois acted on his behalf.

Chapter 19. Hounded

1. Frazier, "The Failure of the Negro Intellectual," 34.

2. Frazier, "The Failure of the Negro Intellectual," 31. Frazier meant this quite literally. He had warned St. Clair Drake to watch out for a mutual colleague who, according to Frazier, was serving as an informer for the State Department and CIA while pretending to be doing research on Africa. (Interview with St. Clair Drake by the author, January 22, 1975.)

3. See, for example, Bud Schultz and Ruth Schultz, *It Did Happen Here: Recollections of Political Repression in America* (Berkeley: University of California Press, 1989); Herbert Mitgang, *Dangerous Dossiers: Exposing the Secret War against America's Greatest Authors* (New York: Ballantine, 1988); Schrecker, *No Ivory Tower;* Franklin, "The Dilemma of the American Negro Scholar"; and Winston, "Through the Back Door."

4. Though Frazier did not try to get *Black Bourgeoisie* published in the United States before being approached by a publisher in Paris, he probably realized from experience that such a book would not make it past an editorial screening. After the book was published in France in 1955 and received sociology's MacIver Award in 1956, it became respectable and was published by the Free Press in 1957.

5. Interview with Herbert Blumer by the author, April 28, 1971.

6. Frazier, "The Role of the Social Scientist in the Negro College," 17. Frazier refused ("I'm no diplomat, I am a social scientist."), and the book was published by Dryden Press in 1951.

7. See, for example, David Garrow, *The FBI and Martin Luther King, Jr.: From "Solo" to Memphis* (New York: Norton, 1981); and Kenneth O'Reilly, *"Racial Matters": The FBI's Secret File on Black Americans, 1960–1972* (New York: Free Press, 1989).

8. On May 26, 1988, I initiated a Freedom of Information–Privacy Acts (FOIPA) request for documents on Frazier held by the FBI. I was informed in July 1988 that the FBI held some eight hundred pages on Frazier. On December 1, 1989—eighteen months after my original request—I received 462 pages on Frazier from the FBI. As of July, 1990, I was still trying to get several hundred classified pages released.

9. The conference was cosponsored by the Joint Committee on National Recovery and Howard's Social Science Division.

10. See Frazier's testimony to SISS, 19.

11. Mordecai Johnson, Howard's president, and other faculty (especially Emmett Dorsey) were targeted by the investigators. For the full seventy-one-page investigation, see U.S. Congress, Senate, *Letter from the Acting Secretary of the Interior.*

12. O'Reilly, *"Racial Matters,"* ch. 1.

13. O'Reilly, *"Racial Matters,"* 19.

14. The following information, unless otherwise noted, is based on information released by the FBI under my FOIPA request. The data are from Frazier's files 101–1603 and 138–825 in FBI headquarters, Washington, D.C. Frazier's records were made available to me by Emil P. Moschella, chief of the FOIPA Section, Records Management Division, FBI. Supporting documents were provided by Clark Dittmer, director of the Diplomatic Security Service, U.S. State Department.

15. The scope of the investigation is described in a letter from E. R. Marlin et al. to the Committee on Subversive Activities, Federal Security Agency, May 27, 1942. The Federal Security Agency was a predecessor to the Department of Health and Human Services. My thanks to Aloha South, Civil Reference Branch, National Archives, for finding and making available this document.

16. Letter from R. M. Barnett to Frazier, August 21, 1942, Frazier Papers, box 131-4, folder 41.

17. SISS, 54–55.

18. House Committee on Un-American Activities (hereafter cited as HUAC), *Investigation of Un-American Propaganda Activities in the United States*, 78th Cong., 2d sess., 1944, vol. 17, 10299, 10301, 10303, 10306, 10340, 10341, 10343, 10344, 10346, 10348.

19. HUAC, *Report on Southern Conference for Human Welfare*, 80th Cong., 1st sess., 1947, H. Rept. 592, 14, 17.

20. HUAC, *Report on the Communist "Peace" Offensive: A Campaign to Disarm and Defeat the United States*, 82nd Cong., 1st sess., 1951, H. Rept. 378, 1, 118, 125, 143.

21. HUAC, *Communist Political Subversion*, 84th Cong., 2d sess., 1956, pt. 2, 7141, 7208, 7798.

22. For a catalogue of Robeson's "subversive" activities, especially his efforts to organize Afro-American support for the peace movement, see HUAC, *Hearings Regarding Communist Infiltration of Minority Groups*, 81st Cong., 1st sess., 1949, pt. 1, 485–493.

23. HUAC, *Hearings Regarding Communist Infiltration of Minority Groups*, 479–483, 459–475. Charles Johnson, now president of Fisk, not only testified as a friendly witness but also made sure that Giovanni Rossi Lomanitz, a young physicist who refused to cooperate with a HUAC investigation, was forced out of his job at Fisk. See Schrecker, *No Ivory Tower*, 146–147.

24. Until 1958, when the Supreme Court took up the issue, the State Department had broad discretion to restrict travel by U.S. citizens.

25. His application for the position was formally acknowledged in a letter from Katherine Goddard (recruiting officer for UNESCO) to Frazier, January 16, 1951, Frazier Papers, box 131-54, folder 18. The Du Bois dinner took place on February 23rd.

26. This anecdote was told to me by St. Clair Drake in an interview (January 22, 1975) and confirmed in my interview with Marie Brown Frazier (November 2, 1975). Frazier had told this story to St. Clair Drake by way of giving him advice about the need to "take the offensive" when trying to get a passport from government bureaucrats.

27. SISS, established in 1951, was the Senate equivalent of HUAC.

28. MBF Interview. A copy of the subpoena, dated March 29, 1955, is in the Frazier Papers, box 131-4, folder 39.

29. SISS, passim. The eighty-one page transcript of the hearing is available in the National Archives.

30. The Supreme Court's decision, declaring school segregation unconstitutional, was issued in May 1954. Ten months later, Frazier was subpoened by SISS. In a letter from Virginia Durr to Frazier (June 27, 1955, Frazier Papers), the writer said that she had just read a story in the local press in Alabama in which "Jim Eastland . . . accuses you of being the chief 'brainwasher' of the United States Supreme Court and then recites the lengthy tale of your sins."

31. SISS, 27, 24, 25, 75, 78, 79, 80.

32. See letters from Alfred Métraux to Frazier, May 4, 1960; from Frazier to Métraux, May 12, 1960; from Métraux to Frazier, May 31, 1960; from Frazier to Métraux, June 8, 1960, Frazier Papers.

33. Letter from Alfred Métraux to Frazier, January 27, 1961, Frazier Papers, box 131-54, folder 19. (All correspondence between Frazier and the United Nations can be found here.)

34. Letter from Frazier to Métraux, February 6, 1961, Frazier Papers.

35. Letter from Métraux to Frazier, March 16, 1961, Frazier Papers.

36. Letters from Virginia Westfall (State Department) to Frazier, March 22, 1961; from Métraux to Frazier, May 4, 1961; from Frazier to Métraux, May 9, 1961, Frazier Papers.

37. Letters from Métraux to Frazier, September 7, 1961; and from Frazier to Métraux, September 12, 1961, Frazier Papers.

38. Letter and interrogatory from Henry Waldman (chairman, International Organizations Employees Loyalty Board, U.S. Civil Service Commission) to Frazier, November 1, 1961, Frazier Papers, box 131-54, folder 20.

39. Letter from Métraux to Frazier, March 13, 1962, Frazier Papers.

40. Letter from Frazier to Métraux, March 23, 1962, Frazier Papers.

41. Interviews by the author with Marie Brown Frazier, November 2, 1975, and with Michael Winston, March 30, 1989.

Epilogue

1. E. Franklin Frazier, Personal Diary (December 1, 1950–December 18, 1950), Frazier Papers, box 131-2, folder 6.

2. Frazier, Personal Diary, entry for December 18, 1950. For the complete text of Carl Sandburg's poem "The Liars," written in March 1919, see *The Complete Poems of Carl Sandburg* (New York: Harcourt Brace Jovanovich, 1970), 192–193.

3. Frazier, "What Can the American Negro Contribute to the Social Development of Africa?" 263–278. As we have seen, Frazier's article was so disturbing to John

Davis, editor of *Africa: Seen by American Negroes,* that he devoted most of his introduction to refuting Frazier. For other articles by Frazier that expressed a similar cynicism, see "The New Negro Middle Class," 26–32; and "The Failure of the Negro Intellectual," 26–36.

4. Frazier, "The New Negro Middle Class," 32.

5. Frazier, "The New Negro," 7–9.

6. Frazier, "What Can the American Negro Contribute to the Social Development of Africa?" 275, 276.

7. Frazier, "The Failure of the Negro Intellectual," passim.

8. Frazier's letter to the editor (March 19, 1956, Frazier Papers) was critical of Faulkner and others for slowing down integration out of "cowardice, ignorance or prejudice."

9. See, for example, his correspondence with Langston Hughes, November 3, 1961; Richard Wright, December 6, 1959; Essien-Udom, December 14, 1962; Raya Dunayevskaya, November 24, 1961; Herbert Aptheker, April 25, 1960; and Benjamin Davis, July 7, 1956, Frazier Papers.

10. Frazier, "The New Negro," 7–9; "New Role of the Negro Woman," 40.

11. Frazier, *The Negro in the United States,* 690–691.

12. Frazier, *The Negro Church in America.*

13. A similar observation is made by Cayton, "E. Franklin Frazier," 137–142.

14. Edwards, "E. Franklin Frazier," 122–128.

15. Frazier, Personal Diary, entry for March 2, 1956.

16. Frazier's alienation from Howard was confirmed in my interviews with Marie Brown Frazier and Michael Winston, plus a personal communication from Alvin Schorr.

17. See, for example, Frazier, "The Role of the Social Scientist in the Negro College," 9–18; "Race Contacts and the Social Structure," 1–11.

18. C. Wright Mills, *The Sociological Imagination* (New York: Oxford University Press, 1959).

19. E. Franklin Frazier, "Presidential Advice to Younger Sociologists," *American Sociological Review* 18 (December 1953):602.

20. Quoted in Odum, *American Sociology,* 238.

21. Frazier, "Theoretical Structure of Sociology and Sociological Research," 310.

22. Frazier, *Race and Culture Contacts in the Modern World,* 31.

23. Frazier, Personal Diary, entries for December 5 and 6, 1950.

24. Frazier, Personal Diary, entry for December 4, 1950.

25. Frazier, "The Role of the Social Scientist in the Negro College," 13–14.

26. See, for example, his views on this in Frazier, "The Present State of Sociological Knowledge Concerning Race Relations," 73–80.

27. Frazier, *The Negro in the United States* (1949), 703.

28. Frazier, *Race and Culture Contacts in the Modern World,* 228.

29. Frazier, Personal Diary, entries for December 1 and December 16, 1950.

30. See, for example, Frazier, "Brazil Has No Race Problem," 363–365.

31. See, for example, correspondence between Frazier and Thomas Cook regarding travel arrangements, October 24 and October 26, 1951, Frazier Papers, box 131-54, folder 18.

32. Frazier expressed all these views in *Race and Culture Contacts in the Modern World,* passim.

33. Frazier, *Race and Culture Contacts in the Modern World,* 334.

34. Frazier, *Race and Culture Contacts in the Modern World,* 335, 337, 338.

35. Frazier, "A Negro Looks at the Soviet Union," 15.

36. Du Bois's statement was read by Shirley Graham Du Bois, who presented Frazier's library to the University of Ghana on July 9, 1963, on behalf of Mrs. Frazier. Nkrumah's personal letter of thanks to Mrs. Frazier (dated December 21, 1962) is available in the Frazier Papers. See "Presentation of E. Franklin Frazier's Library to the University of Ghana, Legon, Ghana" (July 9, 1963), Frazier Papers, box 131-5, folder 24. Du Bois died six weeks later, and Nkrumah's revolutionary government was overthrown in 1966.

Index